Quitting Cocaine

Quitting Cocaine

The Struggle against Impulse

Howard J. Shaffer, Ph.D
Stephanie B. Jones, Ed.D.

Foreword by
Norman E. Zinberg, M.D.

Lexington Books
D.C. Heath and Company/Lexington, Massachusetts/Toronto

Library of Congress Cataloging-in-Publication Data

Shaffer, Howard, 1948–
  Quitting cocaine.

  Includes index.
  1. Cocaine habit—Treatment.   2. Habit breaking.
I. Jones, Stephanie B.   II. Title.
RC568.C6S48   1989   616.86′3   87-45977
ISBN 0-669-17098-4 (alk. paper)
ISBN 0-669-19690-8 (pbk.: alk. paper)

Published simultaneously in Canada
Printed in the United States of America
Casebound International Standard Book Number: 0-669-17098-4
Paperbound International Standard Book Number: 0-669-19690-8
Library of Congress Catalog Card Number: 87-45977

The paper used in this publication meets the minimum requirements of American National Standard for Information Sciences—Permanence of Paper for Printed Library Materials, ANSI Z39.48-1984. ∞™

Year and number of this printing:

90 91 92 93   12 11 10 9 8 7 6 5 4 3

For Phillip, Lillian, Nathan, Eva (HJS),
Donald, and Beverley (SBJ).

Their love will endure always.

Contents

Figures and Tables

Figures

Tables

Foreword

Essential Factors of a Rational Policy on Intoxicant Use

Norman E. Zinberg, M.D.

In my book *Drug, Set, and Setting* (1984) I emphasized the importance of three variables in connection with the use of an intoxicant: the pharmacological properties of the substance itself; the attitudes and personality structure of the user; and the influence of the physical and social setting in which use takes place. When the longitudinal research for that book was begun in 1974, cocaine was hardly a factor. The scant attention that drug was receiving at that time from both the drug-using public and professional researchers can be judged by how little space was devoted to it by the comprehensive and learned report of the National Commission on Marijuana and Drug Abuse of 1972 to 1973. Howard Shaffer and Stephanie Jones have set out to remedy that significant omission.

They recognize, as I did in *Drug, Set, and Setting,* that without knowledge of all three variables, we cannot identify the factors that affect the decision to use, or predict either the immediate effect of use on the individual or its long-term consequences. Because the third variable, setting, was least understood, as described by both me and Shaffer and Jones, we pleaded for its inclusion in future considerations of social policy. Unfortunately, this plea has not been heard. And now, just a few years after the publication of my book, when social policy questions of grave importance are again being considered, the alarmed public is still thinking of drug use (as it did in the mid-sixties) as the most serious domestic problem and is not paying any attention to the social setting in which use occurs. In this forward I will outline the bare bones of a social policy that would take the social setting into account.

Vital changes in this area have taken place since the sixties. One result of the debate at that time between the "heads" (users of marijuana) and the "juicers" (users of alcohol) has been the increased recognition that alcohol, as well as tobacco, is indeed a drug. These two drugs differ from other drugs not only in pharmacological properties and effects but also in legal position; nonetheless, they also have some similar properties and effects, including the development of dependency. Because they are acceptable legally and socially, however, a more moderate, more humane policy has been adopted, which does consider the social setting. Surgeon General C. Everett Koop's recent announcement concerning the addictive properties of cigarettes has elicited a few cries for a "war" on cigarette smoking, but the decisions that have been reached about smoking and health eschew an all-out assault on smokers by separating use from abuse. Controlled users of tobacco—those who enjoy an occasional cigarette, pipe, or cigar in the proper quarters and at the proper time—have not been interfered with. Rather, it is the compulsive smoker, who has trouble observing regulations on airliners or in public places, who is the target of the most recent antismoking rulings. No doubt these efforts will be stepped up, and smoking may be banned on all flights, not only on those lasting less than two hours.

Actions taken against excessive alcohol consumption have followed a similar pattern. Although "war" has not been declared on drinking, and there seems to be little interest in repeating the disaster of the Volstead Act, striking changes have occurred in the public attitude toward driving while intoxicated. Several states have been sufficiently enlightened to mandate treatment rather than punishment, if there is no other violation involved, and attempts are being made to evaluate and improve treatment programs. The cry is being raised to expand employee assistance programs to provide easier access for more workers who are in trouble. The rise in the legal drinking age in most states has been accompanied by an effort to keep this drug out of the hands of young people. These attempts to cope with the public health problems resulting from alcohol consumption do not interfere in any way with those users (who make up 90 percent of all drinkers) who are controlled, who generally follow regulations, and who enjoy their relationship to the substance.

Similar procedures have not been followed in regard to illicit drug users, despite the obvious fact that it is not they but the *licit* drug users who incur the highest costs in terms of health care and drain on the economy. It is estimated that from 200,000 to 250,000 deaths result each year from alcohol use, with a health-care cost of $15 billion; estimates for cigarette smokers show 350,000 deaths per year and a cost of $117 billion. To estimate the cost of illicit drugs to the economy is more difficult; the figure of $50 million to $60 billion is often used, but certainly the cost of law enforcement is far greater. For many years a succession of "wars" has been launched against illicit drugs, all notable chiefly for their lack of success.

Legalization

Recently, because of the failure and high cost of this "war," as well as the generally disruptive and inhumane quality of the warlike stance, demands have been made for the legalization of all drugs so that they can be regulated openly, as are alcohol and cigarettes. It is my impression that this call for legalization has arisen out of sheer frustration and that little serious consideration has been given to the three variables outlined that must be taken into account in determining a realistic social policy, a point abundantly supported by Shaffer and Jones.

First, illicit drugs are chemically and pharmaceutically different, with lesser or greater consequences in terms of toxicity and dependency. Despite the publicity surrounding individual cases, deaths from cocaine caused by heart stoppage are rare; death resulting from heroin overdose is more common; and there have been no known deaths from marijuana use. Whereas at least 95 percent of cigarette smokers are known to be addicted, addiction figures for cocaine, which are hard to garner, are probably between 10 percent and 20 percent, for alcohol 5 percent to 10 percent, and for marijuana 1 percent to 2 percent. Long-term health effects vary similarly. Second, under the conditions of virtually unrestricted availability that would accompany legalization, it would be almost impossible for certain personality types to resist use and reuse. Therefore, at least in the first phase of legalization, use would greatly increase. And, in part because of the third variable, the social setting, the number of casualties would also greatly increase. This variable, which embodies norms, sanctions, and rituals, shows people how to use an intoxicant in a controlled and pleasurable manner rather than destructively. The history of alcohol use in the United States reveals that in certain historical periods this drug has been used in more or less destructive ways, and that it has been especially destructive to the American Indians, whose culture lacks regulatory norms. As recently as the sixties and early seventies the development of social norms and sanctions sharply reduced the casualties from the use of LSD and other psychedelics. Today, however, our society is not prepared for the legalization of cocaine and opiates because the norms and sanctions that would encourage controlled use have not had an opportunity to develop.

A second issue relating to the influence of the social setting on drug use is the attitude of the reigning cultural majority toward illicit drugs. They have been told and often believe that these drugs are not controllable and therefore are far more deadly than the licit drugs. According to public opinion polls and social researchers, the majority also believe that many, if not most, of the users of these drugs are enemy deviants—criminals at best, depraved monsters at worst. They want them removed from society, and therefore they support the unsuccessful "war." Thus even an attempt to legalize marijuana—which according to every scientific study is the least damaging of the illicit drugs, and in all likelihood less damaging (this does *not* mean harmless) than the two licit drugs—could lead to a socially disruptive struggle akin to that surrounding abortion. The proponents of marijuana use—more than 70 million Americans have tried it—could become Wet-style activists, while the opponents—for example, the parent groups—could become diehard antagonists. Both sides could easily line up spokespersons filled with moral fervor, buttressed by sometimes ambiguous but always powerfully stated scientific "facts." In the case of the political and legislative bodies that have so long espoused this war, the even more fervid rhetoric that would be necessary to turn the tide toward legalization could only engender confusion and lead to bitter strife.

War

The war against drugs has been almost totally unsuccessful on the so-called supply side. Drugs are coming into this country at an increasing rate despite the expenditure of hundreds of billions of dollars to stop them. Suppliers of marijuana, the most bulky drug and therefore the easiest to interdict, have moved to production within the United States, and when air patrols become a problem, they simply move production indoors. The effect of law enforcement has not been to reduce supply but to keep up the price, thereby guaranteeing a monopoly and incredibly high profits for those willing to take the risks.

One could argue that keeping up the price has brought some success on the demand side, discouraging some people who would have experimented and might have got into trouble. Nevertheless, it is likely that availability is so great that almost anyone who wants to use can do so. It is true that some use has been prevented by negative attitudes toward use, either personal or social. At the same time, the illicitness of certain drugs interferes with the development of those social sanctions and norms that are the most reliable preventive of destructive use. Whatever the previous arguments about the impact of the war and its continuation and acceleration, conditions have changed so much in the last three or four years that the new situation must be recognized and taken into account.

An interesting and complex paradox has developed. The use of drugs, licit and illicit, is down overall. Cigarette consumption continues to drop slowly. For the fourth consecutive year, more light wines and beer have been consumed than hard liquor, which has never happened before in the history of the United States. The proof of hard liquor remains at 80 in contrast to the 86 to 100 proof of just a few years ago. The age of first use of all intoxicants has been rising for ten years. (It was the drop in age of first use in the early seventies that caused the greatest concern and led to the formation of the parents' movement.) Marijuana use is down, and, more important, the age of users has risen significantly. Heroin use is down too, and for each year of the past decade the age of heroin addicts has risen by almost a year, indicating that there are few new addicts. Cocaine use also is slightly down, and its position in the culture is documented splendidly in this book.

But here is the paradox. An increasing body of evidence indicates a growing class difference in drug use, particularly in respect to cocaine and alcohol. (This has always been true of heroin.) The consumption of light wines rather than hard liquor centers in the middle class and does not extend to the low-skilled working class. Even the growth of employee assistance programs most affects those with regular jobs, and to get into therapy after a driving-while-intoxicated (DWI) conviction one has to have a car. The middle class, actually the upper middle class, fueled the boom in cocaine use in the late seventies and early eighties. It took several years to learn that cocaine, the champagne or caviar of drugs, was powerfully destructive. The initial mild sense of well-being and enhanced performance changed after heavy, continuous use into dissociation, paranoia, sexual perversity, and isolation. By the mid-eighties the members of that initial group were fleeing the drug and filling the treatment centers newly developed for them. At the same time, the use of the drug was rapidly dropping down the social scale. The consumption of crack and other more overtly intoxicating variants of cocaine quickly became associated with the South Bronx, East Los Angeles, and Roxbury. It is true that the continuing residue of heroin addicts, a sizable half million, also comes chiefly from those same areas. But at this time the cocaine drugs are the greatest problem, as Shaffer and Jones show so clearly. The qualifying phrase "at this time" is necessary, for the drug scene can change with surprising swiftness. It is interesting that the learned and comprehensive report of the National Commission on Marijuana and Drug Abuse of 1972 to 1973 hardly mentioned cocaine.

Thus at the moment, when the call for an increase in the war on drugs is at its height, including the unprecedented use of the military and mandatory, random urinalysis on the job, it looks as if these measures are to be aimed largely against a socially excluded and politically underrepresented group of our population. It should be added that the political representatives of these minority groups are mostly behind the war because, while the reigning cultural majority wants these intoxicant users to stop dirtying up their streets and go away, the brunt of drug-related crime, killing, and disorder is borne by the neighborhood. Nevertheless, if this war heats up, it will not be just a war on drugs but a war mobilized by the reigning cultural majority, the franchised and employed, against a minority—an essentially disenfranchised and deeply alienated segment of our society.

Education

Accompanying the war is a call for increased education. This is an old call now, because since the Drug Revolution of 1962, "education" has been promoted, legislated, and relied upon. Like the war on drugs, "education" has been shown again and again to have failed. In fact, several studies have demonstrated that drug education, sometimes called education in decision-making, has usually resulted in an increase in use. The common goal of all these educational efforts has been to prevent all illicit intoxicant use. To my knowledge, no educational program has attempted to separate use from abuse or to indicate how abuse might be avoided by means other than abstinence. Some of the presentations have been less fervid than others, but they have all inculcated the attitude that those who used any drugs at all, and of course those who got into trouble—and it was only a matter of time before the first group became the second—were social deviants and destroyers of the moral fabric of society. The centerpiece of most antidrug campaigns is an ex-addict (almost always male) who describes in graphic detail the horror of his addiction and the terrible things he did to support it. He points to himself as proof that one should never use any drug even once, because a single marijuana joint would inevitably lead to heroin addiction.

Efforts to mount an educational campaign to inform the reigning cultural majority have had a similar flavor. Television has been in the vanguard with such programs as "48 Hours on Crack Street." What is the goal of such a program? Essentially—and here I believe the producers would agree—it is to increase the viewers' perception that all drug use is bad, that the users are or have become degenerates outside the pale of ordinary society, and that we as a nation must redouble our resolve and rid ourselves of this plague. Such programs make nonusers feel more righteous and more resolved to intensify the war. A question that is rarely raised is how such a program affects users, both occasional and addicted. The effect on occasional users is complex, but in essence these programs increase their sense of having to hide their use and not to oppose the party line in public. Studies show that they are already aware of and concerned about controlling their use; certainly this sort of education does not cause them to abandon use. This casual response to educational programs is sharply contrasted by the effect of cocaine use on sports teams, advertising agencies, law firms, and stock brokerage establishments, when a member of the group, a buddy, suddenly falls apart.

As for addicts who come from the already dispossessed minorities, such "education" is further proof that they cannot hope for understanding from the institutions of the cultural majority, especially the law and the media, as clearly demonstrated in chapter 4 of Shaffer and Jones. They can only become further alienated. One of the clearest signs of the hardheartedness of our social institutions in their low investment in treatment. Although it is true that treatment is slow, is much more often maintenance than cure, and frequently fails, it is by any count enormously cost-effective. Yet for years there has been a continuing reduction in public investment in treatment for all groups, and virtually no help is available for cocaine users. That lack can be partially explained by the recent transfer of use from the middle class, whose members have insurance and can afford treatment, to those who cannot. Yet now, when it is clear that cocaine is the chief problem, treatment efforts are still paltry and poorly thought through.

The AIDS epidemic, coupled with the growing awareness that intravenous drug users (IVDUs) are primarily responsible for the spread of the HIV to the heterosexual community, has led to an increase in demand for treatment. Even in the light of the deadliness of this virus, the moral fervor that demands that treatment be done in the "right" way, that is, in the no-condoning-drug-use way, has restricted innovative programs that would offer users bleach, clean needles, or methadone on demand. The answer to the argument that the population of addicts is removed and uneducable has been given by the San Francisco program. This group sent outreach workers into the addict population with a single message: "Use Bleach and Stop the Spread of AIDS." Purposely avoiding messages about treatment, stopping drug use, or morality, they delivered a straight health message, and it seems to be working. This approach is in sharp contrast to antiAIDS programs that have attempted to induce IVDUs into treatment. That form of education tells people in trouble that unless they conform to society's desires they will fail. It is hard to imagine that people from the South Bronx, even those who think they want to stop use, will be willing to come into a system that seems to hate them. Even if they should seek and find treatment, what then? Treatment in this field is not like the treatment for pneumonia. It is the beginning of a process of social rehabilitation. Can people reenter or plan to reenter a social structure that views them as pariahs? The modicum of self-esteem that may have prompted them to seek treatment may make it impossible for them to accept the notion of treatment under current social conditions and attitudes. It is this lesson that educational proponents have so far failed to learn. They do not meet the client where the client is.

Social Policy

The first element in a coherent social policy should be education. Although this would include a form of education for the person in trouble, it would also be directed at the reigning cultural majority. The majority must know about the seriousness and the perniciousness of the problem, not just how deadly it is. They must hear about the terrible difficulty of struggling against addictions and must recognize that we are all addicts. Some of us have chosen a less dangerous and licit drug, such as coffee or tea, while others, for all sorts of social and psychological reasons, have chosen a more deadly and addictive illicit one. Above all, they must learn to differentiate use from abuse and put their money and their humane values to work against the latter. The war, the effort at zero tolerance, goes after the wrong people. Although urine testing is potentially useful in the criminal justice system, it is not useful in the work place. Urinalysis only tests for "have used" in the past, not for impairment, as the breathalyzer does for alcohol. Not only can mandatory random urinalysis interfere with civil liberties, but it costs a fortune to pick up a few cases which usually are not the ones the system is after. If workers, including airline pilots, are impaired, properly trained supervisors can detect it. I would hope supervisors would also look for the other sources of severe nervous strain and debilitation, including alcohol use, which is not picked up by urinalysis.

To pick up a ship, such as the notorious Monkey Business, carrying one twenty-eighth of a gram of marijuana, or the oceanographic vessel from Woods Hole, yielding three joints, is chiefly a symbolic gesture and a very costly one. In part, I think, the purpose of the zero tolerance symbolism is to show that the war is not all class warfare, though here again the relative bulk and easy detection of marijuana make it a ready scapegoat. It probably would be worthwhile, as the education of the majority proceeds, to make symbolic gestures in the other direction to indicate that the majority wants to make sense of the issue, be humane, and recognize human rights, without opening the floodgates by adopting legalization. For example, it has now been shown that in the states that have decriminalized (not legalized) the use of mari-juana, such as Oregon and California, the patterns of use, including its cur-rent reduction, are the same as in those states that have not decriminalized use. Why not, then, enact a federal decriminalization statute that includes a provision for a careful study of the effects of this change in policy? It would not be a cheap project, but it would be cheaper than current law-enforcement prosecution for simple possession and use. In a decade there might be solid information that would make it easier for Mr. and Mrs. Citizen to decide what would be the best way to go.

Above all, we must increase treatment capacity, improve access to treat-ment, and train and pay superior personnel. This too would be expensive, but it would be cost-effective. What would probably be harder to implement are the policy changes necessary to make access to treatment easier. These changes would require more than just the elimination of long waiting lists; they would include a variety of efforts at outreach, unheard of in a system that wants clients to start off by playing the game according to the larger society's rules. For one thing, sterile needles should be given away with the

fewest possible strings attached. Data from England and the Netherlands indicate that not only does providing needles *not* increase use or seem to condone drug use, but participating in a needle exchange program leads those
people who have made this first preliminary attempt to become engaged in
the larger social system and eventually seek out treatment. The same would
be true of the practice of supplying methadone on demand. Any procedure
that would engage the addicts, wean them away from their resentful isolation, should be encouraged. And equally important, the public must be willing to support reasonable salaries and a high level of training for personnel
staffing such sensitive spots.

Outreach should not stop there. Cocaine users, who are our chief target,
are not touched by any of these efforts. Just as we should be doing for IVDUs
and AIDS victims, so we should be sending workers, again properly trained,
onto the users' own turf. And these outreach workers *must* have more to
offer than the simplistic advice to "get treated and straighten out." If society
is to make a dent in this problem, these outreach workers should be able to
lend a sympathetic hand if the drug users try to reenter the society—not only
a society that will offer fewer harsh words but one that will put deeds behind
words by arranging special educational opportunities and job corps, physical
care, and rehabilitation programs. Such ideas are not new. In 1971 the Vera
Institute of Justice developed a supported work program that included many
of those notions and was very successful. Vera recognized that in contrast to
alcoholism, which characteristically develops later in life after its sufferers
have had a chance to learn some skills to which they may return, drug addiction starts early. Its sufferers have had little opportunity to acquire skills or,
for that matter, to learn how to work, to be on time, or to communicate with
others. The program was devised to meet the client where the client was, and
with what we know now we could succeed even better in such educational
efforts.

What is the alternative? If Congress, in its wisdom, approves the use of
the military for operations against crack gangs, will we have soldiers in flack
jackets marching into the South Bronx? One participant in a media program
has already wondered what would happen if the Air Force shot down by
mistake the first dentist who commuted in his own plane between his office
in Miami and his office in Palm Beach and had his radio off at the wrong
moment. At least it is worthwhile trying to find other, less warlike ways to
solve the problem.

These approaches do not exclude law-enforcement efforts. Both James
Q. Wilson and John Kaplan have emphasized the capacity of law enforcement to reengage people with the social system when enforcement is fair,
swift, and effective. The substantial percentage of arrests for other than drug-
related crimes in which heroin, cocaine, and occasionally PCP (in the District
of Columbia and Los Angeles) have been found in the suspect's urine indi-

cates a high level of interaction between the use of these drugs (and alcohol) and the commission of other crimes. The interaction itself is no surprise, but the high rates—72 percent in the District of Columbia, 68 percent in New York, 67 percent in Los Angeles, for an overall average in the large cities of 70 percent—are greater than imagined. The so-called J curve, which shows that a small percentage of the users of any health care system use an enormous amount of the services, is likely to operate here, too, so that a small percentage of users will commit a high percentage of the crimes. Assuming that regular urine testing is legal, it would have a place during pretrial periods and certainly during any probationary period. Years ago George Vaillant, in his studies of people released from U.S. Public Health Service hospitals, concluded that enforced parole is the best way to keep people in treatment. John Kaplan, noting the overcrowding and the poor record of the penal system, suggests short but sure incarcerations following a dirty urine.

In fact, an approach that emphasizes coerced abstinence is not so different from treatment as it might sound. Methadone, for example, acts as a form of coercion in methadone maintenance, and the drug-free programs are well known for their heavy-handed approach to constituents. In an odd way, coercion in the treatment of drug abusers makes theoretical sense, even though it does not in most other treatment situations. In contrast to alcohol users, who can get their drug anywhere, illicit drug abusers take a certain pride in their ability to hustle, survive, and maintain their habit on the street. They cohere around what Erik Erikson calls a "negative identity," and whatever self-esteem they can muster is invested in this antisocial know-how. As mentioned earlier, this source of self-esteem often prevents them from tamely submitting to the dictates of the reigning cultural outlook. They hate to admit that they can't or don't want to hack it on the street any more; giving in and asking for "help" is experienced as weakness or degradation. Being coerced into treatment saves face. "I wouldn't be here if I didn't have to" allows the program person to respond, "Of course not, but as long as you're stuck here, let's see what we can do." Such a stance works in the criminal justice system as well, but it requires greater effort.

Educating the majority to a more humane approach, indicating by a series of symbolic but real gestures that our society is willing to make real changes, beginning to deal with drug abusers in areas other than just their drug abuse, and coordinating these measures with more pragmatic and swift law enforcement—these are the elements of a social policy that could deal significantly with the drug problem. This policy will not win the war and make drug use go away. Nothing will do that. But it would be neither a surrender nor a repetition of an old, unsuccessful policy. The first step in implementing any real change in social policy is to provide solid knowledge to both professionals and the public. This book represents just such a step and does so with clarity and wisdom.

Acknowledgments

This book could not have been conceived and written without the help and assistance of many important people. We would like to thank Leslie Sauer, Candace Jones, and Rick Shaffer, who provided emotional, practical, and intellectual support throughout the development of this work. Dr. David Starkey provided special support and intellectual assistance; he deserves a distinct note of gratitude.

A note of special thanks is also extended to Dr. Daniel Levinson, whose generativity, interest, and personal time donated to this project contributed to the richness of our experience and our perspective on the natural history of human growth and development.

Drs. Ralph Mosher, Hillary Bender, Blase Gambino, Peter Gombosi, Leonard Solomon, and Norman Zinberg all were generous and influential in helping us determine the shape and scope of this book. For all that is successful about this work we owe them; for all of its shortcomings, we accept sole responsibility.

The enormous amount of clinical material that had to be reduced and organized required special help. Michelle Bowdler was influential, exceptional, and persistent in her capacity as editorial consultant during earlier drafts of this manuscript. Judy Burgholzer did a heroic job with all aspects of computer-related services. We also want to thank Diane Jenkins, David Shaffer, Nate Michaels, Tony Violanti, and the staff of Computertown for assisting us with information management and word processing. Liz Hunt, Theresa Lynch, and Sharon Stein served impeccably as reliable research assistants during different phases of this project.

Special thanks to Louise Harrington for coordinating the clinical interviews and making the cocaine quitters feel comfortable coming to our offices. Mia Child, Robin Marks, and Dr. Bob Kennedy were graciously helpful when we needed assistance with the nuts and bolts of interviewee recruitment.

We also wish to extend our thanks to the Harvard University and Andover Town Library systems. Each of these libraries provided the staff support and resources essential to this project. If there are any better library systems, we know not where to find them.

Finally, a very special thanks to those who quit cocaine and then opened their hearts and minds; they enabled us to begin to understand the process of recovery from cocaine addiction as never before.

1

From Cocaine Desperation to Quitting: An Introduction

> Someone saw Nasrudin searching for something on the ground.
> "What have you lost, Mulla?," he asked.
> "My key," said the Mulla.
> So they both went down on their knees and looked for it.
> After a time the other man asked: "Where exactly did you drop it?"
> "In my own house."
> "Then why are you looking here?"
> "There is more light here than inside my own house."
> (Shah, 1983)

This book is about human resilience. It is a study in tenacity and spirit. In it, we offer a consideration of cocaine addiction illustrated with oral histories of those people who courageously confronted one of the most mysterious and challenging forces in the universe: human impulse. The struggle between human impulse and the capacity to control it is epic. The electronic and print media are filled with stories of temptation, seduction, and submission. In this case, cocaine—the "White Lady"—is the temptress.

Instead of assuming, as many before us have, that any cocaine use inevitably leads to compulsive cocaine abuse, we have spent many years interviewing patients who reveal a pattern quite different from that popularly portrayed: "One puff of crack leads to addiction." Our patients taught us that drug use and abuse, in general, and cocaine use and abuse, in particular, often reveal patterns of waxing and waning. Sometimes these patterns alternate in violent shifts of behavior; during other times, the shifts between cocaine abstinence, cocaine use, and excessive cocaine abuse are gentle and subtle. In the pages that follow, we are going to present a wide variety of information. This material is intended primarily to be a starting point. To date, scientific, secular, and religious explanations and interventions fail to provide an adequate understanding of excessive drug use. We hope that this book will help raise consciousness and questions alike. Discovery is most often found in

---

Nothing in this book is intended to promote, condone, or encourage the use of drugs, licit or illicit.

those areas where it is least expected—that is why momentous discoveries are so very rare. If we knew where the light would illuminate "truths" and proffer discovery, than more people would look there. More often, we consider solutions and explanations that are already brightly illuminated rather than risk the search for information found only in the shadows.

Cocaine: A Problem of Desperation

Cocaine became the "champagne of drugs" in the early 1980s. The consequences of its use were occasionally tragic. Individuals with uncontrollable impulses to use cocaine often generate images of broken desolate people who have lost the essence of their humanity and reason, not to mention their relationships, families, vocations, and belongings. Some cocaine abusers outlast this image. Others do not fare as well.

In the presence of desperation engendered by drug abuse, there emerged a purposeful group of health care providers who began to specialize in drug treatment. These individuals were determined to find effective "cures" for cocaine abuse and dependence. They were people who wanted to relieve the desperation and excesses of their patients. Well-intended programs specifically for the treatment of cocaine problems began to flourish during the 1980s. Inpatient and outpatient drug treatment programs became staple units of many hospitals that had been watching their occupancy rates decline. Now, it is a rare mental health center that does not advertise comprehensive drug abuse treatment services.

Drug Treatment and Psychosurgery. If, as the popular wisdom of our time suggests, drug treatment should be mandatory for those who can no longer care for themselves because they suffer from a devastating mental "disease," then the treatment of cocaine abuse parallels the treatment of mental illness in the 1930s and 1940s. During that time, the prevailing wisdom dictated that the most effective treatment for many major mental illnesses was psychosurgery; that is, lobotomy and electrical shock treatment. Between 1948 and 1952, tens of thousands of patients were treated surgically for mental illness (Valenstein 1986). With the advent of psychotropic (mind altering) medications, this practice has all but disappeared as a treatment for mental illness. It also disappeared because clinicians began to consider psychosurgery primitive, excessively invasive, unethical, and medically clumsy.

Addictive behaviors also can be seen through dark glasses. Orford (1985) reminds us that treatments equally radical to those offered for major mental illness have been extended to the addictive behaviors: ". . . the implanting of Antabuse as a deterrent to drinking . . . , intestinal by-pass surgery and jaw-wiring in the treatment of obesity . . . , brain surgery in a case of 'compulsive gambling' . . . , and quite recently in Czechoslovakia, brain surgery in a number of cases of 'chronic alcoholism'—the rationale in this case being that 'alcoholism' indicated 'compulsive hedonism' or a pathological desire for pleasure due to an abnormality in the hypothalamus" (p. 248). One can only speculate as to how these "interventions" will be judged by society in the future.

The psychosurgery of the 1930s, 1940s and 1950s did not prosper as a consequence of a primitive dark time in the history of psychiatry. Psychosurgery was an expression of the conventional wisdom of its time. Similarly, "interventions" are a part of the prevailing wisdom of our drug treatment time. The use of cocaine interventions suggests that there is no reasonable alternative for those who are desperate about someone else's drug abuse even if the identified drug abuser is not as concerned or troubled by it. Consider the following description of the intervention process: "Intervention is a process by which the harmful, progressive, and destructive effects of chemical dependency are interrupted and the chemically dependent person is helped to stop using mood-altering chemicals and to develop new, healthier ways of coping with his or her needs and problems. It implies that the person need not be an emotional or physical wreck (or 'hit bottom') before such help can be given. There is a shorter, simpler way to define intervention: presenting reality to a person out of touch with it in a receivable way" (Johnson 1986, 61). In other words, those who conduct an intervention are confident about their reality and that the results of their act will benefit the person upon whom they intervene—the drug abuser. The drug abuser, according to this view, has lost the ability to understand or perceive these actions as helpful precisely because of his abuse.

The notion of being out of touch with reality is a consistent concern among those who assess and treat mental illness as well as addictive behavior. When excessive behavior patterns are denied and drug abuse continues in spite of adverse consequences, treatment providers raise the spectre of reality testing and psychotic denial. Betty Ford, and others less well known, have promoted the use of "interventions" for those who deny their own drug abuse problems. Endorsements of psychosurgery were equally common between 1940 and 1952. An intervention is intended to bring family, friends, and often a guiding professional together with a substance abuser in order to help her or him recognize the extent of the problem. An intervention is considered maximally successful if an individual agrees to enter an inpatient treatment program. A moderate success would be if an individual agrees to enter an outpatient program, and a slightly successful intervention would be one in which the family were to agree to a contract which, if violated, leads to treatment or jail.

Early psychosurgeons made exaggerated claims about the effectiveness of their "interventions" (Valenstein 1986). Likewise, intervention specialists in the drug field have exaggerated the efficacy of their intercessions. Consider, for example, the following: "Of the referrals we make to treatment, seven or eight out of every ten emerge successful" (Johnson 1986, 9). A scholarly review of the treatment effectiveness literature, however, concluded that ". . . follow-up success rates at 6–12 months after treatment mostly lie within the range 20–45 percent, averaging around one-third . . . When those receiving treatment have been randomly assigned to different forms of treatment, or when groups receiving different treatments have been carefully matched, the large majority of findings have been uniform, i.e., different treatments tend to produce very similar results" (Orford 1985, 249).

Bolstered by exaggerated claims, we should not be surprised that Johnson (1986) boasted, ". . . the process of intervention . . . has gained such widespread acceptance as to be practiced at virtually every economic and social level in the United States" (p. iii). The fact that intervention is practiced almost everywhere by numerous clinicians without question[1] suggests that practitioners are looking for simple solutions to admittedly difficult problems. These solutions have been guided by convention and custom; signposts such as these tend to simplify problems by focusing our gaze sharply. As a consequence, these models blind us to alternative explanations. The results are that prevailing practice is sustained and discovery is abundantly absent by contrast.

Cocaine and other drug abuse, without question, can present serious social problems. Yet, as this book will reveal, some drug abusers are resilient and—left solely to their own devices, without intervention—recover from addiction. As we will illustrate, drug use and abuse is not as desperate a predicament as it has been portrayed. It may not be necessary to intervene with those individuals who do not want help. When the notion exists that drug abuse is uncontrollable, the only viable treatment responses become rooted in an escalating cycle of desperation; under these conditions, coercion and duplicity become treatment allies. The presence of natural recovery and the history of psychosurgery should remind us that it is unnecessary to coerce unwilling patients into "treatment."

Drug Use as Predicament

In the midst of a contemporary trend to urge a drug-free America, the conventional wisdom has been to view all drugs as inherently addictive. This view suggests that all drugs quickly and automatically produce physical dependence; dependent states are thought to remove human reason and respon-

---

[1]It seems vital to examine the potential for and existence of adverse consequences associated with interventions and other coercive drug treatment tactics; however, to the best of our knowledge, these questions have not been investigated. Further, those who raise such questions have been, on some occasions, referred to as apologists for intoxicant abusers.

sibility, leaving victims helpless in the wake of a complex set of biological and psychological impulses that are out of control. This perspective has been responsible, in part, for the notion that "just one puff" of crack (a concentrated form of cocaine ready for smoking) can lead to addiction, or the maxim that "anyone who says that cocaine is not addictive, lies." Facts about cocaine use and abuse tell a different story, however: of the 10 percent of the American population estimated to have tried cocaine, 5 percent to 10 percent seem to be at risk for continued use and approximately 2.5 percent of those who have tried it become involved destructively with the substance (Abelson & Miller 1985; Clayton 1985).

Because we are dealing with an illicit substance and a questionable reporting system, it is possible to debate the accuracy of these statistics; in fact, we are willing to accept these estimates as extremely tempered (Clayton 1985). Even a conservative estimate of the extent of the cocaine abuse problem in the United States suggests that cocaine use reflects a very real social and personal predicament (Shaffer 1987), and not some pattern of mental illness. It is impossible by current scientific and lay standards to predict who will and who will not become troubled by cocaine use. Thus, any cocaine use must be considered a potentially dangerous situation, or, in other words, a predicament. Considering cocaine use as a predicament, with all its inherent dangers is a departure from the customary and widespread notion that cocaine (or other illicit drug) use reflects an underlying disease process.

Natural Cocaine Recovery

A very special group of people stands as direct evidence that drug use reflects a social, personal, and biological predicament rather than a disease. This group has been thought by many who subscribe to the orthodox drug wisdom of our time to be nonexistent. It is comprised of people who have seriously abused and become dependent on the excessive use of cocaine but managed to stop without medical or self-help treatment interventions. This finding stands in direct opposition to the notion that cocaine (or any other psychoactive drug) creates a dependence against which humans have no defense. The identification of natural recoverers is not anomalous and should not be dismissed casually. The professional literature contains significant and meaningful evidence documenting the spontaneous recovery of groups of alcoholics and narcotic addicts. These groups have much to teach those who are willing to learn. In order to learn, however, one must first believe that groups such as these exist. The present volume presents the story of just such a group of people, illustrated with their own words.

Our goal is to provide lessons about the effective struggle against impulses for those who have been less victorious in their own battle against personal impulse. When we began this project, we were interested in learning how some very significant human struggles were won and what factors characteristically were associated with the development and maintenance of impulse control.

This book is dedicated to all those people who struggle against their impulses, and on special occasions demonstrate that one can be victorious in that encounter.

The People Who Knew How to Quit: Their Cocaine-Using Patterns

The oral histories that illustrate the second part of this book were obtained from a wide variety of cocaine quitters. Their words are presented here exactly as they were spoken. For this book, we have adopted the convention of presenting oral histories by setting apart the statements from the rest of the text with quotations and no specific reference to the speaker. This style best permits us to protect the anonymity of the quitter while concurrently presenting their words with precision.

We offer the material in this book not as a scientific study of cocaine quitting but rather as direct clinical evidence that the phenomenon exists and that we can learn much from those people who know how to quit. We include a great deal of scientific information; furthermore, we are certain that more systematic scientific evidence will follow. However, there is no evidence that can change those who already have their minds set, just as there are set minds that cannot change the evidence.

All of the people interviewed for this book were volunteers. They were not remunerated in any way. Their motivation was intrinsic. The typical cocaine quitter wanted—even felt compelled—to tell us his or her story. In the section that follows, we have summarized the drug abuse characteristics of those remarkable people whose oral histories illustrate this book.

Types of Cocaine-Using Patterns

There are, perhaps, as many different types of cocaine abuse patterns as there are individual users. Some cocaine quitters[2] binge on cocaine. Others use heavy amounts of cocaine constantly throughout the day and night ("dealers' habits"). Still other cocaine quitters maintain relatively "light" use patterns. Cocaine quitters also vary according to the route and method by which they administer cocaine. For example, snorting or sniffing cocaine represents a

---

[2]Throughout this text, we refer to cocaine quitters. The notion of a cocaine quitter is specific to this text and identifies those who have successfully achieved cocaine abstinence even though they may have been cocaine abusers during previous drug episodes.

different route of administration than smoking it (for example, "freebasing" cocaine). Richard Pryor's movie *Live on Sunset Strip* depicts a man who is addicted to freebasing cocaine; Pryor describes his "pipe" calling to him—to the exclusion of everything else in his life. The multiplicity of cocaine use patterns are important because the presence of different abuse styles implies the likelihood of different quitting styles.

Heavy Cocaine Abusers. There are many variables that quantify the size and extent of a cocaine habit. These variables include: the frequency of use each week; amounts used in terms of grams or cost of cocaine per week; duration of cocaine use or the time span of cocaine use (for example, two years from start to finish) and the primary mode of administration. The case illustrations throughout this book reflect a group of cocaine users who had been abusing cocaine at least weekly. These abusers had relatively heavy cocaine histories and, therefore, were more likely to have a harder time quitting cocaine.

Frequency. Some cocaine quitters binge by doing cocaine in "runs" for several days and then not using for more extended periods of time. For example, people may binge on cocaine during the weekends and then stay away from the drug during the work week. Often the definition of "weekends" would be stretched out to include Friday and Monday. Others use relatively smaller amounts of cocaine daily while still others maintain constant intoxication throughout the day.

Amount. It is difficult to determine the precise amount of cocaine used during the heaviest episodes of a cocaine abuser's career. The cost and quantity (grams) of cocaine, however, provides a rough estimate. Approximately half of the oral histories in this book reflect cocaine quitters who used more than one thousand dollars' worth of cocaine a week. These amounts represent "dealer" habits; the heaviest users tend to be dealers as well. It is difficult to measure the size of a dealer's weekly habit because he or she does not go through middle managers and is able, therefore, to obtain cocaine at a reduced price. Furthermore, the cocaine is not "cut" or "stamped on" (no additives) and is more pure per gram than street cocaine.

The dealers in this book spent an average of fifteen hundred dollars per week on cocaine, or approximately twenty-three grams. The highest cocaine amount used was three thousand dollars or fifty-six grams per week (ingested by freebasing). For the other individuals who bought their cocaine, the average street cost was one hundred dollars a gram. The medium-level users spent an average of $350 a week or 3.8 grams, ranging from two hundred to seven hundred dollars. The lightest abusers spent less than $250 for their weekly cocaine supply. The range for this group was between two hundred and 350 dollars.

Duration. The duration of cocaine abuse varied from case to case. At least half the cocaine quitters in this book had histories of cocaine involvement that stretched decades. In fact, when long-time abusers terminated cocaine, approximately half their lives had been spent involved with the drug. Not surprisingly, cocaine dealers comprised the majority of this group. All our cocaine quitters have been abstinent for at least six months; the quitter with the longest period of cocaine abstinence stopped more than eight years ago. The average cocaine quitter included in the book has been abstinent from the drug for approximately three years.

Other Drug Experience. The oral histories that illustrate this text represent cocaine quitters who were familiar with licit and illicit drugs before their cocaine initiation. Alcohol, marijuana, caffeine, and nicotine were used by these individuals in a regular fashion; that is, these drugs were built into their lifestyle in a patterned way. It is important not to be misled, however. The regular use of alcohol, marijuana, and tobacco is not unique to cocaine abusers.

Audience and Organization

Audience

This book is intended for the reader who is interested in understanding the struggle against impulse. It is offered for those who want to learn lessons about how to change their own behavior; in addition, it is hoped that this book will raise new questions and ideas for clinicians who are thinking about how to improve treatment programs. Finally, this book should interest those who are curious about human beings—their weaknesses as well as their re-markable capacity for resilience.

Organization

This book is organized in several ways. Part 1 is a primer in cocaine, cocaine abuse, and the addictions field. Part 2 deals directly with the major question at hand: quitting cocaine. The first part of this book can be used to review the vast array of issues and concerns that influence our understanding of cocaine and how people come to engage in addictive patterns of behavior. The second part illustrates how some people become addicted to cocaine and then managed to stop these patterns.

The chapters in this book can be read in any order, though we suggest the order presented. Each chapter is self-contained. Interested readers can jump to the chapters that are of most interest to them. Following chapter 1, the introduction, Part 1 begins with a chapter devoted to essential information about cocaine, its chemical qualities, and social influences. The third chapter, Understanding Addiction, is designed for the theoretically uninitiated; it provides a sampling of the major theoretical positions offered to explain the phenomenon of addiction in general. For those well schooled in the models of addictive behavior, it may be nonessential reading. However, that chapter does offer a larger view of theoretical models that deal specifically with anomalous data and how it is ignored. The discussion might be interesting even for the experienced theorist. The fourth chapter on cocaine and the media focuses on how the media have influenced and been influenced by our perceptions of cocaine. Chapter 5, Natural Recovery, completes Part 1 and examines how people have stopped a variety of addictions (including cocaine) without treatment. It establishes the phenomenon and reviews the evidence that is currently available.

Part 2 begins with the chapter on cocaine initiation and the shift that often occurs when users become abusers. That chapter, the sixth, marks the beginning of a sequence of chapters illustrated in more depth with the oral histories of cocaine quitters. Chapter 7 describes the active quitting strategies and tactics often employed by successful quitters. Chapter 8 explores how new quitters manage to stay quit and prevent relapse. Chapter 9 summarizes the lessons that successful quitters have to offer by organizing their experiences into a model of quitting. The model is discussed and the learned lessons are then applied to other aspects of drug treatment and prevention. Finally, in an Afterword, we shift gears, step back, and discuss some of the lessons generated by a broad-based perspective on the pharmecology of intoxicant use. This viewpoint emphasizes the need to reevaluate how we think about drugs and our attempts to control them.

Part I

When your only tool is a hammer, then every problem is a nail.
—Mark Twain

2
Understanding Cocaine

This chapter will examine cocaine from a variety of perspectives: historical, biological, epidemiological, psychological, and social. It is intended to provide the reader with an overview to cocaine as a psychoactive drug as well as a psychosocial object.

Cocaine is a powerful central nervous system stimulant with a short duration of action. The pharmacologic effects vary with site and route of administration (Kauffman, Shaffer & Burglass 1985). Historically, the two most socially prevalent and approved central nervous system stimulants are tobacco and caffeine; cocaine represents another energizing drug that American society recognizes as the third most popular stimulant behind these two legal substances. Recently, cocaine use has received widespread publicity and exposure, despite its extreme cost and illegal status. According to a recent national household survey on drug abuse (NIDA 1983), cocaine has become one of America's favorite illicit substances (along with marijuana) and is considered the "Champagne Drug" of drugs. During the early and middle 1980s, cocaine carried the implicit message that "things goes better with coke."

History of Cocaine

Cocaine is derived from the coca plant. "The coca plant, Erythroxylon coca, is a bush four to six feet in height, similar to our Blackthorn" (Freud 1884/ 1974, 49). Cocaine has been used for thousands of years in the Andes and Amazon regions of South America. Dyke (1981) claims there is evidence that the Inca Indians were chewing coca leaves as far back as 2500 BC. Cocaine made its first appearance in the Western world during the nineteenth century.

The nineteenth century history of cocaine has been chronicled in detail (for example, Gay, Sheppard, Inaba & Newmeyer 1973; Dyke 1981; Grinspoon & Bakalar 1985). For our purposes, a brief review of the major historical events should suffice for a basic understanding of how this drug ascended to the position of popularity and attention that it now holds.

Cocaine had its contemporary beginnings in 1860 when a European scientist, Alfred Niermann, extracted an alkaloid from the coca plant and called it cocaine. In 1873, cocaine's anesthetic property—that is, its capacity to block sensory information—was discovered. One year later, a friend of Sigmund Freud, Carl Koller, used cocaine as an anesthetic for eye operations. Between 1884 and 1887, Freud helped to popularize the drug by writing many enthusiastic articles on cocaine; these now-classic works are entitled "Uber Coca." Freud, through self-experimentation with cocaine, was the first to describe the psychological effects of cocaine in humans.

In 1885, "the great cocaine explosion" (Gay et al. 1973, 1032) occurred. During this period, cocaine was used commercially in Europe and the United States; cocaine was put into tonics, elixirs, and wines for its medicinal and stimulating properties. Coca Cola, which removed cocaine from its list of active ingredients just after the turn of the twentieth century, was advertised as a "tonic for elderly people who tire easily" (Gay et al. 1973, 1032) or for "young persons afflicted with timidity in society" (Grinspoon & Bakalar 1985, 20).

The uninhibited use of cocaine in American products was limited in 1906 by the Food and Drug Act. In 1914, the Harrison Tax Act required that all "narcotics" (cocaine was classified as such at the time) be monitored and recorded. The Harrison Act marked the beginning of the end of America's love affair with cocaine—at least for that historical period. Dispensing cocaine was outlawed and the drug went underground. Cocaine reappeared in the 1960s when it was used mainly by American "bohemians." By 1970, patterns of cocaine use had shifted, and the drug was used once again by "White Middle America" (Gay et al. 1973, 1032).

Cocaine use has changed dramatically since the 1960s. During that time, large-scale drug experimentation took place in the American population. A broad spectrum of the society was exposed to drug use as a direct consequence of increasingly liberal sociocultural folkways and mores; in fact, there was a national climate that seemed to promote drug experimentation (Smith & Wesson 1985). The increase in cocaine use reflected a cultural revolution: the illicit use of psychoactive drugs was becoming, for better or worse, normalized. Drug use was becoming part of the American culture.

Though such drug use remains illicit, the current generation of cocaine users has not been restricted to those who, during earlier times, comprised the majority of drug users: "jazz bohemians" or "sociopathic personalities" (Zinberg 1984). As illicit psychoactive drug use became increasingly prevalent, cocaine users began to represent every type of personality, social class, and economic level. They became less deviant than their cocaine-using predecessors (Smith & Wesson 1985). By 1982, 28 percent of young adults had tried cocaine at least once (National Institute on Drug Abuse 1983/84).

Cocaine Effects

In spite of the erroneous but popular belief that each drug has the same effect on every user under diverse sets of conditions, there are many important distinctions that must be considered in order to describe the effects of cocaine. For example, it is essential to consider the confluence of physiological and psychological factors, route of drug administration, size of dose, acute and chronic effects of cocaine intoxication, occasional, habitual, or chronic use patterns, etc. (Grinspoon & Bakalar 1985). There are countless factors that interact to produce a response to drug taking. The following description, therefore, will describe a general, if not stereotypical, response to the use of cocaine. Individual experiences may differ.

The use of cocaine results in an increase of energy and mood, for example, euphoria and exhilaration. The duration of these effects ranges from twenty minutes to an hour; the most powerful subjective experiences occur within minutes and last typically only five to fifteen minutes. As a result of the powerful, subjective sense of well-being, competence, and mastery, as well as the relatively short duration of action, cocaine is one of the most powerful reinforcers available on the menu of psychoactive substances.

Interestingly, cocaine's reinforcing properties have been compared to tobacco smoking (Zinberg 1984). Cigarettes produce a very quick reaction, have a short duration of effect, and typically provide the experienced user with the much-sought-after confluence of energy (pharmacologic effect of nicotine) and relaxation (consequence of deep breathing). Tobacco and cocaine are both short-acting drugs that require frequent application in order to avoid abstinence symptoms. As a result, each of these drug experiences is practiced within a wide range of physical and emotional contexts. Consequently, both tobacco and cocaine have a powerful capacity to generate positive experiences that can lead to addictive patterns of behavior; contemporary society has not been able to control the use of either tobacco or cocaine as effectively as alcohol (Zinberg 1984). Although cigarettes can be powerful reinforcers, they still do not possess the inherent subjective reinforcing potential of cocaine or amphetamines, which are more potent (Jaffe 1985, 555).

Crack. Crack, also known as "rock," has recently become a popular form of cocaine. In this form, cocaine is administered by smoking through a pipe or similar device. Smoking rock cocaine generates a very rapid and powerful response. Simply stated, the process of converting cocaine hydrochloride, the powdered or crystal form of cocaine, to crack entails the elimination of hydrochloride through the use of baking soda or ammonia, water, and heat. This process eliminates many of the contaminants that were involved originally in the production of cocaine. The common procedures for converting cocaine hydrochloride to more potent forms (such as crack or freebase) can be very dangerous because one of the common processing methods involves ether and heat, a volatile combination, rather than baking soda and heat. In the absence of a secure working environment and strictly controlled protocols, the use of ether or other flammable material is extremely dangerous and has been responsible for countless injuries to "basers." We will discuss freebase and cocaine smoking in more detail later.

The strategies to market crack illegally have been as cleverly devised as any Madison Avenue product promotion. Crack is precooked, sold in ready-to-use packages and costs between five and ten dollars for one to two doses. This product form no longer requires the more expensive preparation protocol that was responsible for extremely high cocaine prices. Consequently, as prices have moved lower, cocaine costs no longer serve as a source of external control that limit its availability to the wealthy few. Instead, crack effectively has found a way around the "price barrier." Crack has been marketed and sold like a fast food product: it is relatively consistent in quality, portable, easy to access, and affordable to most consumers. Like a "Big Mac," crack is precooked, prepackaged, relatively inexpensive, and always available in major cities. Newsweek (Merganthau, Greenberg, Murr, Miller & Raine 1986) reported that some ice cream trucks in New York City have been selling crack along with ice cream. These franchises have been called "cop and shop."

Crack looks like candle slivers and is smoked in a pipe or cigarette paper. Presumably, crack got its name from the crackling sound generated by the burning bicarbonate. Because crack is smoked, it provides an almost instant "rush" as it passes through the blood-brain barrier in approximately six seconds (NIDA 1986b, 1986c). Crack highs are "higher" than intranasally or orally ingested cocaine and its lows (cocaine "crash" or "blues") are lower. Crack encourages the user to reapply cocaine dosages more often because of the drug's brief duration of action; furthermore, the withdrawal process or crash can be temporarily staved off with another dose.

The problems associated with cocaine smoking cluster around four major factors: (a) the rapid delivery system that produces almost instant intoxication, (b) lower costs, (c) a general increase in cocaine purity, and (d) the ease with which crack can be prepared. These elements have been responsible for the emergence of crack as a very popular street form of cocaine. These influences also have increased crack's capacity to produce adverse physical reactions. Finally, David Smith, founder of the Haight-Ashbury Free Medical Clinic of San Francisco, speculates that crack availability has lowered the age of first cocaine use, and, therefore, increased the incidence of adolescent cocaine addiction (Smith 1986).

Freebase and Cocaine Smoking. Cocaine freebase is extracted from street co-caine (cocaine hydrochloride) through a variety of methods. Each method separates the psychoactive cocaine ingredient from the chemical base that serves as its conduit; hence, the name freebase. Cocaine hydrochloride, paste, and freebase have all been smoked. Siegel (1982) published the most thor-ough account of cocaine smoking to date. His work, which is considered classic, includes a history of cocaine smoking. A brief summary of these high-lights is included for the interested reader.

According to Siegel (1982) cocaine smoking was observed first during the turn of the twentieth century; however, this phenomenon gained popu-larity during the 1970s and 1980s. This activity was first observed in 1885 when Dr. F. E. Stewart smoked coca-leaf cigars in Philadelphia. Between 1885 and 1906, the American patent medicine industry promoted the smok-ing of coca leaves, cigars, cheroots, and cigarettes. Various subcultural groups have been considered the first cocaine hydrochloride smokers in America dur-ing the 1950s. In Peru, during 1971, the first patient description of coca-paste smoking occurred. In 1974, the first documented account of cocaine freebase smoking in California was observed and the first hospital admission for this behavior was recorded. In 1976, the first scientific papers about cocaine smoking were published. Between 1979 and 1980, cocaine smoking para-phernalia was advertised, clinical health warnings published, public hearings conducted, and dire warnings of a cocaine smoking epidemic forecast.

Factors Leading to Increased Cocaine Use

Norman Zinberg (1984) organized the multideterminants of drug effects into three interactive categories: *set, setting,* and *substance.* These concepts have proved extremely useful to addiction treatment specialists, theorists, and re-searchers. A brief introduction to these concepts is presented here; a more detailed discussion of these factors will be presented later in the afterword on pharmecology.

"Set" represents the personality and expectations of the drug user; "set-ting" consists of the social and cultural milieu that surrounds the drug and drug user; and "substance" refers to the pharmacological and physiological characteristics of the drug. The confluence of set, setting, and substance is responsible for the effects achieved by a user (for example, mood, level of euphoria or dysphoria) as well as his or her overall attitude toward the drug experience. Although the emergence of crack represents a meaningful shift in the form of cocaine, and users have come to think about cocaine in ways quite different from their counterparts of only a decade ago, the most signif-icant historical change influencing cocaine effects is the shifting social environment or cocaine "setting." Economic and social trends have been responsible for cocaine's increased appeal to more considerable groups of users. In the following sections, we will examine the interactive evolution of cocaine's "substance" and "setting."

Evolving Cocaine Use: Substance and Setting. The preparation and purchase of street cocaine is not what one might consider an "exact science." Drug dealers mix look-a-like additives into pure cocaine as a means of increasing their profits. In 1981, the purity of cocaine was approximately 27 percent. More recently, the purity of street cocaine has increased to between 40 percent and 70 percent (1-800-COCAINE 1985). In addition to more pure concentrations of cocaine, the overall price of the drug has decreased as well. "The world cocaine glut has brought prices down—a gram of cocaine now sells for about $50 in New York City—less than an ounce of marijuana. . . ." (Beck 1985, 23). In terms of accessibility, users and abusers have reported that cocaine is significantly easier to obtain than marijuana (a drug considered by many to be less socially deviant). As a consequence of these social and economic developments, expense and accessibility no longer serve as important social factors that naturally limit the use and abuse of cocaine.

As "crack" became a popular form of cocaine, it influenced the drug-using patterns of many. Crack is more affordable than traditionally prepared cocaine. To younger, less affluent consumers it was (and is) perceived as an attractive and interesting alternative. As a result of its diminished cost and increased availability, cocaine is being used at an earlier age than ever before (Gold 1986). Younger populations tend to become involved compulsively with psychoactive drugs more rapidly than older cocaine users, even if the drugs are applied using less potent forms of administration (Smith 1986).

Before crack became popular, the most common way to use cocaine involved sniffing or "snorting." With the emergence of crack, the most frequent route of administration became smoking. Smoked cocaine, as opposed to nasally sniffed cocaine, enters the bloodstream more rapidly, and as a consequence, produces a more intense sense of intoxication. Smoked cocaine enters the bloodstream in eight seconds: this is at least equal to (or even more rapid than) intravenous administration (Smith 1986). Crack not only enters the central nervous system more quickly than powdered cocaine but also enters the bloodstream in more concentrated amounts. Preliminary data (for example, Siegel 1982) indicates that the time period between first use of cocaine via smoke inhalation to compulsive use is shorter than the time period for nasal or oral administration of cocaine to compulsive patterns of abuse.

The route of administration of any drug may be more important than the quantity and purity of the drug used in terms of determining its effect and potential for abuse. Thus, a person's response to any drug may be more the result of the rate that the drug enters the bloodstream rather than the absolute concentration of the drug in the bloodstream at any particular moment.

With the growing acceptance, accessibility, and more potent forms of administration, there has been a corresponding increase in cocaine morbidity and mortality. Further, increasing numbers of abusers are seeking treatment for their cocaine-related problems. Emergency rooms are reporting increased visits because of adverse cocaine reactions. Psychiatric, physical, vocational, and social complications are frequent correlates of cocaine abuse. Some examples of the psychological, medical, and social consequences of cocaine abuse are the development of (1) a toxic cocaine psychosis that mimics major thought disturbances, (2) medical problems including respiratory and circulatory difficulties (such as heart attacks), and (3) a loss of or threat to job or career functioning and family stability.

Although the number of cocaine-related and cocaine-abuse deaths has risen in this past few years in the United States, this figure pales in comparison with alcohol- or tobacco-related deaths. The deaths of prominent athletes and celebrities (such as Len Bias and John Belushi) precipitated extensive media coverage and, some would argue, an exaggerated sense of cocaine's presence. The inflated fear and anxiety stimulated by unprecedented media coverage also influenced individuals to seek treatment for their cocaine use. In the sections that follow, we will examine the prevalence of cocaine use and abuse. In addition, we will provide a context within which cocaine use can be compared with other drugs.

Cocaine Use Prevalence

Cocaine use is extensive in the United States. Cocaine has penetrated "mainstream" America. Its popularity is evident by the acceptance of its usage among large segments of the population. The National Institute on Drug Abuse (NIDA) produces the most representative data for national norms on drug use prevalence. NIDA's latest National Household Survey on Drug Abuse in the United States was based on data obtained between 1974 and 1982 (NIDA 1983)[1] in a survey consisting of 5,624 randomly selected American citizens. Therefore, for the most up-to-date cocaine use patterns, a variety of research data from different sources will be reported as well as displayed in table format. In spite of the efforts of many researchers at NIDA and elsewhere, it is important for the reader to remember that it is difficult to estimate with great precision the current cocaine-use rates because of co-

---

[1]Although NIDA has recently completed another household survey, as this book goes to press, the data have not yet been analyzed or made available to the public.

caine's illegal status. Furthermore, estimates of cocaine-using patterns can be confusing and controversial depending on the source of the data. For example, according to the 1982 National Household Survey, an estimated 21.6 million people used cocaine at least once, 10 million people used cocaine in the last twelve months and 4.2 million people used cocaine one or more times in the last month (Abelson & Miller 1985). Data derived from 1-800-COCAINE[2], a cocaine helpline and research facility in New Jersey, reflect an even higher rate of cocaine use among the population. Instead of the 21.6 million figure given above, 1-800-COCAINE increased its estimate of those who have used cocaine at least once to 25 million people. In other words, this evaluation claims that one out of every ten Americans has tried cocaine (Gold 1986, 1). This estimate of cocaine use prevalence suggests that the percentage of Americans who have tried cocaine at least once equals the entire population of Canada (currently 25.3 million) (Paxton 1987). It has been calculated that between three thousand (Gold 1986) and five thousand (NIDA 1986b) new users try cocaine each day in the United States. Of the 25 million people who have tried cocaine at least once in their lives, about 1 million are judged to be compulsive cocaine abusers (Gold 1983, 2).

Clayton (1985, 13) claims there is an "underestimation" of persons who are thought to be cocaine dependent. He hypothesizes that 2.5 percent of the 21.6 million Americans judged by NIDA to have tried cocaine progress from experimental drug use to abuse. Clayton's calculation of abusers may be conservative given the recent decrease in cocaine prices, increase in cocaine purity, and influx of "crack" introduced and marketed in affordable units to the public.

Figure 2–1 compares NIDA's population estimates of cocaine prevalence data with statistics obtained from 1-800-COCAINE.

As we mentioned earlier, smoking cocaine tends to be more potent, both physically and psychologically, than sniffing or snorting. It also serves as a more potent reinforcer. Therefore, cocaine smoking presents greater physical and psychological risks to the user than cocaine sniffing. This higher risk of dependence and addiction has been confirmed by hotline data gathered in May 1986 by another 1-800-COCAINE random survey. This survey found that one-third of the 458 consecutive callers, who were twenty years old and older, were "crack" involved. These callers asked for information or help in overcoming crack-related problems. Eighty-one percent of them had snorted cocaine and said their use rapidly escalated after using crack. Fifty-four percent reported a "love at first smoke" phenomenon with this form of cocaine (Gold 1986).

The widespread use of cocaine is also demonstrated by data that revealed

---

[2]This toll-free telephone hotline has received as many as twelve hundred callers a day requesting information and assistance regarding cocaine.

NIDA:

Lifetime Prevalence	21.6 million
Used in Last Year	10.0 million
Used in Last Month	4.2 million
Compulsive Users	≤1.0 million
Projected New Users Per Day	5,000

Source: Total Population from Household Survey (1972–1982)

1-800-COCAINE Hotline

Lifetime Prevalence	25.0 million
Used in Last Year	———
Used in Last Month	4–5.0 million
Compulsive Users	≤1.0 million
Projected New Users Per Day	3,000

Source: 1-800-COCAINE Estimates (1986)

Figure 2–1. Comparison Between the National Institute on Drug Abuse's Household Survey/and the 1-800-COCAINE National Hotline Survey

that approximately 30 percent of all graduating high-school seniors had tried cocaine (Johnston, O'Malley & Bachman 1986). This cocaine-use pattern was identified in spite of the concurrent finding that high school and college students, as well as other young adults, demonstrated an overall *decrease* in drug-using patterns (Johnston et al. 1986).

Cocaine Use Demographics. Cocaine use is more common among whites than nonwhites and is predominately a male activity. For example, in the 1982 Household Survey, nearly 70 percent of those questioned who had ever used cocaine or used it in the last twelve months were male (NIDA 1986e, 2). Interestingly, this gender gap is fading and women are catching up with men (Gold 1984, 1–3; Ray & Braude 1986). For both sexes, drug use is more common within urban areas on the East and West coasts than in other parts of the United States.

Cocaine Emergencies and Deaths. Statistics available from NIDA's Drug Abuse Warning Network (DAWN) reveal recent trends in drug-related emergencies and deaths. DAWN collects data from emergency rooms in twenty-one metropolitan areas. For example, Boston, Massachusetts has thirty-eight emergency rooms and thirty of them participate with the DAWN program (NIDA 1986a). The number of cocaine-related emergencies has increased from approximately three thousand to ten thousand in the past four years (NIDA 1986e). In 1977, fewer than one percent of the cocaine-related emergencies were caused by smoking the drug. Recently collected data suggest that

Table 2–1
Cocaine Abuse Deaths and Cocaine-Related Deaths Reported by the Drug Abuse Network (DAWN) for 1981–1984

	1981	*1982*	*1983*	*1984*
Cocaine–Related Deaths:	195	217	323	578
Cocaine–Abuse Deaths:	——	115	——	294

14.3 percent of those who visited the emergency room in 1986 for cocaine-related problems reported smoking as their primary route of administration (NIDA 1986e, 4).

Mortality rates for cocaine-abuse deaths and cocaine-related deaths are collected by medical examiners in metropolitan cities in the United States. The difference between a drug-abuse death and a drug-related death can be understood as follows: "A drug-abuse death is any death involving a drug 'overdose' where usually a toxic level is found or suspected. A drug-related death is any death where the drug usage is a contributory factor, but not the sole cause (for example, accidents, diseased state, withdrawal syndrome, etc.); causation of death by the drug is not implied" (NIDA 1986a, 82). In 1984, 578 cocaine-related deaths were reported; in 1981, 195 deaths were recorded. Similarly, between 1982 and 1984, cocaine-abuse deaths have more than doubled, increasing from 115 to 294, respectively. These data do not include New York City, which would increase this mortality index still further (NIDA 1986a, 1986e). Table 2–1 provides a summary of the types of cocaine deaths that occurred between 1981 and 1984.

Prevalence of Cocaine Abuse. Cocaine use tends to begin during young adulthood (that is, eighteen to twenty-five years old), a transitional time when individuals must negotiate the move from adolescence to entry and participation in the social tasks of adulthood. Although cocaine is a drug that appeals to a wide age-range, most abusers are between the ages of twenty-five and forty. The average cocaine abuser is approximately thirty years old.

As we noted earlier, 2.5 percent to 5 percent of the total population of people who try cocaine become cocaine abusers (Clayton 1985). If we accept the 5 percent value to represent the rate of cocaine abuse, we find an incidence that is similar to alcohol abuse: ". . . 69 percent of the adult population (eighteen and over), or nearly 102 million Americans, drink more or less regularly [and] only 5 to 10 percent overdo it. . . ." (Koffend 1979, cited in Zinberg & Bean 1981, 1). Similarly, there are 5 million occasional heroin users and five hundred thousand compulsive heroin abusers (Trebach 1982). Such estimates of abuse potential to particular drugs suggest that 5 percent to 10 percent of the general population tends to develop pathological abuse patterns regardless of the type of drug involved (except for nicotine). As a rule, the vast majority of the population manages to avoid compulsive drug use.

Cocaine and Secondary Drug Use

Cocaine use and abuse is often associated with secondary drug abuse and/or polydrug abuse (Chitwood 1985, 116–117; Burglass 1983, 1985). Drugs often used in combination with cocaine include alcohol and other sedative-hypnotics (drugs that depress the central nervous system), marijuana, cigarettes, and caffeine. These "secondary" drugs function to regulate—some would argue that they medicate—the side effects of cocaine. For instance, the use of alcohol counteracts or "takes the edge off" the stimulating effects of cocaine so that needed sleep is possible. Sedatives are also used to soften the cocaine "crash" or the withdrawal symptoms. It is safe to conclude that a person who abuses cocaine exclusively is the exception rather than the rule; cocaine abusers commonly use a host of drugs as adjuncts to their primary drug—cocaine. Thus, the process of multiple simultaneous drug abuse with cocaine is not unusual because the use of one drug (such as cocaine) creates a disequilibrium within the pharmacological ecosystem (also known as Pharmecology; see the Afterword) of the individual user and the resulting imbalance stimulates other drug seeking behavior.

This phenomenon of pharmecology can be illustrated by considering the delicately balanced ecosystems of the natural environment. For example, when pesticides are used to depopulate a geographic area of a particular insect, its prey—without a natural enemy—multiply without regulation and overpopulate the region. Consequently, another insecticide is often implemented to limit the side effects of the first pesticide application. The introduction of one event, then, can produce effects that ripple throughout an ecosystem. Similarly, cocaine can create a chemical imbalance leading to the use of a second drug to offset the effects of the first. The recognition that compulsive cocaine abusers may be dependent on secondary drugs is crucial. For example, in terms of detoxification treatment, cocaine withdrawal is usually not life-threatening and typically occurs on an outpatient basis. If a secondary dependence to sedative-hypnotics (such as alcohol) is present, however, the withdrawal syndrome can be life-threatening. These detoxifications require careful monitoring and ordinarily should be accomplished in an inpatient medical facility.

Cocaine and alcohol can present a particularly lethal combination, especially if a user is driving under their interactive influence. Simultaneously ingesting cocaine and alcohol allows the user to drink beyond her or his normal capacity and masks the drunken effects of the alcohol. Unfortunately, the effects of cocaine wear off more rapidly than the intoxicating effects of alcohol, leaving the user extremely drunk. When behind the wheel of a car, intoxicant users in general, and polydrug users in particular, risk their lives and the lives of others.

Putting the Cocaine Problem in Perspective

Although the media provide frequent and spacious coverage of cocaine and related stories, it is important to keep this particular drug problem in perspective. Even though the past decade has shown an overall decrease of drug taking (except for cocaine), drug use in America is still relatively high. Americans use a variety of drugs, alone and in combination with others (such as cigarettes, caffeine, alcohol, sedatives, marijuana, cocaine). In the sections that follow, we will examine two of the legal drugs of abuse that contribute to America's drug problems.

Alcohol. Licit or legal drugs are still the great American killers. For example, there are at least 250,000 alcohol-related deaths a year (Seixas 1981) and more than 13 million alcoholics and problem drinkers (Wisotsky 1986). Annually, half of all arrests (5.5 million) are associated with alcohol use; two-thirds of all assaults involve alcohol; half of the murders in America and one-third of all suicides are committed under the influence of alcohol (Berger 1981). Alcohol contributes to a deregulation or disinhibition of the aggressive and sexual drives; its use has been associated often with incest and violence. It has been estimated that half of all incest victims come from alcoholic homes (Black 1982).

Like other drug abuse, alcohol abuse affects relatives, friends, and workers of the alcoholic: "More than 75 million Americans are affected by the disease, and it cost this country more than $120 billion in 1983" (Gravitz 1985, 3). The damaging effects on the family from excessive alcohol use are so profound that there is a demand for therapy/recovery groups specifically tailored to adult children of alcoholics (ACOA). Mothers Against Drunk Drivers (MADD) and the Massachusetts Governor's Highway Safety Bureau report that one of every two traffic deaths in the United States is caused by a drunk driver. Drunk drivers killed twenty-six thousand people in 1986. Finally, according to the Eunice Kennedy Shriver Center in Waltham, Mass., alcohol use/abuse during pregnancy (which is responsible for producing the Fetal Alcohol Syndrome) is one of the leading causes of mental retardation.

Tobacco. Each year in this country the mortality rate associated with tobacco is estimated to be between 250,000 and 350,000. Currently, the National Cancer Institute says that 25 percent to 30 percent of Americans are still smoking—approximately 56 million people as of December 11, 1986. The cardiovascular and cancer-related health hazards associated with smoking are well documented and readers interested in these health issues are encouraged to contact their local heart and lung associations for more detailed information.

In sum, of the five hundred to six hundred cocaine-related deaths that occurred in 1984, a large majority of deaths involved cocaine use in combination with other drugs. This figure still represents a small sum compared to alcohol- and tobacco-related losses. The mortality associated with cocaine can be best understood within the context of the variety of other drugs that are used regularly.

Media Hysteria and Cocaine

From all available accounts, it does appear that compulsive drug use is a serious problem for this country. Isolating one drug like cocaine, however, and designating it as the most dangerous drug, is misleading. This nation seems to have a hunger and thirst for multiple drug and alcohol use. Advertising that floods consumers with messages that "we haven't got time for the pain" stimulate and maintain drug—particularly analgesic—craving. Over-the-counter drugs are also advertised and abused heavily.

To suggest that one drug is responsible for "society's drug problem" is a curious form of scapegoating. Cocaine has become the receptacle for ". . . a murky cloud of symbolically projected passions" (Grinspoon & Bakalar 1985, 239). A Newsweek editor, Tony Fuller, said in an interview that ". . . crack was the biggest story since Vietnam" (Gladwell 1986, 10). The comparison between crack and the Vietnam War is strangely disproportionate, and reflects the "hysteria" surrounding the cocaine issue. Although we recognize the tragedy associated with even a single cocaine-related death, the number of cocaine deaths in this country is minuscule when compared to the fifty thousand Americans killed during the Vietnam war. Add to this the number of Vietnamese and Cambodians killed during the war and the evidence is overwhelming: any comparison between crack and Vietnam is unwarranted, inappropriate, insulting, misleading, and irrelevant.

In spite of the attention cast upon cocaine, tobacco and alcohol are still the most widespread drug problems in this country. More people die each year from tobacco-related problems than the number of people in total that die from all other drug abuse combined. Alcohol abuse continues at an enormous rate. "Although alcohol is now sometimes rhetorically and correctly proclaimed to be the biggest drug problem of all, practically no one acts on this assumption. The alcohol problem has proved uncontainable by the combined powers of law and medicine, but physicians should at least consider what it implies about the disproportionate attention and emotional fervor devoted to controlling other drugs. Moderate use of alcohol, unlike moderate use of cocaine and other drugs, has fallen into the category of fun rather than vice or crime. . . ." (Grinspoon et al. 1985, 264–265). Unfortunately, the media's tendency to exclusively focus on cocaine has obscured the total drug picture by sensationalizing the illicit and headlining the "sexier" drug crack instead of covering the more complex and less exciting issues of tobacco, alcohol, and the addictions in general. ". . . the press has overdosed on the drug issue of cocaine and crack" (Gladwell 1986, 11).

The topic of media hype and hysteria is so important that we have dedicated an entire chapter to it. A more detailed account of the media's role in our perception of drug use and abuse can be found in chapter 4 on cocaine and the media.

Cocaine Abuse as a Human Problem

Loss of Control. In general, most people who experiment with cocaine do not cross the line—the difficult-to-specify line—that separates recreational, experimental use from compulsive, dependent use. As we stated earlier, between 2.5 percent and 5 percent of cocaine users are estimated to develop problematic cocaine use patterns. This means approximately one million people struggle against intense impulses to use cocaine; these feelings of loss of control are often accompanied by an inability to discontinue the use of cocaine, even though the experience is associated with adverse consequences.

Health Consequences. The chronic cocaine abuser commonly reports problems with sleep, fatigue, headaches, coughing, and nosebleeds (Gold, Washton & Dackis 1985, 135). More adverse physical/overdose effects of cocaine range from elevated blood pressure and increased pulse rate to episodes of unconsciousness, seizures, strokes, convulsions, and possibly fatal reactions such as circulatory arrest, respiratory arrest, and cardiac toxicity (Goodman & Gilman 1985; Isner et al. 1986).

The adverse psychological effects of chronic cocaine abuse include a response range that spans from relatively benign common reactions to more life-threatening events. Gold et al. (1985) studied five hundred cocaine abusers and found that over 80 percent of them complained of depression, anxiety, and irritability. Over 60 percent reported apathy, paranoia, and difficulty concentrating, and 50 percent or more described problems with memory, sexual interest, and anxiety. The progressive stages of cocaine abuse typically begin with euphoria, leading over time to dysphoria, paranoia, and cocaine psychosis (Post 1975). The psychiatric signs and symptoms associated with the latter stages can also include depression, delusional thinking, and acute suicidal or homicidal thoughts; after the individual ceases to use the substance, these signs usually remit within several days.

Cocaine and AIDS. Cocaine has often been used as an aphrodisiac. Male drug users have reported the experience of prolonged sexual activity while under the influence of cocaine; in addition, many users relate a heightened sense of sensuality and tactile sensitivity. Given the omnipresent threat of AIDS in contemporary society, the relationship between cocaine and AIDS deserves detailed attention. A full description of this relationship is beyond the scope and purpose of this book; however, some of the key factors will be considered.

The use of cocaine at low dose levels can serve to stimulate and disinhibit socially sanctioned behaviors. For example, individuals who are consistently careful to practice "safe sex" may concede these behaviors when under the influence of cocaine. Sexual contact is not an altogether uncommon consequence of sharing cocaine in a social setting. Compromised sexual practices among partners who are less than careful increases their chances of contracting the AIDS virus. This risk is exacerbated further because some cocaine users apply this drug, as well as other drugs, intravenously. If needles are shared, the risk of infection from the AIDS virus is significant. Finally, if users continue to ingest cocaine at moderate to high dose levels, they risk the onset of a cocaine-induced psychosis (a toxic reaction). This experience can jeopardize the user's judgment entirely; if dirty needle use and/or "unsafe" sexual practices result, the outcome may be lethal.

The presence of psychosis among cocaine abusers reveals another complicated connection between cocaine and AIDS. Shaffer & Costikyan (1988) were the first to identify the diagnostic dilemma faced by clinicians who work with cocaine-involved drug abusers. Recent findings (for example Faulstich 1987; Perry & Jacobsen 1986) reveal that neuropsychiatric complications may appear as manifestations of AIDS, ARC, or direct central nervous system involvement of the AIDS virus (HIV) itself. These complications may predate seropositivity for HIV and mimic many functional psychiatric disorders ranging from mild chronic dysphoria to acute psychosis. Early symptoms of such complications include many of the same experiences associated with advanced cocaine psychosis: depression, impaired memory, agitation, panic attacks, anorexia, tachycardia, seizures, impaired concentration, insomnia, delusional and/or disoriented thinking, and hallucinations (Faulstich 1987). In short, HIV psychiatric impairment that *predates* seropositivity can produce symptoms similar to those observed among chronic high-level cocaine abusers.

Perry & Jacobsen (1986) contend that organicity (that is, impairment of the central nervous system) should be suspected in the mental changes of all AIDS and ARC patients. Marmor, Des Jarlais, Freidman, Lyden & El-Sadr (1984) reported data about the seroepidemiology of AIDS among New York intravenous drug abusers. They found that 58 percent of patients entering a drug detoxification program had antibodies to the core protein of lymphadenopathy associated virus (LAV/HIV). Although lower rates of seropositivity may be found elsewhere, HIV is expected to be found in an increasing number of intravenous drug abusers (Knox 1987). The complications in accurately distinguishing between and diagnosing both AIDS-related dementia and cocaine psychosis converge to complicate an assessment process already clouded by perceptual distortion (countertransference) (Shaffer & Costikyan 1988; Sargent, Shaffer & Lawford 1986).

Cocaine Abuse as a Social Problem

Social and Interpersonal Consequences. For those struggling against their own impulses to use, chronic cocaine abuse can be devastating. For these individuals, cocaine abuse can progress to a point where every aspect of one's life is profoundly and negatively affected. The dysfunctional cocaine abuser can experience interpersonal disruption and loss, financial and occupational ruin, adverse physical and psychological effects, and severe legal ramifications. Interpersonally, the compulsive cocaine abuser often alienates and/or loses her or his spouse, children, family, and established friendships. In order to maintain a cocaine habit, the abuser may be forced to lie, conceal, and steal from family and intimates. Financially, the individual may be ruined by the costly habit. In terms of occupation, the addict may lose her or his job or career, professional status, and license.

Cocaine and the Job. Eventually, chronic and excessive cocaine abuse can remove some people from the work force. Perhaps more troubling than the unemployment caused by cocaine abuse are the problems of concurrent drug abuse while employed. This issue raises additional social and ethical concerns. Researchers at the 1-800-COCAINE hotline surveyed drug use at the workplace in March 1985. The survey took place over a six-week period during which 227 subjects were interviewed randomly. Ninety-two percent of the subjects reported that they had been under the influence of a drug at some point during work; forty-five percent stated the use of drugs at work on a weekly basis. Eighty-three percent reported that cocaine was their drug of choice. Sixty-four percent said they thought their work suffered because of drugs and 18 percent cited on-the-job accidents as a consequence of drug use.

To summarize, nearly half the cocaine hotline callers reported using drugs (most often cocaine) at the work site weekly. It is reasonable to assume that some working drug-takers represent regular cocaine users as well as chronic cocaine abusers. Cocaine-impaired workers will manifest physical and psychological dysfunction at work as well as in other areas of their life.

Cocaine abusers whose occupations involve responsibility for the safety of other peoples' lives and who continue to practice their vocation under the drug's adverse effects constitute a very real social—rather than individual—problem; people other than the abuser are placed at risk. Cocaine may be more insidious than alcohol because it is odorless and, in low doses, quite invisible to the casual observer.

David Smith says that during the 1980s there has been a ten-fold increase in the number of addicted health professionals (1986). Physicians, for example, cannot afford to have memory loss and impaired cognitive function while performing in a professional capacity. Interestingly, to date, there are no established criteria for determining the range of acceptable cognitive and intellectual performance among physicians and the many assorted professionals who are responsible for the well-being of others. Without such guidelines it is difficult, if not impossible, to determine the level of disability or impairment associated with cocaine and other drug abuse. Perhaps it is time for the professional disciplines to begin the arduous task of establishing cognitive and intellectual criteria for their members.

Cocaine: Classification and Crime. Often, the general public confuses cocaine's pharmacological properties and nomenclature; for example, "Isn't cocaine a narcotic?" Why a stimulant like cocaine should be considered a narcotic appears to be the result of historical accident. In 1914, the Harrison Narcotic Act was passed by Congress mandating that everyone who produced or distributed opiates and cocaine had to register all transactions with the government (Musto 1973, 8–9). Consequently, over time, cocaine erroneously became merged into a drug classification that included narcotics.

The federal drug laws place cocaine in the schedule II category. These are defined as psychoactive substances with high abuse potential that may lead to physical or psychological dependence but clearly possess medical uses for treatment; for example, opiates and cocaine (Drug Enforcement Administration 1977). The legal penalties for possession of, or intent to distribute, cocaine are the same as those for narcotics such as heroin. Similarly, cocaine receives the same drug enforcement treatment as narcotics.

Penalties vary for cocaine possession. The criminal penalties for trafficking a schedule II drug are the following: "For narcotics (cocaine) in schedule I and II, a first offense is punishable by up to 15 years in prison and up to a $25,000 fine. . . . It must be emphasized that possession for one's own use of any controlled substance is always a misdemeanor on the first offense, punishable by one year in jail and up to a $5,000 fine" (Drug Enforcement Administration 1977, 32).

Cocaine and Government. The fall season of 1986 saw the initiation of President Reagan's "War on Drugs" (Thomas 1986). The consequent public concern mounted to the point where suggestions were made in the Senate that the death penalty be applied to drug dealers.

Cocaine's classification as an illicit drug has contributed to—some would argue created—criminal activities ranging from street crime to international drug trafficking, murder, violence, and political corruption. "There was a time when cocaine was seen as relatively harmless compared to heroin. No more. The issue is not simply one of measuring the danger to the health of individual drug abusers, but of correcting a threat to the welfare of entire governments" (Anderson et al. 1985, 18).

Gold (1983, 2) says that each year fifty tons of cocaine enter the United States and yield $25 billion to $30 billion in business. Clayton (1985, 14) posits that the cocaine industry is valued at an even higher estimate of $50 billion to $70 billion a year. Regardless of the exact figures, it is safe to conclude that cocaine is big business.

There was a sudden increase in murders from 1985 to 1986 and some criminologists consider that this increase might have been caused by drug violence; in particular, they attribute this increase to cocaine-related activities. For example, New York City had 1,384 deaths in 1985 and 1,461 in 1986; Boston had 87 homicides in 1985 and 106 in 1986 (Johnson, Lubenow, Miller, Gonzalez & Carroll 1987). The cause of the violence appears to be the result of illegal drug trafficking rather than adverse effects stemming from the drug's pharmacological properties.

Cocaine & Politics: Wars on Drugs, Drug Wars, and Drugs for War

Drug abuse is a strange but common pattern of human behavior. Political pundits might argue similarly about the nature of politics. It is easy for politicians and governments to take the position that drugs are bad and people should treat these substances with great respect and care. Things are not always as they seem, however. For example, governments with a stated purpose of protecting the welfare of their citizens are widely considered to be against drug abuse and drug trafficking. Governments, as we will see, sometimes compromise the safety of their citizens when political priorities change.

Any serious discussion about addiction, in general, and drug abuse, in particular, must include an examination of the political forces that have influenced the field.[3] Musto (1973), for example, recognized that narcotics control is more than a medical or legal problem; it is a political concern. The political influences affecting the use and abuse of cocaine cover such an extraordinary range of topics that a complete analysis of these factors is beyond

---

[3]Readers interested in a classic and comprehensive treatment of narcotics control in the United States should see Musto (1973).

the scope of this book. A brief discussion of the relationships among the war on drugs, drug wars, and drugs for war is warranted, however.

The War on Drugs. Wars against the use and trading of illicit drugs have been launched several times during the twentieth century. These wars on drugs remind us of the tendency to anthropomorphize. We wage war against drugs as if *they* were *motivated* to *seduce* humans and then, following the seduction, forcibly *take* away our freedom and material belongings. Drugs, however, are inert substances without human motives. Cocaine cannot be held responsible for an Orwellian future where human behavior is restricted by external forces. More accurately, our relationship with drugs reflects a Huxleyan *Brave New World* where, for a variety of complicated reasons, people willingly subscribe to and endorse their influence.

Absent an understanding of this distinction, wars against drugs are likely to continue with no noticeable effect on the ingestion of psychoactive substances around the world with one exception: when the availability of one drug is restricted, another less popular drug will ascend. For example, when the United States government limited the availability of marijuana, cocaine became more available; when powdered cocaine was being sniffed out by law enforcement officers, dealers were making the transition to rock cocaine, which proved easier to transport and more difficult to detect. Rather than fight against a substance that is essentially lifeless, it may be more useful to come to some understanding of the human desires and motives that affect cocaine. It may prove more fruitful to make peace with cocaine instead of war. As the following accounts depict, undertaking a war against cocaine (McDonald 1986) may not be as straightforward as it seems.

Drug Wars. We often think of wars against drugs. Sometimes, however, attempts to restrict illicit drug trade actually lead to civil war. Consider the following: "Enrique Camarena Salazar had just left the U.S. Consulate in Guadalajara to keep a lunch date with his wife. As he walked away from the building, the 37-year-old U.S. drug-enforcement agent was intercepted by four gunmen who shoved him into a getaway car and rapidly drove away. Three hours later, Alfredo Zavala Avelar, a Mexican pilot who flew occasional missions for the American Drug Enforcement Administration, set off to drive home from the airport. He, too, was snatched at gunpoint. Neither man has been seen since" (Anderson et al. 1985, 14). United States drug enforcement agents have been getting caught between drug lords and war lords. They have become objects both of those who would disrupt and those who would maintain the international trafficking of cocaine.

United States drug agents are not the only ones caught in a drug war predicament; civilians are as well. For example, in January 1985, ". . . in the wake of the extradition of four suspected Colombian drug figures to the

United States, Colombia was suddenly a very dangerous place for Americans. The powerful Colombian cocaine mafia had already threatened to kill five U.S. citizens for every alleged drug trafficker extradited, and intelligence sources indicated that they even planned to go after the children of American diplomats. That report sparked the evacuation last week of all the children— and many spouses—of U.S. government personnel. . . . Given their immense wealth and private armies, the cocaine kingpins seem almost as powerful as the Colombian government. That is precisely why the government believes that the war against them must go on" (Drugs and a U.S. Pullout 1985, 37). The relationships among governments, government officials, and cocaine-dealing groups is fascinating and complex.

Ryser & Javetski (1986) revealed that several South American governments may be dependent economically upon their cocaine trade. If these countries accept military and financial aid from the United States, they risk violence in the streets, political protestations, and labor union opposition. If these countries do not accept outside assistance, Ryser & Javetski suggest that they may not be able to recover from their cocaine dependence. This situation is complicated further because of the strings attached to United States foreign aid dollars. For example, the $58-million financial aid package provided by the United States to Bolivia links the use of drug suppression money with rural development monies (Anderson et al. 1985). In other words, although the United States provides foreign aid to limit the flow of cocaine from South America, the government fails to recognize that some of these foreign countries require drug traffic in order to survive economically. In order to subsist, drug trade has to be maintained; civil wars emerge as the consequence of drug wars.

In 1985, the U.S. State Department issued an international narcotics control strategy report. This report concluded that "worldwide production of illicit opium, coca leaf and cannabis is many times the amount currently consumed by drug abusers. Some governments do not have control of the narcotics growing regions, and prospects in several countries are dampened by corruption, even government involvement in the narcotics trade" (Iyer 1985, 26). The notion that governments and/or government officials participate in drug trafficking is not new or isolated. The United States has threatened to cut off aid to South American countries if they cannot limit graft and corruption among public officials: ". . . $25,000 in cash is said to be the going rate for persuading a police commander to turn a blind eye to the three-day job of stomping and processing coca and loading the paste onto a plane. At such lofty prices, corruption is almost impossible to curb. And the police aren't the only officials who are susceptible. Some senior politicians and judges are routinely linked to the drug trade" (Ryser & Javetski 1986, 44).

Mills (1986) compiled a remarkable account of international drug trade among governments and their agents. According to him, "The inhabitants of the earth spend more money on illegal drugs than they spend on food; more than they spend on housing, clothes, education, medical care, or any other product or service. The international narcotics industry is the largest growth industry in the world. Its annual revenues exceed half a trillion dollars—three times the value of all United States currency in circulation, more than the gross national products of all but a half dozen of the major industrialized nations. . . . The statistics on which the above statement are based appear in classified documents prepared with the participation of the Central Intelligence Agency and the National Security Agency. These studies are circulated in numbered copies with warnings of 'criminal sanctions' for unauthorized disclosure. Why is this information withheld from public view?" (1986, 4).

Cocaine involvement has not been restricted to international government officials (Miller 1985). Prominent city officials (Charleston mayor admits cocaine guilt 1987), police officers (Slice of vice: more Miami cops arrested, 1986), professional athletes (Keteyian 1987), and financial (From hot tips to hard drugs, 1987) and business executives (Flax 1985; Cocaine in the executive suite?, 1985; Too little kick from champale, 1985) have also been associated with the business of cocaine. It does seem that cocaine use and even cocaine trade is an integral part of contemporary life at the highest levels.

The airlines have gotten into the cocaine business as well. In February of 1985, a 747 jet belonging to the Columbian airline Avianca was seized when it was learned that one thousand kilos of cocaine estimated to be worth $600 million (Iyer 1985) was hidden within a shipment of cut flowers. Similarly, in 1986, Eastern Airlines baggage handlers were involved in a sophisticated cocaine smuggling scheme (Shannon 1986).

Drugs for War. In addition to the civil wars that emerge as a consequence of wars against drugs and drug wars, drugs may have been used to wage war. For example, the spectra of cocaine trafficking have been raised with regard to the Iran-Contra affair (Nordlund 1987). One possible scenario goes like this: The airplanes that lifted weapons to the Contra rebels may have been used to return cocaine cargos that could then be sold at handsome profits; these profits could then be used to further subsidize the purchase of arms. Given the secrecy that surrounds the covert policies involved in the Iran-Contra affair and who said what to whom, with all the politically necessary lapses in memory, we may never know the full extent to which our government could not "Just say no" to cocaine.

In 1988, what appeared to be one of the most fascinating—and perhaps hypocritical—examples of the political version of "do what I say and not what I do" found General Manuel Antonio Noriega, the highest ranking Panamanian government official, indicted on drug trafficking and racketeering charges. News reports indicated (Kurkjian 1988) that the general was paid $4.6 million to protect cocaine shipments that passed through Panama on the way to the United States. Noriega also arranged for the sale of ether and acetone, two substances often used in the freebase preparation of cocaine. General Noriega ". . . received more than $5 million to protect a drug cartel said to be responsible for 80 percent of the cocaine imported into the United States . . ." (Kurkjian 1988, 1).

Senator John F. Kerry of Massachusetts accused the Reagan administration of ". . . intentionally moving slowly in pursuing allegations against Noriega. Kerry, whose Foreign Relations subcommittee will begin hearings . . . on Noriega's links to international drug trafficking, said the administration had failed to pursue Noriega because he had made secret deals with the White House aide, Lt. Col. Oliver L. North, and William Casey, the director of the CIA, to provide the support for the Nicaraguan rebels" (Kurkjian 1988, 24). Apparently, Noriega was paid two hundred thousand dollars a year by the CIA to provide intelligence information from the region (Kurkjian 1988, 24). In addition, it has been estimated that Noriega's monthly drug trade profits averaged about $10 million.

Obsessed with providing Contra aid, the Reagan administration enabled the use of drugs by American citizens. While foreign policy covertly used cocaine to wage war internationally, domestic war was being waged overtly against cocaine and other drugs.

The politics of war—cocaine wars in particular—are complicated and confusing. Various attempts to stop the cocaine trade have met with opposition and generated counter wars. When political aspirations and financial profits are high and the world economy in need of resources unavailable through traditional channels, governments seem to have turned to cocaine trafficking to achieve their ends. The ends, however, do not justify the means. It is unreasonable to expect young people to rally around "Just say no" campaigns when the government seems to "just say yes." Ambiguous political strategies[4] send potent and perplexing messages to those who are thinking about using intoxicating drugs. Drugs are important international assets, yet they are to be avoided because they are also illegal and dangerous. Public policy based on this logic increases the international value of drugs as resources. As drugs increase in worth, their social importance escalates. This situation, in turn, encourages and perhaps even perpetuates drug use among those who, uncertain of their social allegiances, are enticed by the stimulation of risky, dangerous, antisocial activities.

---

[4]The anticocaine campaign, "Cocaine, The Big Lie," has been co-opted by an even bigger lie. The American government has used cocaine money for its own covert purposes as well as ignoring international drug traffickers. Perhaps the war against drugs is simply a political maneuver designed to distract the American public from more dangerous global political activities.

Cocaine Abuse Treatment

Just as governments have been unable to avoid "using" cocaine to fulfill social policy, drug-using trends in America through 1986 reflect an increase in cocaine use (Johnston, et al 1986) from previous decades. Demands for treatment tend to lag behind increases in drug use. In several years, a small but meaningful proportion of those who became new cocaine users will likely progress from experimental use to more chronic cocaine abuse; they will need and many will demand treatment. Clayton (1985) theorized that the elapsed time between when one begins to abuse cocaine and when one initially begins the treatment seeking process is approximately four years. Therefore, as a result of time and increased levels of cocaine use, substance abuse specialists will have an increasing wave of cocaine abusers in need of treatment services. Unfortunately, cocaine treatment has not been explored and developed sufficiently to meet the current (and future) influx of cocaine abuse victims.

The study and treatment of alcoholism and tobacco abuse have been examined extensively and a wide range of treatment approaches and services are available. Cocaine treatment, however, is still in an early stage of development and available treatment methodologies and services for cocaine problems are primarily borrowed from the field of alcoholism. Clinical awareness and treatment models specific to the unique requirements and needs of the cocaine abuser are vital; yet, very few, if any, effective treatments for cocaine dependence exist in spite of the tendency to demonstrate technological and pharmacological advances (for example Baxter 1983; Boza, Milanes & Flemenbaum 1986: Jordon 1985).

In the next chapter we will examine the theoretical explanations that have been offered to explain drug abuse, addictive behavior in general, and cocaine abuse in particular. These models provide the landscape against which these peculiar, potentially self-destructive behaviors can be observed and understood.

3
Understanding Addiction

History, Science, and the Addictions

I n this chapter, we will review a sampling of the major theoretical models
that have been offered to explain substance abuse and addictive behavior
patterns. We will emphasize those theories that are particularly relevant
to the abuse of cocaine and the notion of natural recovery. To fully understand these models, they will first be presented in their cultural and historical
context. An essential requirement for any type of drug investigation is the
recognition of the extent and types of biases present in the field. These biases,
in part, are caused by the "immaturity" of the addictions field as a scientific
discipline. This immaturity is complicated by the high level of emotion associated with the topic, as well as the lack of conceptual clarity among workers and theorists in the field.

The Emotional Context of Understanding

Many researchers have described the intense emotions that usually surround
any discussion of drug use and abuse. Grinspoon noted that these exchanges
are less academic and more like "political debates" (Grinspoon & Bakalar
1985). Stanton Peele recognized this: "Drug and alcohol use are emotional
topics, particularly in the United States today. Those who study and treat
substance abuse must navigate extremely tricky waters" (1986, 149). Andrew
Weil acknowledged that "unconscious bias is as common among proponents
of drugs as among opponents" (1972, 6). Weil cautions further that "unconscious biases act like filters between our perceptions and our intellects. They
enable us to screen out observations that do not fit in with our preconceived
notions and to see causal relationships where none exist. Worst of all, they
blind us to their own presence so that we are quick to defend our erroneous
hypotheses with shouts of 'I saw it with my own eyes!' " (p. 9).

Some of the contemporary "unconscious or conscious biases" that per-
meate the field of addictions are particularly relevant to the present discussion. For example, some authors in the field of substance abuse take a moral
position with regard to drug use. On the one hand, drugs, especially cocaine,

are at fault, and are described in value-laden terms, for example, as an "evil seductress" or "vamp from Hell" (Green 1985). On the other hand, drug abusers are often blamed and described in perjorative language. Consider, for example, professional terminology like "impulse-ridden sociopath" or "addictive personality." Street jargon also has a perjorative cast, as in "coke freak," "dope fiend," or "junkie."

Youthful Fields and Conceptual Confusion

The field of the addictions is very young, and marked by controversy, zealous emotion, and confusion. It is precisely this chaotic state of affairs that Shaffer (1986; Burglass & Shaffer 1983; Shaffer & Gambino 1979, 1983) observed when he argued that the field of addictions is in a preparadigmatic period and in the midst of a conceptual crises. The developmental immaturity of the addiction field is evident by the presence of intensely conflicting and polarized explanations of its identity and purpose, anomalous research findings, and few facts (Shaffer 1986).

A paradigm, according to Thomas Kuhn (1962), is essentially the framework, or perspective, that defines the rules and standards of practice for a particular scientific community of workers (such as physicists, psychiatrists, and psychologists). Individuals working in the field of addictions do not share a unitary set of rules or standards for the treatment of dependence disorders; in fact, there is controversy as to whether these disorders are multi- or uni-dimensional. For example, as some clinicians who treat addictive disorders debate the efficacy and morality of drug treatment (such as methadone) versus drug-free treatment, and whether psychotherapy can proceed or be useful while a patient is using a particular substance, other clinicians and researchers argue the utility of abstinence or controlled use as treatment outcomes.

Similarly, there is little agreement as to the etiology of addictive disorders. For example, pharmacologists understand the addictions as a set of pharmacological problems involving such categories as drugs, tolerance, or binding sites. Psychologists and psychiatrists typically are willing to read into the phenomenon of addiction those problems of learning, compulsion, or ego function. Physiologists posit problems of withdrawal, metabolism, or target organ effects. Sociologists see processes of social regulation, peer pressure, and/or environmental forces. Politicians, lawyers, and law enforcement agents view addiction problems as involving controlled substances, criminals, and/or deterrence. At present, no single theory dominates the field of addictive behaviors or comprehensively informs clinical interventions. "Nonetheless, current theory and practice, despite the extreme diversity and often strident discord in the field, reflect a growing consensus on the importance of using scientific methods in both research and practice, and on modeling the older, established scientific disciplines" (Burglass & Shaffer 1981, xxi).

Complicating the lack of agreement among addiction workers is the underdeveloped scientific state of knowledge in the addictions. This circumstance is characterized by an inability on the part of addiction treatment specialists to tolerate or even evaluate alternative theories with the prevailing wisdom of our time. Currently, for example, it is pedestrian to consider addiction the consequence of biological, medical, or disease processes. Alcoholism is viewed as a disease: a primary condition, biologically based, that is irreversible, incurable, and progressive if not arrested. Such a condition will, according to its followers, lead to premature death. Not only do champions of this model believe that the disease leads to inevitable premature death among addicts, but some believe that the disease is present among family members as well. These advocates have suggested that the "disease" can lead to premature death among those significant others who are not drinking and drugging themselves. Consider, for example, the position taken by Young (1987). She proposed that "co-alcoholism [the addiction to have control over people, places, and things], like alcoholism, is a primary addiction requiring a primary diagnosis. . . ." and ". . . produces a chronic physical, mental, emotional and spiritual deterioration, which if left untreated can lead to premature death . . . and recovery from co-alcoholism requires a system shift at a characterological level" (Young 1987, 257).

Throughout history, research and theory anomalous to the prevailing wisdom tend to be suppressed, oppressed, and even censured. Peele (1987), an impassioned opponent of the disease model of addiction, recalled his own and other prominent investigators' experiences generated by their research and publication of alternative (in this case, unpopular) theoretical perspectives. Peele described some of the mechanisms of social suppression designed to restrict his alternative position; these included the use of smear tactics, publication and grant restrictions, allegations of fraudulent research data, and social ostracism.

In science, when anomalous data are ignored, denied, or suppressed, current ways of knowing are maintained and a crisis averted. When findings that differ from the conventional view cannot be ignored or explained, however, a crisis has occurred. Consider the impact of Galilean, Darwinian, or Freudian ideas on the conventional thinking of their time; their positions precipitated enumerable debates that were argued against the landscape of emotional orthodoxy in an attempt to suppress and deny these new ways of understanding. In the addictions, we are presently in the midst of a similar conceptual crisis. There are several examples to illustrate this dilemma: the research of Davies (1962) and Sobell & Sobell (1973, 1976) have challenged the dominant notion that the only treatment outcome possible for alcoholics is total abstinence; Peele (1986) has questioned both the research and logic that has accepted a genetic component or predisposition to alcoholism and other addictions; Shaffer (1985) has suggested that the disease model of addiction is simply a metaphor for a commonly observed process and that this metaphor should not be casually substituted for a primary biological process. Taken together or separately, these positions, representative of numerous other anomalous findings, both reflect and fuel the conceptual crisis in the addictions. As a result of the shifting conceptual tides, even devotees of the disease model (such as Pace 1984) have altered their positions so that more adaptive and behavioral approaches have become acceptable.

It is important to recognize that suppressive forces are not evil and ma-levolent by nature—though they can be expressed and experienced as such. Rather, they are part of the machinery that ever so slowly advances scientific thinking (interested readers should see Shaffer 1986 for a detailed account of this process in the addictions).

Twentieth Century History and Models in the Addictions. With its roots firmly placed in witchcraft, medicine, psychology, sociology, biology, chem-istry, physiology, political science and law, a rich historical progression of theories and explanations about addictive behavior has advanced during this century. In the early 1900s, the dominant theory of the times emphasized "personal responsibility." Drug dependence was viewed as spiritual weakness and evidence of moral turpitude. By the 1920s, drug disturbances, for the first time, were regarded as an indication of psychological defects. In the aftermath of the Depression and World War II, an appreciation of societal influences on individuals began to appear and by the 1940s and 1950s, the popular theories of addiction emphasized social and environmental factors. The "science" of behaviorism was applied to the study of addiction and by the 1960s behavioral theories represented the prominent explanations of ad-dictive behavior. The 1970s and 1980s have demonstrated a theoretical pref-erence for physiological explanations of addiction (for example, the disease model of addiction, including genetic and/or chemical predispositions to ad-diction) (Shaffer & Burglass 1981; Shaffer 1986).

Recently, historical and theoretical trends in understanding addictive be-haviors have moved away from interpretations based solely upon personal responsibility and toward explanations based upon involuntary determinants that victimize individuals. It is interesting to note, however, that in spite of this theoretical trend, physicians, psychiatrists, and lay people alike have demonstrated a consistent tendency to hold a combination of medical and moralistic beliefs that underlie their behaviors toward drug-using individuals (Caetano 1987; Orcutt 1976; Rohman et al. 1987; Shaffer 1987).

Definitions and Concepts in the Field of the Addictions

Because the scientific study of addictive behaviors is in a "preparadigmatic" stage of development, confusion and crisis surrounds the field's explanatory concepts and definitions. To reduce this confusion and provide some internal consistency for this text, the following discussion will review the definitions of "drug," "addiction," "dependence," and "drug abuse."

What is a Drug? A drug is any chemical agent (natural or synthetic) that affects living processes (Shaffer & Kauffman 1985, 38). For drugs of abuse, there are six basic categories: (1) narcotics and related analgesics; (2) sedative-hypnotics (including barbiturates, non-barbiturate sedatives, minor tranquilizers, and alcohol); (3) stimulants (including amphetamines, cocaine, and others); (4) hallucinogens, and others like (5) phencyclidine; (6) cannabis and inhalants, which do not readily fit the other categories (Kauffman, Shaffer & Burglass 1985). Under most circumstances, it is simpler, though less precise, to organize commonly used drugs by considering them to reside within one of three categories: depressants, stimulants, and hallucinogens.

What is Addiction? The concept of addiction has undergone many revisions. Because of the absence of unity in the field, many archaic definitions are still widely held among professionals and the public. For the most part, the word *addiction* is too elastic and, therefore, devoid of meaning; for example, "work addiction" and "love addiction." Sometimes the concept of addiction is misused when it is applied strictly in the medical sense and substituted for the concept of physical dependence. Physical dependence, as evidenced by tolerance and physical withdrawal symptoms, refers to a physiological condition that is often correlated but not identical to addiction.

For the past two decades, a distinction has been maintained between physiological and psychological addiction (Burglass & Shaffer 1983). Psychological dependence has referred to a state in which a drug user *believes* he or she requires the effect of a drug in order to function "normally." Physiological dependence is an altered physical state produced by the repeated administration of a drug, which necessitates the continued administration of the drug to prevent the appearance of a stereotyped syndrome of unpleasant effects characteristic of the particular drug—that is, the withdrawal or abstinence syndrome. The development of physical dependence is facilitated by the phenomenon of tolerance. A tolerant state has developed when, after repeated administration, a given dose of a particular drug produces a decreased effect. Conversely, tolerance exists when increasingly larger or more frequent doses of the drug must be administered in order to obtain the effects observed with the original dose (Shaffer & Kauffman 1985). Heroin addicts, for example, avoid physical withdrawal by increasing their drug intake gradually as their level of tolerance develops. If withdrawal does occur, the symptoms include a flu-like illness with physical complaints such as nausea and chills. Although physical withdrawal from heroin (or narcotics in general) is not life-threatening in the absence of complicating medical conditions, heroin addicts will go to great lengths to avoid the experience of withdrawal; such addicts regularly report a belief that narcotic withdrawal would kill them.

Cocaine, unlike heroin, was considered a drug that did not produce physical tolerance or withdrawal symptoms. Cocaine withdrawal symptoms are not necessarily obvious to an observer, or, in some cases, the user—for example, sleep disturbances, changes in rapid eye movement (REM) sleep, fatigue, and depression; consequently, cocaine dependence was assigned only to the category of psychological dependence. This narrow definition of addiction is one of the reasons cocaine had been misrepresented as a "safe" drug by many of its users. Many still believe cocaine to be nonaddicting.

The addictions field, led by the World Health Organization (WHO), has started to revise the concept of addiction. Currently, for example, addiction is considered to represent a *quantitative* pattern of behavior. That is, addictive behaviors are characterized by a high frequency of occurrences; they are recognized as having a much higher value than other behaviors previously thought to be more important. In other words, addictive behaviors are identified by their frequency, not by the presence of physical dependence. The notion of addiction is now thought to reside along a continuum. This gauge has been referred to as the "dependency syndrome." This syndrome does not require all its elements to be present at the same time or with the same intensity for it to be identified. Furthermore, the concept of neuroadaptation has been offered to serve as the generic shelter for physical dependence, tolerance, cross-tolerance, and so on. The notion of dependence will be discussed in more detail in the next section.

The Dependence Syndrome Concept. The dependence syndrome is a new concept and will likely replace the term addiction. It incorporates the quantitatively defined patterns of behavior, neuroadaptation (as evidenced by tolerance or withdrawal syndrome), and the phenomenon of psychological drug craving or "dependence." In 1969, the World Health Organization considered dependence as a state, psychic and sometimes also physical, that results from the interaction between a living organism and a drug. This state is characterized by behavioral and other responses that always include a compulsion to take the drug on a continuous or periodic basis in order to experience its psychic effects, and sometimes to avoid the discomfort of its absence. Tolerance may or may not be present. A person may be dependent on more than one drug.

In 1981, the World Health Organization redefined dependence as ". . . a syndrome manifested by a behavioral pattern in which the use of a given psychoactive drug, or class of drugs, is given a much higher priority than other behaviors that once had higher value. The term syndrome is taken to mean no more than a clustering of phenomena so that not all the components need always be present with the same intensity" (Burglass & Shaffer 1983, 28). The newer World Health Organization definition recognized the complex nature of drug dependence and redefined addiction as a combination of behavioral and contextual symptoms, existing on a continuum rather than falling into discrete categories. The World Health Organization produced yet another definition of addiction in its 1981 Memorandum. This more recent definition reduced the term to an even lower common denominator found in all psychoactive drugs by introducing "neuroadaptation" as part of the dependence syndrome. Neuroadaptation refers to drug-induced changes in the chemistry of the brain, specifically at the single cell or neuronal level. The emphasis by the WHO on a *syndrome* of dependence recognizes the inefficiency and futility associated with trying to determine the distinction between psychological and physiological dependence.

According to Edwards, Arif & Hodgson (1982), the dependence syndrome can be identified by the presence of seven factors. These are as follows:

1. a subjective awareness of compulsion to use a drug or drugs, usually during attempts to stop or moderate drug use;
2. a desire to stop drug use in the face of continued use;
3. a relatively stereotyped pattern of drug-taking behavior;
4. evidence of neuroadaptation (that is, tolerance and withdrawal symptoms);
5. use of the drug to relieve or avoid withdrawal symptoms;
6. the salience of drug-seeking behavior relative to other important priorities;
7. rapid reinstatement of the syndrome after a period of abstinence.

The 3-Cs. Dependence has also been defined by the 3-Cs: Continued use in the face of adverse physical or psychic reactions; Compulsion to use the drug; and, a feeling of being out of Control regarding the drug use. In other words, the 3-Cs suggest that drug addiction is the continued use of a drug or drugs in an uncontrolled and compulsive manner in spite of the adverse consequences associated with such use (Gold, Washton & Dackis 1985; Smith 1986).

The experience of craving includes feelings that a drug is necessary for normal or optimal levels of functioning. This feeling can range from a mild desire to an intense drug hunger. When this craving remains unsatisfied, adverse reactions are often experienced by the sufferer and sometimes are evident to observers. These reactions may be perceived as unusual agitation, anxiety, depression, and/or acting out.

The Concept of Drug Abuse. Drug abuse is defined as ". . . the use, usually by self-administration, of any drug in a manner that deviates from the approved medical or social patterns within a given culture. The term conveys the notion of social disapproval, and it is not necessarily descriptive of any particular pattern of drug use or its potential adverse consequences" (Jaffe 1985, 532).

In the American culture, any use of cocaine is considered abuse because cocaine is illicit. Throughout this book, however, the term "drug abuse" or "cocaine abuse" will be used to recognize and identify a pattern of drug use that negatively affects the physical or mental health and/or safety of the drug user. In short, drug abuse will be used synonymously with one end of the drug abuse spectrum—that is, compulsive drug use.

Like addiction, the term "abuse" is applied inconsistently and can mean anything from one-time experimental use of an illicit drug to drug dependency (Jaffe 1985). With any type of psychoactive substance, there exist various patterns of usage. This range includes experimental, occasional, social, recreational, and compulsive drug use (Siegel 1985). As we mentioned in chapter 1, only a small group of users within the cocaine-using culture—as is true with users of any dependence-inducing substance—progress from experimental to compulsive drug abuse. The compulsive abuser or "coke-aholic" (Stone, Fromme & Kagan 1984, 145) does not merely use cocaine but abuses it.

Cocaine Abuse. The diagnostic criteria from the third edition of the Diagnostic and Statistical Manual of Mental Disorders (DSM-III 1980) of the American Psychiatric Association fail to contain a category for cocaine dependence. The distinction between cocaine abuse and cocaine dependence has been recognized in the revision of DSM-III (DSM-III-R 1987). This revision expands the definition of cocaine use disorders and, in making the distinction, emphasizes a definitional shift that suggests a new course that proceeds from use to abuse and dependence.

Cocaine *dependence,* defined by DSM-III-R, is present if at least three of the following nine characteristics apply:

1. The drug user ingests more cocaine than intended;
2. The user is unable to reduce use in spite of attempts to do so;
3. The user devotes significant time to procuring, using, and withdrawing from cocaine;
4. Intoxication and/or withdrawal symptoms interfere with activities of daily living;
5. Noncocaine-related life activities (social, occupational, and recreational) are reduced or eliminated in preference to the drug activities;

6. The user persists in the face of known causes and related adverse consequences (such as social, psychological and/or physical problems);
7. The user takes more cocaine to achieve the same effects;
8. The user experiences withdrawal symptoms;
9. The user takes the drug to medicate or ward off withdrawal symptoms.

Cocaine *abuse* is present, according to DSM-III-R, when at least one of the following characteristics applies:

1. Continued cocaine use in spite of adverse consequences;
2. Continued use of the drug in situations where such use presents physical danger to the user;
3. Never met the criteria for cocaine dependence.

The problems associated with cocaine dependence must be present for at least one or more months. Although the signs and symptoms of cocaine abuse must endure for the same length of time as for cocaine dependence, the diagnostic difference between abuse and dependence rests simply on the number of criteria observed. In other words, cocaine abuse is less pervasive than cocaine dependence, though not less dangerous or severe.

The DSM-III-R definition captures the quality of continued cocaine use in the face of adverse physical, psychological, social, and financial consequences. Furthermore, DSM-III-R, in keeping with newer notions of addiction, does not require evidence of physiological withdrawal.

In conclusion, drug abuse, dependence, and addiction are complex concepts that set the stage for how we identify, understand, and react to drug-involved people. In the sections that follow, we will provide (1) an overview of the major models that contribute to the foundations of our understanding of drug use/abuse and (2) an impression of how these models have served as the focus of contemporary treatment interventions.

Models for Understanding Addictive Behaviors

The chief theoretical models of addiction can be readily organized into the following models of addiction: (1) psychological; (2) social; and (3) biological.[1] Each of these conceptual approaches will be examined below.

---

[1] Readers should note that this organizational schema corresponds with Zinberg's tripartite model for understanding drug effects (that is, set, or psychology of the user, setting or sociocultural context of the user, and substance or biochemistry of the drug used). Interested readers should see chapter 1 of this text and Zinberg (1984) for a more detailed account of these factors.

Psychological Models of Addiction

Psychoanalytical Theories

Psychoanalytic literature reviews suggest consensus among various theoretical perspectives in support of the notion that drug use is seen as a vehicle to correct or compensate for defective ego functions (Treece 1984; Treece & Khantzian 1986). In other words, drug use is an adaptive solution to an internal problem of ego deficiency. These "ego functions," which drug use substitutes for or augments, consist of ego defenses, self-esteem, regulation and management of overwhelming affect, self-care, and object relations (for example relationships with people). These factors can be reduced to three major conceptual categories: (1) nonspecific cravings; (2) affect deficits; and (3) self and object deficits.

Nonspecific Craving. Psychoanalytic theories of drug abuse have moved away from almost exclusive focus on libidinal drives and oral dependency as explanations for drug hunger. Recently, the trend has been to view excessive appetites as representative of major deficits in ego development (Frosh 1985). The early literature on addictive behaviors stated that nonspecific drug cravings and drug use represented a direct drive (libidinal) or instinctual gratification for the acquisition of pleasurable feeling states, for example, "pharmacogenic elation" (Rado 1933). This thinking has changed dramatically; drug use is not commonly viewed as a pleasure-seeking activity but rather as a means of reducing emotional pain. Specific drugs are chosen by different individuals for their specific pharmacological properties and capacity to reduce psychological distress (Khantzian 1975).

Affect Deficits. Drug use and the management of painful emotional states may be interconnected. Psychoactive drug use can regulate emotional states by altering or modifying feelings. According to this model, the regulation obtained from the use of psychoactive drugs is not unlike how the well-functioning ego provides protection from emotional intensity and pain. If the ego is deficient in providing emotional regulation, than an individual must look elsewhere (outward) for support. The concept of addiction as adaptive implies that drug use is ego supportive and represents a defense mechanism in relation to an internal problem or conflict. Consider, for example, one user's explanation of drug abuse as an adaptation. "Cocaine was a way of numbing out feelings. . . . Being stoned is like having a layer between me and reality, like doing things with gloves on. I dealt with emotions by avoiding them. Cocaine, I think, allowed me to avoid dealing with the root of the problem."

According to this psychoanalytic model, what was initially employed as an adaptive coping mechanism can readily turn into a maladaptive, destructive activity. Shaffer called addiction "a two-edged sword; it serves as it destroys" (Milkman & Sunderwirth 1983, 38). In other words, addictive behaviors may have adaptive purposes that serve the ego well; however, they concurrently extract penalties.

According to the "adaptive" psychoanalytic model of drug abuse, individual drug users will "self-select" a drug or combination of drugs for their particular pharmacological properties in order to medicate or relieve the discomfort associated with specific internal states or external events.[2] The process of self-medicating with a specific drug or drugs was named the "drug-of-choice" phenomenon by Wieder & Kaplan (1969).

Throughout an individual's drug-using career, he or she may be exposed to a significant portion of the psychoactive drug smorgasbord, and eventually, through experience and elimination, select those drugs and drug effects that most efficiently help reduce personal distress. There are particular emotional states that certain people find very difficult to tolerate; drugs with specific pharmacological properties tend to reduce the discomfort from these feelings. This model argues that these drugs will be consistently selected, by the abuser, to modify distressful feelings. Thus, current psychoanalytic theory maintains that there is a meaningful relationship between a drug of choice and the user's state of ego functioning.

Milkman & Frosch (1973) examined the relationship between personality and drug of choice. They identified three coping styles, each associated with a particular drug category. Milkman & Sunderwirth (1983) later named these three coping styles as satiation, fantasy, and arousal. Opiates, for example, depress the central nervous system, reduce sensitivity to stimulation, and slow us down; these drugs facilitate a satiation style of coping. According to this view, the opiate user seeks to cope with "negative feelings by reducing stimulation from the external or internal world" (Milkman & Sunderwirth 1983, 38). Khantzian (1985) claims that opiate use specifically aids the user in the management of aggressive drives by dampening or reducing impulsive energy.

The hallucinogens similarly assist with a "fantasy" mode of coping. This appeals to personality types who ". . . experience a sense of disconnection from their internal experience or from their relationships with others. Pharmacologically, hallucinogens 'crack the autistic shell' (Wieder & Kaplan 1969) so that the person is able to discover new worlds both within and outside himself" (Brown & Fromm 1987, 191).

Lastly, the stimulants, such as cocaine, encourage the "arousal" mode of adaptation. These drugs attract individuals who use physical and mental activity as a means of coping with intrapsychic feelings and conflicts. Pharma-

---

[2]Interested readers are encouraged to see the works of Khantzian 1975 and 1985, and Khantzian & Treece 1985 for more comprehensive discussions of this phenomenon.

cologically, stimulants have energizing properties that promote an active stance of acting out overwhelming affects (such as rage or aggression). In addition, depressed individuals may seek cocaine and other stimulants as a way of providing needed energy to their depleted mood and apathy.

Self and Object Deficits. Deficits in ego functioning can occur when early relationships with others are somehow inadequate. Disruption of early life development is the basic assumption of object relations theory. In particular, cocaine addicts can be seen as individuals who suffered major difficulties during the separation/individuation stages of development, which occur during the first three years of life. The tasks of these developmental stages are to establish separateness from the mother (or major caretaker) and develop intrapsychic images of the mother and other significant people in the infant's world. The "normal" infant initially experiences that the mother exists only when she is with the infant. The infant lacks a sense of permanence with regard to people. By experiencing the mother's repeated comings and going, the child learns that she exists even when not in sight. To minimize the fear of the mother's loss or disappearance, the child creates an inner world of images that represent the mother and other loved people (or "objects"). These images, or "internalized objects," give the infant the illusion of their existence, or continued presence, even when absent. This acts as a sort of self-soothing function, thereby diminishing the child's typical fears and insecurities.

Additionally, the infant not only internalizes the mother, but also internalizes some of the functions she provides. If the infant can internalize a "good enough" caretaker, this can form the basis for a positive sense of self and provide the foundation for further personality development. Before the infant builds up a store of internalized images, however, he or she frequently makes use of transitional objects, which symbolize the mother or caretaker and provide a soothing function. A teddy bear or special blanket may serve as companions that help the child tolerate periods of emotional discomfort during mother's physical absence.

The cocaine addict, according to the object relations perspective, has not internalized adequately the "good enough" caretaker during the separation/individuation stage of development and, as a result, does not have the ego functions sufficient to regulate day-to-day stress and discomfort. Cocaine, then, often becomes the transitional object. The object deficit view posits that the drug user requires external aid to maintain a sense of well-being. Cocaine provides the ego functions lacking in the user; the results are elevation in self-esteem, the ability to manage and control painful affects, and energy.

Khantzian & Mack (1983) suggest that among addicts there is a failure to internalize certain aspects of self-care from the early environment and, in particular, from the caretaker. "In searching to identify and understand impairments in survival skills and self-care, we have stressed a developmental perspective focused upon how early nurturing attitudes and the caring and protective functions of parents, particularly the mother, are internalized and transformed into positive attitudes of self-regard and adequate structures and functions assuring self-care and self-protection" (Khantzian & Mack 1983, 229).[3] Drug users frequently show a deficiency of appropriate apprehension regarding the consequences of drug use. This deficiency is also linked to generalized difficulties in self-care. These individuals fail to care for and protect themselves; this can perpetuate drug involvement. Perhaps in individuals with better self-care functions, drug use would be terminated before problematic use evolved; possibly illicit drug use would not even begin.

Jones, Treece & Hoke (1981) reviewed the psychoanalytic literature and concluded that analytic theorists also speculate that the lack of a sufficiently nurturant environment during early life can lead to "narcissistic vulnerability." This vulnerability includes low self-esteem and a low estimate of self-worth. Wurmser (1974, 1978) describes what he calls the "narcissistic cycle." He suggests that a life crisis, arising from internal or external events, activates unresolved conflicts about one's self-esteem and self-image. The pharmacological properties of cocaine counteract low self-esteem and depression. Cocaine produces a sense of grandiosity, a feeling of being empowered and in control, mastery, and self-sufficiency. Vulnerable individuals often search for an external solution to an internal problem (that is, the "addictive search"). If drugs are available at this juncture, the beginning of a compulsive drug-using cycle can be set in motion. In other words, the chemically addicted represent individuals with severe narcissistic impairment, and drug use is a means of self-medicating the painful affect associated with narcissistic injuries to self-esteem and disappointments with the self or outer world. Weider & Kaplan (1969) similarly view the use of drugs as a means of providing the user with "soothing and protecting" drug-induced effects to buttress the defective ego.

Difficulties in object relationships inevitably lead to problems with intimacy. In other words, when one has little life experience relating to others during developmental years, relating intimately during adulthood can be most difficult. The use of narcotics to cope with the anxiety associated with intimacy, especially during adolescence, has been stressed by several theorists. Holmes & Rahe (1967), for example, found that interpersonal crises frequently preceded one's first use of narcotics. Hendin (1974) also noted that

---

[3]It is easy to see why some people have criticized psychological theory for being too critical of mothers!

beginning intense, heterosexual involvements often precede the first use of narcotics. Hendin suggests that heroin may be used in these circumstances to reduce the anxiety related to the fears of potential abandonment and disappointment that often come with new relationships. We can speculate that intense homosexual relationships may create anxiety and, therefore, precede narcotic use as well.

Finally, according to the object deficit component of the psychoanalytic perspective, drug use can also be an expression of a wish to reexperience a lost stage of life (Gombosi 1987). Gombosi mentioned, for example, that drug use may be an attempt to experience the symbiotic union with the mother. It is unlikely that stimulants serve this purpose, however; pharmacologically, depressant drugs (such as narcotics and sedatives) are more likely to reproduce the sensations associated with the early experience of parental merging and orality.

In summary, Hartmann (1969) abstracted the four basic tenets of psychoanalytic models of drug abuse.

"1. There is a basic depressive character with early wounds to narcissism and deficits in ego development.

2. There is an intolerance for frustration and pain with a constant need to change a 'low' into a 'high.' This may come from an early lack of satisfying object relations.

3. There is an attempt to overcome the lack of affectionate and meaningful object relations through the pseudocloseness and fusion with other drug takers during their common experience.

4. The artificial technique of maintaining self-regard and satisfaction with drugs, of avoiding painful affects, and alleviating symptoms results in a change from a reality-oriented to a pharmacothymic-oriented regimen. This leads to severely disturbed ego functions and ultimately to conflict with reality. Eventually, the drug taking becomes a way of life" (cited in Frosh 1985, 31).

The Behavioral Approach

In this section, we will review the major conceptual underpinnings of the behavioral approach to addiction. In particular, we will focus on the work of Abraham Wikler. Historically, Wikler has had the most influence on behavioral models of addiction. This review is by no means exhaustive; there is a plethora of materials available that describe behavioral approaches in detail. Our goal is simply to provide some of the basic canons of this approach.

Behavioral psychology means many different things to different people. Behaviorism is not, nor was it ever, a monolithic theoretical concept or treatment approach. Nonetheless, current behavioral theory and practice, despite extreme diversity and often strident discord among adherents, reflect agreement regarding the importance of using scientific methods in research, assessment, and practice in the field of addictive behaviors.

By the 1950s, psychoanalytic approaches had failed to solve the riddle of addiction. As a result, there was a growing dissatisfaction with this perspective. At about the same time, behavioral theories boasted the virtues of employing a more empirical and scientific approach to human behavior; these models began to gain popularity, though not without dissent from competing theoretical camps.

The behavioral perspectives were spawned from classical (or respondent) and operant (or instrumental) conditioning paradigms developed by Ivan Pavlov and B. F. Skinner, respectively. These models generated the view that psychopathology is a learned set of dysfunctional behaviors rather than the result of deepseated psychological trauma or physical illness. Thus, the disordered thinking, feeling, and acting were conceptualized as maladaptive responses to environmental events which, once learned by the individual, are maintained by reinforcing contingencies.

Behavior therapies are based on the assumption that the individual and the environment are an interacting system of events and that the developing person reacts from birth to external conditions in the physical and social environment. Therefore, individual behavior is influenced—that is, altered or maintained, in predictable ways. On the basis of experience with the external world, people acquire consistent patterns of reacting to new conditions as they develop through the life cycle. Finally, according to behavioral theory, individual behavior, modified and/or maintained by experience, should be the major focus and subject matter of scientific and clinical inquiry.

Conditioning Factors in Addiction. In 1965, Abraham Wikler published a chapter on conditioning factors in opiate addiction and relapse. As a result, Wikler emerged as a pioneer in behavioral theory. That paper was the first to consider the roles that operant and classical conditioning played during the process of addiction. Wikler's thinking predated contemporary cognitive-behavior modification theorists and practitioners by analyzing the relationship between cognitive and behavioral phenomena. Wikler's view, unlike many behavioral models, considered the drug user as an active, self-determining individual who was not simply a victim of circumstance or conditioning. Addicts were human beings with feelings, thoughts, motives, and ideas, all of which were considered to come into play during the acquisition, maintenance, and extinction of addictive behavior.

As a result of (a) Wikler's concept of conditioned dependence and (b) that "typical" substance abusers continue to spend a great deal of time in the environments that had previously been associated with substance use, naltrexone treatment has been used to extinguish the bond between conditioned stimuli (such as the environment) and conditioned responses (such as opiate use). Naltrexone blocks the reinforcing properties of narcotics so that drug-taking behavior will be extinguished. Wikler's two-stage approach to substance abuse (figure 3–1) perhaps best illustrates the application of classical behavior theory to an understanding and treatment of addictive behavior.

The theoretical explanations that most cogently explain the clinical application of naltrexone and Antabuse as pharmacologic treatments for drug abuse are largely based on Wikler's two-stage conditioning model. Naltrexone's action, that of a narcotic antagonist, essentially eliminates the unconditioned reinforcing properties of narcotics by blocking their action. Conversely, Antabuse punishes the use of alcohol by inducing a noxious syndrome; this syndrome—according to behavioral theory—should reduce the use of alcohol. It should be readily apparent to supporters and critics of behavioral theory alike that these interventions, like other treatment approaches, are effective on some clinical occasions and not on others.

Wikler's conditioning model of addiction has been supported by data obtained primarily in animal laboratories. Because generalization of animal data to humans is equivocal, at best, Wikler's propositions are in need of additional empirical support. Nevertheless, by considering addiction as the

STAGE ONE: ACQUISITION SEQUENCE (classical conditioning)

---

1. conditioned stimuli (works, room, thoughts, feelings)
2. unconditioned stimulus (narcotic)
3. unconditioned response (narcotic euphoria, "rush," nausea)
4. soon tolerance develops and the UCS no longer elicits the UCR

STAGE TWO: MAINTENANCE SEQUENCE (operant conditioning)

---

1. withdrawal syndrome (unpleasant effects of narcotic abstinence)
2. application of narcotics ("shooting-up")
3. negative reinforcement (cessation of withdrawal syndrome)

---

[14]Adapted from Shaffer and Schneider 1985.

Figure 3–1. Wikler's Simplified Two-Stage Model of Conditioned Dependence

consequence of learning, Wikler's formulations permit the development and implementation of precise treatment techniques—for example, the extinction of specific conditioned responses that maintain a pattern of drug dependence. It is curious, however, that relatively few practitioners have implemented treatment programs based on the sophisticated theoretical perspectives originally furnished by Wikler. We can speculate that his theoretical concepts were too complex, perhaps, for most practitioners to use within the typically spartan settings reserved for the treatment of opiate dependence. Wikler's models have yielded numerous progeny, many of which are not readily recognizable because of the changes that characterize contemporary behavior therapy.

Wikler's Legacy: Contemporary Behavior Therapy. Today, behavior therapists engage in different clinical activities from their counterparts of ten to fifteen years ago. The full scope of the techniques practiced by contemporary behavior therapists is beyond the purview of this discussion. One of the trends revealed by a survey of contemporary behavior therapists is the shift in focus from solely external, observable behaviors to behaviors that are more cognitive and, hence, internal (Gochman, Allgood & Geer 1982).

Gochman et al. (1982) demonstrated this cognitive trend during a recent survey of the American Association of Behavior Therapists. They reported that 63 percent of the respondents were somewhat eclectic in their practices; only 27 percent were strictly behavioral. In addition, this study found that, of the behavior therapists surveyed, 84 percent used systematic desensitization and 84 percent employed cognitive restructuring as techniques in their practices. In fact, these were the most popular procedures reported by the behaviorists. Not so long ago, only desensitization would have been reported as the most often used behavioral technique. Finally, and perhaps more surprising, 76 percent of the respondents were using contingency contracting, while only 73 percent and 71 percent were using modeling and shaping, respectively. To even discuss these techniques dominating the practice of behavior therapy would have been considered heresy just a few years ago. Yet, in his conditioning models, Wikler included perceptual and cognitive factors; his thinking was twenty years ahead of his contemporary counterparts surveyed by Gochman et al. (1982).

Adult Development Models of Addiction

Adult Development Theory. Developmental theories articulate the natural history or process of human growth from birth to death. Studies of life development investigate what individuals have in common with one another over time. Like many other behaviors, drug use changes drastically over the course of a lifetime. As a result, it is useful to consider the psychological explanations offered to explain these "life transitions" and changes.

Levinson (1978) defined the "life structure" as alternating stable and transitional periods throughout the life span that progress in an age-linked sequential order. His basic theory posits that human life has a developmental structure and Levinson begins by examining the human life cycle as a whole. "First there is the idea of a process or journey from a starting point (birth, origin) to a termination point (death, conclusion) . . . Second, there is the idea of seasons: a series of periods or eras within the lifecycle. . . . There are qualitatively different seasons, each having its own distinctive character" (Levinson 1978, 6). The four seasons of life are (1) childhood and adolescence, (2) early adulthood, (3) middle adulthood, and (4) late adulthood. Although, of course, there are individual variations, Levinson claims that, barring early death, we all go through the four seasons and that these seasons are sequential and age-linked. During the lifespan, specific developmental tasks are accomplished typically within particular periods of time. A transitional period begins when major developmental tasks predominate, such as when a young adult separates from parents and leaves home. According to Levinson, life's overall tasks involve career/work, family, love, friendship, politics, leisure, and ethnicity. Transitional periods require termination of the previous period and initiation into a new one. Transitional phases usher forth feelings of loss, separation, and tension as well as the challenge of goal formation and change (Bocknek 1980). Stable periods represent a time of "structure building" and consolidation rather than shifting tasks.

Levinson postulates the following developmental periods within the life structure:[4]

Childhood and Adolescence	= 0–17 years
Early Adulthood Transition	= 17–22 (+ or - 2 years)
Entering the Adult World	= 22–28
Age Thirty Transition	= 28–33
Settling Down Period	= 33–40
Midlife Transition	= 40–45
Entering Middle Adulthood	= 45–50
Age Fifty Transition	= 50–55
Culmination of Middle Adulthood	= 55–60
Late Adult Transition	= 60–65
Late Adulthood	= 65–?

[4]The Novice Phase of Adulthood = Early Adulthood Transition, Entering into Adulthood and Age Thirty Transition, e.g., seventeen to thirty-three, plus or minus two years at either end. Most cocaine users/abusers fall within the Novice Phase age range.

Levinson's theory of human development was based on a male subject pool. His forthcoming book will discuss women's life transitions. Levinson (1987) noted that "the sequence of periods for women is the same as that for men, but women have a different place in society, build different life structures, and go through the transitional periods in somewhat different ways. The gender similarities and differences are equally important."

Cocaine Use among Young Adults

Much has been inferred about drug use among young adults and adolescents. In this section, we will provide some of the available data regarding cocaine and other drug use among different age categories; the primary focus, however, will remain on the young adult population. Following the data presentation, we will discuss some of the research that has focused on cocaine and other drug use among young adults.

Within the general population, "young adults" (that is, eighteen to twenty-five years of age) comprise the largest group of cocaine users. These data are from the National Institute on Drug Abuse (NIDA). The percentage of young adults who have used cocaine at least once (that is, lifetime prevalence) increased from 9 percent in 1972 to a high of 28 percent in 1982.

Table 3–1 presents NIDA's Household Survey figures for cocaine patterns from 1972 through 1982. This table organizes the findings within three age

Table 3–1
NIDA's Household Survey Regarding Cocaine Trends for 1972–1982
(estimated percentages)

	1972	1974	1976	1977	1979	1982
Age 12–17 (Youth)						
Lifetime Use	2.0%	4.0%	3.0%	4.0%	5.0%	7.0%
Used/Past Yr.	2.0	3.0	2.0	3.0	4.0	4.0
Used/Past Mo.	1.0	1.0	1.0	1.0	1.0	2.0
Age 18–25 (Young Adult)						
Lifetime Use	9.0%	13.0%	13.0%	19.0%	28.0%	28.0%
Used Past Yr.	N/A	8.0	7.0	10.0	20.0	19.0
Used Past Mo.	N/A	3.0	2.0	4.0	9.0	7.0
Age 26–34 (Older Adults)						
Lifetime Use	2.0%	1.0%	2.0%	3.0%	4.0%	9.0%
Used Past Yr.	N/A	<0.5	1.0	1.0	2.0	4.0
Used Past Mo.	N/A	<0.5	<0.5	<0.05	1.0	1.0

groups:[5] youth (twelve to seventeen), young adult (eighteen to twenty-five) and older adult (twenty-six to thirty-four). Cocaine use is categorized by life-time prevalence (any use, if ever), yearly use (used during the past twelve months) and use in the past month (used during the past thirty days). Cocaine use in the past year for young adults has increased from 8 percent in 1974 to 20 percent in 1979.

Recently, NIDA released its most up-to-date drug abuse report surveying high school seniors, college students[6] and young adults—that is, one to eight years after high school (Johnston, O'Malley & Backman 1986). Table 3–2 depicts cocaine-use trends between 1975 and 1985 among these populations. Young adult cocaine use exceeds that of both college students and high school seniors. Up to a point, cocaine use appears to increase with age. For example, by age twenty-seven, four of every ten young adults will have tried cocaine at least once, two of the ten adults will have used cocaine in the last year and one of the ten young adults will have used the drug in the past month (Johnston et al. 1986, 160).

Table 3–3 also compares cocaine use for high school seniors, college students, and young adults with other popular licit and illicit substances of abuse. It is interesting to note that both illicit and licit drug use peaked around 1980 and then started to decline steadily for all but the stimulant drugs. The trend toward decreased drug use stabilized in all three age categories by 1985. The small difference between 1984 and 1985 drug use/abuse levels suggests that drug use/abuse may have reached a plateau. This finding is particularly interesting in light of the enormous amount of media coverage and political rhetoric directed at the level of drug abuse in America. As we noted before, this topic is of sufficient importance that we have provided a separate chapter devoted to media hype and its consequences.

Table 3–2 reveals that the largest increases in cocaine use prevalence between 1984 and 1985 were limited to 1 percent for high school, college, and young adults in the "last year" category; high school students also increased 1 percent or less in the "lifetime," "past month," and "daily use" categories of cocaine prevalence. Interestingly, the plateau interpretation is supported by the decreased level of cocaine use observed among college students in the "past month" and "daily use" categories. Perhaps, as young people gain experience with cocaine (that is, increased prevalence of lifetime use), their regular and repeated use of the drug diminishes. It may be that drug users simply

---

[5]NIDA's category of "Young Adult" (eighteen to twenty-five years of age) corresponds with Levinson's "Early Adulthood Transition" (seventeen to twenty-two, plus or minus two years).

[6]High school seniors and college students fall within Levinson's category of "Early Adulthood Transition."

Table 3–2
NIDA's National Trends: Cocaine Use Among High School Seniors, College Students, and Young Adults for 1975–1985

Cocaine Use for High School Seniors

	1975	1976	1977	1978	1979	1980	1981	1982	1983	1984	1985
Lifetime	9%	10%	11%	13%	15%	16%	17%	16%	16%	16%	17%
Past Year	6	6	7	9	12	12	12	12	11	12	13
Past Month	2	2	3	4	6	5	12	5	5	6	7
Daily Use	0.1	0.1	0.1	0.1	0.2	0.2	0.3	0.2	0.2	0.2	0.4

Cocaine Use for College Students (1–4 Years Post High School)

	1975	1976	1977	1978	1979	1980	1981	1982	1983	1984	1985
Lifetime	------	------	------	------	------	17%	16%	17%	17%	16%	17%
Past Year	------	------	------	------	------	7	7	8	6	8	7
Past Month	------	------	------	------	------						
Daily Use	------	------	------	------	------	0.2	0.0	0.3	0.1	0.4	0.1

Cocaine Use for Young Adults (1–8 years Post High School)

	1975	1976	1977	1978	1979	1980	1981	1982	1983	1984	1985
Lifetime	------	------	------	------	------	------	------	------	------	19%	20%
Past Year	------	------	------	------	------	------	------	------	------	9	9
Past Month	------	------	------	------	------	------	------	------	------		
Daily Use	------	------	------	------	------	------	------	------	------	0.2	0.2

acquire a variety of alternative interests over time and their attention to and reinforcement from drugs diminishes.

Unlike many other patterns of drug use, cocaine experimentation tends to continue after high school. Table 3–3 demonstrates that, in spite of the media hysteria and government "war" against drugs, the evidence—obtained from government sources—indicates a clear and consistent trend toward a reduction in both licit and illicit drug use, with 1 percent increases in cocaine use among high school seniors, college students, and young adults as the only categorical exceptions.

Table 3–3
National Drug Use Trends Among High School Seniors, College Students, and Young Adults (1975–1985)

High School Seniors

	1975	1980	1984	1985	Trend
Alcohol					
Lifetime Use	90%	93%	93%	92%	Down[11]
Past Year	85	88	86	86	Down[12]
Past Month	68	72	67	66	Down
Daily Use	6.0	6.0	5.0	5.0	Down
Cigarettes					
Lifetime Use	74%	71%	70%	69%	Down
Past Year	N/A	N/A	N/A	N/A	N/A
Past Month	37	31	29	30	Down
Daily Use	27	21	19	20	Down
Marijuana/Hashish					
Lifetime Use	47%	60%	55%	54%	Down[13]
Past Year	40	49	40	41	?
Past Month	27	34	25	26	Down
Daily Use	6.0	9.0	5.0	5.0	Down
Stimulants					
Lifetime Use	22%	26%	28%	26%	Down
Past Year	16	21	18	16	Down
Past Month	9.0	12	8.0	7	Down
Daily Use	0.5	0.7	0.6	0.4	Down
Cocaine					
Lifetime Use	9.0%	16%	16%	17%	Up
Past Year	6.0	12	12	13	Up
Past Month	2.0	5.0	6.0	7.0	Up
Daily Use	0.1	0.2	0.2	0.4	Up

College Students

	1975	1980	1984	1985	Trend
Alcohol					
Lifetime Use	N/A	N/A	N/A	N/A	N/A
Past Year	N/A	91%	90%	92%	Up
Past Month	N/A	82	79	80	?
Daily Use	N/A	7.0	7.0	5.0	Down
Cigarettes					
Lifetime Use	N/A	N/A	N/A	N/A	N/A
Past Year	N/A	N/A	N/A	N/A	N/A
Past Month	N/A	26%	22%	22%	Down
Daily Use	N/A	13	10	9.0	Down
Marijuana/Hashish					
Lifetime Use	N/A	N/A	N/A	N/A	N/A
Past Year	N/A	51%	41%	42%	Down
Past Month	N/A	34	23	24	Down
Daily Use	N/A	7.0	4.0	3.0	Down
Stimulants					
Lifetime Use	N/A	N/A	N/A	N/A	N/A
Past Year	N/A	22%	16%	12%	Down
Daily Use	N/A	0.5	0.2	0.0	Down
Cocaine					
Lifetime Use	N/A	N/A	N/A	N/A	N/A
Past Year	N/A	17%	16%	17%	Same
Past Month	N/A	7.0	8.0	7.0	Same
Daily Use	N/A	0.2	0.4	0.1	Down

Young Adults (1–8 Years Post-High School)

	1975	1980	1984	1985	Trend
Alcohol					
Lifetime Use	NA	NA	NA	N/A	N/A
Past Year	NA	NA	90%	90%	Same
Past Month	NA	NA	76	76	Same
Daily Use	NA	NA	7.0	7.0	Same
Cigarettes					
Lifetime Use	NA	NA	NA	NA	N/A
Past Year	NA	NA	NA	NA	N/A
Past Month	NA	NA	33%	33%	Same
Daily Use	NA	NA	26	26	Same

Table 3–3 continued

	1975	1980	1984	1985	Trend
Marijuana/Hashish					
Lifetime Use	NA	NA	NA	NA	N/A
Past Year	NA	NA	40%	40%	Same
Past Month	NA	NA	25	25	Same
Daily Use	NA	NA	5.0	5.0	Same
Stimulants					
Lifetime Use	N/A	N/A	N/A	N/A	N/A
Past Year	N/A	N/A	16%	14%	Down
Past Month	N/A	N/A	6.0	5.0	Down
Daily Use	N/A	N/A	0.4	0.2	Down
Cocaine					
Lifetime Use	N/A	N/A	N/A	N/A	N/A
Past Year	N/A	N/A	19%	20%	Same
Past Month	N/A	N/A	9.0	9.0	Same
Daily Use	N/A	N/A	0.2	0.2	Same

[11,12,13]Since 1980

Drug Preferences and Combinations. Table 3–3 shows the order of drug preferences among age groups. In addition, table 3–3 highlights the fact that several drugs are taken concurrently. Alcohol is abused most often, followed by cigarettes, marijuana, cocaine, and stimulants. Although drug use has diminished in this country, there is an increasing trend toward using multiple drugs among the younger half of the American population.

Chitwood (1985) sampled nearly two hundred subjects from treatment and nontreatment populations who said cocaine was their primary drug of choice. He found that the first use of cocaine occurs largely between the ages of sixteen and twenty-two (the early adulthood transitional period, according to Levinson). His findings also indicate that polydrug use is common among cocaine users. Over 50 percent of his cocaine-using sample were also using marijuana; 75 percent of the time marijuana use occurred concurrently with cocaine use. One-third of the subjects used alcohol simultaneously with cocaine.

Kandel, Murphy & Karus (1985) sampled more than one thousand young adults and found similar patterns. Alcohol and cigarettes were the two most prevalent legal drugs used by their subjects. Marijuana and cocaine followed and represented the two most commonly used illicit drugs. It is safe to conclude that cocaine use and abuse does not represent "a separate drug-using syndrome" (Backman, O'Malley & Johnston 1984). Instead, cocaine appears to represent only one of the items chosen from a large network of available drugs.

Developmental Risks for Drug Abuse. Developmentally, there are particular times when individuals are at greater risk for drug abuse. The transitional periods, using Levinson's schema, appear to be the most vulnerable times for the emergence of substance abuse. For example, Jones et al. (1981) interviewed a sample of heroin addicts and found that, although they had been exposed to heroin for several years, the subjects' first heroin use usually did not occur until they were involved with their first important heterosexual relationship (mean age approximately seventeen). About two-thirds of the subjects (N = 40) volunteered one or more precipitating life events they associated with the onset of narcotic abuse.

According to Jones et al. (1981), the largest category of major life event was the loss of or threat to important relationships; for example, separation, death, or divorce of parents. Many of the major life changes represent typical transitional tasks in the course of adolescence and young adulthood, such as leaving home, going to college, marriage, and change in living arrangements. Furthermore, the subjects who initiated heroin use at the time of situational stress or major life changes were more likely to progress rapidly to regular narcotic use. The age-linked developmental tasks of separation from home, initiation of intimacy and career pursuits may have increased the subjects' psychological dysphoria and, therefore, increased their receptivity to narcotic initiation for the psychic relief of external and internal stresses.

Backman et al. (1984) studied young adults during the first three years after high school. This time is one of transition and separation from home and is marked typically by changes in living arrangements that correspond to changes in drug-using patterns. For example, young adults who stay at home show little change in their drug use and those who marry evidence a decrease in drug use. Young adults, however, who leave home for another residence such as a dormitory, and those who move in—in the absence of marriage—with a partner of the opposite sex exhibit an increase in drug use. In short, separation from home and the associated tasks of forming relationships and starting careers are primary tasks that are often confronted during the young adult transitional period. There appears to be evidence of an association between leaving home, changes in living situations, and increases in drug use. It is difficult, however, to determine whether the developmental tasks described above are the cause or consequence of drug use.

Kandel et al. (1985) investigated the more specific relationship between cocaine use and developmental issues; in particular, this study focused on the transitional period between adolescence and young adulthood. Their research found that both men and women begin to use cocaine around the age of twenty or twenty-one. The authors say this is a high-risk time for drug use/ abuse. A "risk period" or "transitional period" requires individuals to participate in the new social roles of adulthood. These roles require movement toward interpersonal experiences (such as intimate relationships) and the resolution of intracultural expectations (the formation of a career and family). In spite of the apparent importance of the relationship between developmental tasks and substance abuse, Kandel concluded, "No systematic longitudinal analyses have yet been carried out in young adulthood to determine whether cessation of use follows or precedes entrance and exit from certain social roles" (Backman et al 1984, 642).

Social Models of Addiction

While the psychoanalytic literature emphasizes the personality and motivational issues associated with drug use, for example, the "set," the social models of addiction focus on the importance of physical and environmental determinants, for example, "setting." Often, sociological theories focus on the interaction between external setting variables with internal set variables in order to understand the complexity of drug use/abuse. This section will review the salient social learning theories under three major headings: (1) social learning, (2) peer group, (3) social predisposition, and (4) controlled substance use theory.

Social Learning Theories

The question, "What causes addiction?" is a chicken-and-egg problem. It is impossible, for example, to separate precisely environmental from genetic influences. Is there an "addictive personality"? Are there predisposing characteristics that make specific individuals prone to chemical abuse? Alternatively, we can ask whether addiction is the consequence of the social conditions that surround various individuals and their lifestyles.

Gendreau & Gendreau (1970, 1971) rejected the concept of the "addictive personality" after extensive methodological research. They say support for this personality type has not been based on any factual evidence but rather is an artifact of faulty research methods. Zinberg (1975) suggested that the regressed and "deteriorated ego state" of the addict is a consequence of cynical social conditions rather than a result of predisposing psychopathology. He maintains that the social milieu is crucial if one is to understand drug use and abuse.

Peer Group

It is impossible to have an educated discussion of peer groups and their influence without referring to the work of Chein, Gerard, Lee & Rosenfeld (1964). Their work, *The Road to H,* now almost twenty-five years old and somewhat limited in its demographic perspective, still stands as a classic that provides us with large-scale data within a psychologically meaningful framework. With respect to initial drug experimentation, Chein et al. (1964) stressed the easy availability of narcotics within a deviant peer group milieu as the major determinant to drug use initiation. Subsequent authors examined narcotic use across a broader sociological spectrum. These researchers also acknowledged the importance of exposure and access but attributed a more active role to individual motivational factors during the initiation process. Both Kandel (1978) and Robins (1974), for example, stress the role of peer influence during drug initiation. Kandel (1978) differentiated factors relevant to common licit drugs (tobacco, alcohol) and illicit drugs (marijuana). Poor relationships with parents, psychological distress, and more deviant personal characteristics distinguish between those who move away from socially popular drugs to those that are illicit (Jones et al 1981).

The social influence of peer drug-using groups, as well as other social variables, contribute to cocaine's popularity. The following are specific social factors associated with contemporary cocaine use patterns:

1. *Exposure*: The media continue to cover and sensationalize cocaine, and perhaps indirectly create an even larger cocaine market.
2. *Widespread Use and Social Acceptance*: The homogenization of cocaine (no longer the exclusive domain of the affluent) into all social classes provides equal opportunities for cocaine abuse among the entire spectrum of the population.
3. *Availability and Access*: The street price of cocaine has decreased while the quality has increased. Cocaine is affordable, relatively pure, and readily available in spite of the government's efforts to interdict.
4. *Misinformation*: The historical misconception by many that cocaine is without danger and therefore "safe" deceives curious people with a naive sense of confidence; this information can blind users to the warning signs of cocaine abuse.

Social Predisposition

One way of attempting to understand the social predisposition model of cocaine use and abuse is to apply the "drug of choice" theory to the United States. In other words, what is it about cocaine that the nation has found so appealing? In this section, we will speculate about how cocaine became Americans' illicit drug of choice.

Currently, it appears that our society favors the stimulants or energizing drugs; drugs representing other categories are experiencing diminished popularity. Although alcohol still remains the most widely used and abused drug in America, cocaine seems to represent the newest "opiate" of the masses. For example, according to law enforcement officers and public health officials in Massachusetts, cocaine has been considered the drug of choice (Foreman 1986). Cocaine may represent a continuation or extension of the widespread use of licit stimulants like cigarettes and caffeine.

In the recent past, the wholesale advertising of coffee (not linked to a brand name, but simply presented as a generic substance) appeared repeatedly on television. These advertisements are usually upbeat, fast-tempo music videos with cameo appearances of superstars endorsing coffee (a similar ad format is still used for caffeine-containing products like Coca-Cola and other soft drinks). The advertisements' slogans are "The Coffee Generation" or "The Coffee Achievers."

This achievement-oriented context of the 1980s may provide the influential setting for stimulant use and abuse. The American work ethic and Type A pressures of the current generation no longer are driving people to drink but rather to smoking, sipping, snorting, and sniffing. ". . . In its pharmacologic action cocaine, perhaps more than any other of the recognized psychoactive drugs, reinforces and boosts what we recognize as the highest aspirations of America: initiative, energy, frenetic achievement and ebullient optimism" (Newmeyer 1987).

The stimulating effects of cocaine appeal to, compliment, and are reinforced by, sociocultural values. America treasures productivity. In the face of trying economic times and mounting international economic challenges, American citizens are being asked to increase production. The consequence can lead to a stress response syndrome, for example, "burnout." Cocaine abuse often occurs in individuals who maintain high-functioning jobs. The stimulating effects of the drug are a means of energizing an exhausted autonomic nervous system. Freud often described the effects of cocaine as ". . . exhilaration and lasting euphoria." He added that "long-lasting, intensive mental or physical work can be performed without fatigue; it is as though the need for food and sleep . . . were completely banished. . . ." (Gay, Sheppard, Inaba & Newmeyer 1973, 1029–1030).

Controlled Substance Use Theory

As we discussed earlier, the best available evidence indicates that only a very small percentage of those who use cocaine lose the capacity to control their use. The ability to control psychoactive substance use is an idea readily accepted among Europeans; however, in America, such a point of view directly contradicts the "all or nothing" view[7] of the addictions that tends to dominate the thinking of the public as well as contemporary drug treatment specialists. The presence of "chippers" (occasional, nondependent users) and those who spontaneously recover from excessive, compulsive drug use, for example, challenges directly the basic tenets of the disease model.

Chippers are drug users who consume dependence-producing substances in a controlled manner. They are able to avoid physiological dependency or compulsive use (Harding 1983). Prior to Zinberg, Harding & Winkeller's (1977) work with heroin chippers, it was often thought that heroin use would inevitably lead to abuse, dependence, and addition. "Formerly, research was strongly influenced by the reigning stereotypic and moralistic view that all illicit drug use is bad and inevitably harmful, addictive, and that abstention is the only alternative" (Zinberg & Harding 1982, 13). Consequently, drug abuse researchers ". . . tended to equate use (any use) with abuse, and . . . seldom took occasional and moderate use into account as a viable pattern" (Zinberg & Harding 1982, 13). The capacity to control powerful psychoactive drugs is thought to be possessed by few. The observation that heroin cannot be used in a controlled way has been generalized to cocaine. The fact of the matter, though, is that the vast majority of people use cocaine in a controlled way without progressing to abuse (Chitwood 1985): 25 million people have tried cocaine and the majority have discarded it without crossing over the line to addiction (Smith 1986).

Proponents of the disease model argue that controlled use is: (1) an anomaly of our perception and does not really exist; (2) an exception rather than a rule, or (3) evidence of a transitory condition marking the beginning stages of a cocaine career. According to this view, controlled users inevitably become abusers and addicts. Nevertheless, there is a growing body of evidence that indicates that certain people ("chippers") can use psychoactive drugs that are capable of producing physical dependence in moderation— that is, use patterns that avoid addiction (Zinberg & Harding 1982; Zinberg 1984; Maloff, Becker, Fonaroff & Rodin 1982).

Zinberg et al. (1977) investigated heroin chippers over time to determine if they represented a discrete subgroup of individuals who were indeed able to avoid developing addictive drug careers. These researchers did, in fact, identify such a subgroup of drug users. They learned that social mechanisms serve an important regulatory function that helps to control intoxicating drug use. In another now-famous study by Robins, Helzer, Hesselbrock & Wish

---

[7]The disease model will be described more fully in the section on "biological models of addiction." This perspective is primarily responsible for the idea that drugs cannot be controlled by those individuals who are predisposed, either for genetic, psychologic, or biologic reasons, to uncontrolled drug use.

(1977), it was demonstrated that returning Vietnam veterans with heroin addictions were able to quit or moderate their heroin use once they returned home. Only 50 percent of the addicted Vietnam veterans used heroin at all once they returned to the States and just 12 percent relapsed into heroin addiction within the first three years after their return. These findings stand in direct contradiction to the finding that heroin addicts typically relapse at a rate between 60 percent and 80 percent (Orford 1985). Robins et al.'s findings suggest that drug abuse can be controlled more easily once situational stress (and accessibility of the drug) is removed.

A similar example of time-limited drug dependence occurs with hospital patients who are introduced to narcotics postoperatively (as pain medications) for a period of time sufficient to produce the characteristic withdrawal syndrome upon cessation. Most of these hospital patients develop "chronic morphinism" (physical dependency); yet termination of the medications are uncomplicated and withdrawal and craving nonexistent at discharge (Lindesmith 1981, 207). Lindesmith referred to the small percent who remained addicted to their postoperative medications as "morphinomanes" (morphine maniacs). He further noted that less than 10 percent of those patients who experience narcotic dependence become iatrogenically (medically) addicted.

Controlled Drinking and Intoxicant Use. Another aspect of the controlled substance use model concerns whether individuals who have experienced alcoholism can return to "social" or controlled drinking (Heather & Robertson 1981; Miller 1985). Conventional beliefs have argued energetically and emotionally that such a return is not only impossible, but dangerous and life-threatening as well. It is difficult, if not pointless, to determine precisely what percentage of chronic alcoholics are able to return to controlled drinking; questions of research strategy and methodology consistently arise. For example, opponents of the controlled substance use model argue that if one returns to social drinking, he or she could not have been diagnosed accurately as alcoholic. Similarly, opponents of this model argue that those who are offered as illustrations of controlled drinking do not actually control their drinking but that the reporting mechanisms are flawed and if we just wait, the individual will return to uncontrolled or alcoholic drinking patterns.

Davies (1962) reported that 15 percent of his alcoholic subjects who were followed for seven to eleven years were able to return to normal drinking; that is, noncompulsive and moderate drinking. Some studies report only 1.6 percent of chronic alcoholics were able to return to drinking "normally," while other researchers say as many as 18.2 percent of alcoholics achieve nonproblem drinking (Miller 1985, 207). Helzer et al. (1985) followed 1,289 alcoholics who were treated for alcoholism (a two-year program) by examining their fifth- to seventh-year outcome status and monitoring their alcohol consumption. The research revealed that "only 1.6 percent of the subjects met our definition of stable moderate drinking at follow-up, 15 percent had been totally abstinent, and 4.6 percent were mostly abstinent with occasional drinking" (Helzer et al. 1985, 1678). In other words, 6.2 percent of the sample were controlled drinkers, 15 percent were abstinent, and the rest of the subjects continued alcoholic drinking patterns. The "controlled drinkers" consisted of the following two groups: the "occasional drinker" and the "moderate drinker." This area of research is particularly interesting in light of current debates regarding whether there is even the possibility that controlled substance use—regardless of substance—can be achieved after a period of compulsive use.

The Heresy of Controlled Use Theory. The contemporary "disease controversy" between controlled substance use and disease model theorists is so heated a topic that research data tend to be obscured by fundamentalist passion and theory loyalty. Disease model proponents have more than pride and scientific status to lose by controlled substance use research. Their premise—that addiction is progressive and irreversible—is directly challenged by even the possibility of evidence that some individuals return to controlled substance use after a history of compulsive abuse. The controlled substance use theorists argue that the data speak for themselves and say they are being censured informally. The process of challenging conventional wisdom is part of the history of scientific development. When Galileo, Einstein, and Freud revolutionized their fields, they were also treated as heretics whose work was to be suppressed; the history of science teaches us that those who challenge the dogma of addictive disease will be treated similarly.

Given the available clinical and research evidence, it does seem that return to controlled, moderate alcohol or intoxicant use is possible for only a very small minority of those who experienced "out-of-control" compulsive using patterns. Conceptually, however, the numbers are less important than the fact that anyone can return to controlled use. The disease model of addiction suggests that any return to controlled use is impossible because the disease is progressive even in the substance's absence. According to the disease model, if one returns to alcohol use after a period of abstention, he or she will drink and suffer the ravages of alcoholism at the same level (or worse) as if he or she had been drinking all along. The fact that even *one* person can return to controlled drinking challenges the basic premises, concepts, and explanatory power of the disease model. This statement is made in spite of the fact that this model can and has pragmatically guided the recovery of many. In the same way that metaphorical "spring fever" is unrelated to febrile diseases, alcoholism may be unrelated to a primary "disease" process.

Mechanisms of Control. How people control their substance use has been examined by a number of researchers (for example, Apsler 1982; Maloff,

Becker, Fonaroff & Rodin 1982). Apsler demonstrated the presence of five different control styles that can be placed under two major categories: external and internal. The external standard of control relies on something outside of the individual's control to regulate substance intake. For example, the substance user: (1) uses the amounts others are using; (2) uses a regular amount that is commonly used (for example, one pack of cigarettes), or (3) uses the amount specified by somebody else. The internal standards of control include two major styles: the user (1) uses until he feels the way he wants to feel, and (2) uses until he gets a strong feeling to stop.

Maloff et al. (1982) described informal mechanisms of substance control that are usually built into the fabric of society. These mechanisms, or informal social controls, serve as "cultural recipes" learned through association with others in the community. Some examples of these "recipes" are "sumptuary rules" (for example, age requirements), and "sanctions" (for example, social consequences of unacceptable use) that help the user rehearse and use the substance in the presence of experienced users—somewhat like a substance-use apprenticeship. In sum, studies that focus on control mechanisms emphasize the interactive influences of forces that promote and restrict substance use.

Cocaine and Informal Social Control. Unlike alcohol, there are few informal social control mechanisms to regulate the use of cocaine; the few that may be available have not evolved rapidly enough to keep pace with cocaine's relatively recent and active growth. The social rituals and sanctions that have evolved to regulate the use of alcohol (such as cocktail hour, drinking with food, and social prescriptions such as "don't drink and drive") are unavailable for cocaine users. Because of its illegal nature, mechanisms of cocaine control are not taught through formalized networks within the user's social milieu (such as family or school systems). Mechanisms that might regulate cocaine use have not been transmitted from one generation to the next, nor have social sanctions and rituals been built into the user's social matrix. The usual social safeguards that protect individuals against addictive behavior remain underdeveloped for cocaine; this situation yields a high national potential for abusive cocaine use.[8]

In conclusion, to understand drug abuse, one cannot focus on the drug alone, nor solely on the personality of the drug user. It is essential to recognize the powerful influence of the social/cultural landscape against which drug use occurs and in which the drug user resides. Griffith Edwards, director of the intoxicant research center at the Maudsley Hospital in England, is one

---

[8]A more thorough discussion of social control mechanisms can be found in the afterword on pharmacology.

who clearly understands this complex interaction. Edwards once remarked in pointing out the fallacy of trying to separate the specific incident of drug-taking from its social matrix, "One could not hope to understand the English country gentleman's fox-hunting simply by exploring his attitude toward the fox" (Edwards 1974; cited in Zinberg & Shaffer 1985, 72).

Biological Models of Addiction

The biological component of chemical dependency emphasizes the "substance" component of Zinberg's "set," "setting," and "substance." This section will examine the biological theories of addiction. These discussions will include addictive "disease," "genetic" or hereditary, "chemical" or neuro-transmission, and "systemic imbalance" models. Finally, there will be a very short section on animal studies and addiction.

Disease Model

The disease model currently represents the most popular model of addiction in the United States. Interestingly, it is not the most dominant worldwide explanation for understanding addiction. As we said before, disease theory considers chemical dependency and "addictive disease" as a primary, predisposing disease that is progressive, incurable, and ultimately fatal if not arrested. In Alcoholics Anonymous (AA), for example, the first step in recovery is to admit being "powerless over alcohol." For the alcoholic, ". . . alcohol is a poison" and the only medicine for its remission is total lifelong sobriety. Even with long-term abstinence from alcohol the individual is not considered to be recovered but "recovering"—once an alcoholic always an alcoholic— because alcoholism is a progressive disease. The disease of alcoholism existed before the alcoholic ever took that first drink; an alcoholic is predisposed to become an alcoholic if he or she drinks (AA 1939/1976). Lifelong abstention is the only way to avoid the disease entirely.

Alcoholics Anonymous has been relatively successful in helping many overcome the devastation of alcohol dependence. "The therapeutic success of AA is difficult to evaluate. . . . But the available data suggest that although AA may only reach 5 to 10 percent of alcoholics, for those who attend meetings on a regular basis it is the most effective means of maintaining sobriety currently known. . . ." (Mack 1981).

In theory, the disease model shifts personal accountability from the individual to some external agent, thus reducing individual guilt and remorse. What had been associated previously with purposeful behavior can now be seen as the result of sickness. Acceptance of the disease model diminishes the harsh moralistic tone associated with both public attitudes toward alcoholics as well as how alcoholics view themselves. In short, the disease model of alcoholism allows blame or responsibility for the condition to reside outside of the afflicted "victim." If embraced, this view permits more individuals to make their closet sickness public, and receive treatment without fear of scorn and ridicule. In practice, however, the disease model is interpreted to mean that although the alcoholic suffers from an illness, the individual is personally and morally responsible for contracting the disease. If one accepts the moral position that "badness" coexists with "illness," it is easier to understand why alcoholics are willing to place themselves in the hands of others, such as AA, to ensure commitment to the cure. At this stage, the physician is no longer required as part of the equation—if the physician was ever necessary at all.

Recent evidence (Caetano 1987; Rohman et al. 1987; Shaffer 1987) has revealed that although the public and the medical profession are willing to call chemical dependency, cocaine abuse, and alcoholism diseases, this view continues to rest on a foundation of harsh moralistic judgment. This research has demonstrated that although people may be quite willing to comply with the convention of calling addiction a disease, underneath this veneer they do not seem to believe it. They do not consider addiction a disease in the same way they do for biologically based sicknesses such as cancer, malaria, measles, scarlet fever, or AIDS (Shaffer 1987).

Even the most strident disease model disciples are unsure of what they mean by disease. For example, in a recent letter to the editor of the Boston Globe, Comella (1987), an AIDS Action Committee drug treatment specialist and public health nurse, described her concerns about methadone maintenance and how the specter of AIDS was complicating drug treatment. She wrote ". . . I support the goal of drug-free living for all sick and suffering addicts. I believe in the unlimited potential of the human spirit and one's ability to change behavior with appropriate motivation and modeling. . . . Addiction is a disease. . . . When approached from this perspective, a person can be challenged to attempt a different way of coping with the support of people who help addicts to deal with their feelings. The addict may increasingly rely on support rather than utilizing a medication (methadone) that deadens feelings. . . . Methadone does not reduce the desire to get high. Methadone does not take the larceny out of the addict's heart: it does not address the denial of the disease, nor does it allow one to feel. Treatment must confront behavior. . . . human interaction yields change; methadone is ultimately an enabler in the disease of addiction" (p. 20).

Comella's letter illustrates the confusion and nexus that exists between the addiction-as-disease and addiction-as-immoral behavior approach. The primary objective of the addictive disease model has been to eliminate personal responsibility for developing and resolving substance dependence problems. The moral model located responsibility both for the cause and the cure of addiction within the individual (Marlatt, Baer, Donovan & Kivlahan 1988). Comella, like many other disciples of the disease model, argues that addiction is a disease; however, she then suggests that behavioral methods be used to help challenge and confront addicts so that they can cope more effectively. She also wants the addict to change—not only the behavior she says is central to the disease of addiction—but also what is in their hearts: larceny and denial. It seems Comella wants us to adopt the view of addicts as diseased, hold them responsible for their disease, and then treat them as if they were scoundrels. The confluence of the moral and disease models is self-evident. Taken to its logical conclusion, this treatment of disease would result in the moral condemnation of victims of cancer, heart disease, tuberculosis, epilepsy, or AIDS. One can only speculate about the heartfelt motives that Comella would like to excise in these patients.

Although the disease model of addiction has been useful in helping many excessive drug users get on the road to recovery, it has been challenged conceptually by many theorists, researchers, and clinicians in the field as unscientific and theoretically weak (Marlatt et al. 1988). Disease model disciples, like Comella, have managed to confuse others, and perhaps themselves, by suggesting that certain socially unacceptable behavior patterns are the result of disease processes (such as addiction) while others are not (such as forgery).

During an examination of the foundations of mental illness and addictive disease, Szasz noted that "the modern concept of 'mental illness' . . . progressively metaphorized disagreeable conduct and forbidden desire as disease—thus creating more and more mental diseases; second, they literalized this medical metaphor, insisting that disapproved behavior was not merely *like* a disease, but that it *was* a disease—thus confusing others, and perhaps themselves as well, regarding the differences between bodily and behavioral 'abnormalities' " (Szasz 1974, 5). Addiction is a social phenomenon that mimics contagious disease. It appears to "spread" to hosts that are vulnerable and affect them adversely. In this sense, the metaphor of addictive disease is useful to map the phenomenon under examination. We must not confuse the map with the territory or else we risk eating the menu instead of the meal (Shaffer 1985). Physicians who mistakenly fail to understand disease in the metaphorical sense could find themselves writing prescriptions for the treatment of spring fever or performing bypass surgery on "larcenous hearts."

Genetic Theory

Recently, Collins (1985) reviewed the essential literature concerning genetics and alcoholism. His analysis of how alcoholism is transmitted within families suggests that children of alcoholic parents have a two to four times greater probability of becoming alcoholics than the general population (that is, children from nonalcoholic parents). Adoption studies also indicate that adopted children with alcoholic biological parents had four times a greater incidence of alcoholism than adopted children who had nonalcoholic biological parents (for example, Goodwin 1979).

It is extremely difficult for scientists to separate hereditary and environmental factors in their research. Those who argue against genetic predisposition for addiction suggest that the negative results of being reared in a dysfunctional, chemically abusing family may sufficiently impair offspring and produce a vulnerability to alcohol/chemical dependency. This argument does little to offset the importance of the adoption studies mentioned above, however. The "nurture versus nature" dichotomy is ultimately a straw man. Environmental and genetic factors are always confluent in effect; the weight of their interaction represents shifting influences on human behavior. Many adoption studies, for example, neglect to inform the reader of "nurture" influences that may have affected the subjects studied. Consider the importance of an adopted child's exposure to a biological parent who is addicted. Heath (1987) recognized that all models that stress the role of genetics in determining alcoholism also stress the interaction of this factor with individual, social, and other environmental factors.

Vaillant's (1983) longitudinal study of the natural history of alcoholism found that Irish Americans were much more likely to become alcoholics than Southern Europeans. This finding can easily be interpreted as confirmation that alcoholism or other chemical dependencies are genetically based. Peele (1984) noted, however, that American Indians and Chinese Americans—two groups recognized for their shared and exaggerated metabolic reactions to alcohol—manifest very dissimilar rates of alcoholism. Although similar in biological predisposition, these different rates of alcoholism seem to reflect the dissimilar social mechanisms responsible for their respective styles of drinking.

Heath (1987) summarized the problems associated with a strict genetic explanation of addiction: "It has been recognized since ancient times that something like what we call 'alcoholism' tended to 'run in families'—but so does speaking Swahili, eating with chopsticks, attending Oxford University, being a bank president, or a number of other behavior patterns that no one would think of calling genetic" (p. 21). "The popular misconception of the meaning of 'alcoholism as a genetic disease' harms not only the social sciences (by inappropriately discrediting the relevance of environmental factors), but it also is prejudicial to most approaches toward prevention, and may even undermine treatment for many who need it. Until gene splicing becomes routine, far too many people view genetics as destiny, unalterable so that the quest for a 'marker' becomes viewed as a hope of labeling incipient alcoholics at an early age, and anyone who ignored that warning would certainly be trapped. Such labeling and such resignation may be harmful to any number of individuals who might otherwise enjoy the benefits of drinking along with other aspects of a more 'normal' life" (p. 30).

Chemical Receptor Site Theory

There are important biochemical mechanisms that influence the subjective effects of psychoactive drugs. In this section, we will explore briefly some of these structures and examine cocaine's influence on brain chemistry to better understand its effects (Eckholm 1986; Bardo & Risner 1985; Gold et al. 1985).

All drugs alter the brain's chemistry within the central nervous system. First, the drug (for example, cocaine) enters the blood-stream of the user via various routes of administration (such as through oral, intranasal, intravenous administration, or by smoke inhalation and "freebasing"). Orally ingested drugs take the longest to be absorbed by the bloodstream; drugs that are smoked (tobacco and "freebased" cocaine) or injected intravenously are more rapidly absorbed. Once the drug is in the bloodstream, it penetrates the blood-brain barrier. This barrier is where the drug joins with the brain's neurochemistry. Chemical messengers called neurotransmitters are altered by the presence of a drug.

The effects of drugs on biochemical and neurotransmitter processes are very complicated and will be described only in a most elementary form. Each chemical message travels through and along a nerve cell, or neuron, to a location at the end of the nerve known as an end foot or presynaptic terminal. Every neuron ends at a gap that marks the end of one neuron and the beginning of the next; this gap is known as the synapse. An electrical charge that spreads down the neuron causes the neurotransmitters to be released, along with their messages, into the synapse. Three things can happen to a neurotransmitter once it has entered the synapse: (1) it can attach itself to the neuron located on the other side of the synapse (that is, the postsynaptic membrane); (2) it can be deactivated or neutralized by metabolic process; or, (3) it can be retrieved or taken back to the first neuron in the presynaptic membrane or end foot area. This process of retrieval is referred to as a "reuptake" mechanism.

Cocaine specifically blocks the reuptake of three neurotransmitters: dopamine, norepinephrine, and serotonin. These neurotransmitters are associated with feelings of euphoria (for example, dopamine) and other functions of the autonomic nervous system. If the process of reuptake is inhibited, more neurotransmitters than normal are available within the synapse. Both amphetamine and cocaine increase dopamine's availability, although via different mechanisms. Amphetamines stimulate the release of dopamine; cocaine blocks dopamine reuptake.

Initially, the physical effects of cocaine are dilation of the pupils, narrowing of blood vessels, increased heart rate and blood pressure, and decrease in appetite. These physical responses to cocaine also occur when the sympathetic nervous system is activated as in a "fight or flight situation" (Kauffman et al 1985). With repeated use of cocaine, neurotransmitters can be depleted by what we can consider a burning of the chemical candle at both ends. Without the availability of essential neurotransmitters, the user does not have the ability to maintain a normal mood; a chemical depression with concurrent anxiety and cocaine cravings typically follows neurotransmitter depletion. This cocaine depression is called "crashing" or "cocaine blues" by the users. "The same process—blockage of neurotransmitter retrieval—can cause brain convulsions, an increase in heart rate, constriction of blood vessels and increased blood pressure, which may account for some of the cardiovascular deaths among cocaine users" (Eckholm 1986, 24).

Chronic cocaine abuse eventually depletes the brain's capacity to manufacture these indispensable neurotransmitters on its own. Thus, the artificial substance (cocaine) is needed to continue "normal" chemical functioning in the brain. In short, chemical receptor site theory suggests that self-induced changes in neurotransmission are responsible for addictive behavior (Milkman & Sunderwirth 1983).

Chemical receptor theorists speculate that some individuals have a deficiency of certain chemicals in their brain. Rather than becoming addicted because of the depleting effects of chronic drug abuse, it is hypothesized that these people do not produce sufficient supplies of opiate-like chemicals naturally produced by the brain, (that is, endorphins). Therefore, it is argued, individuals who are chemically deficient in their brain chemistry seek external chemicals to compensate for their internal biological inadequacy.

Systemic Imbalance Theory

Systemic imbalance theorists postulate that a predisposing biochemical imbalance exists in the chemically dependent person and that "relief" can be obtained by the application of cocaine or other psychoactive substances. Khantzian & Treece (1985) examined 133 opiate addicts and found that 60 percent of them suffered from depression or described a history of depression. Mirin & Weiss (1986) studied the biological correlates of substance abuse and found that a substantial minority of drug users experience psychiatric problems that preceded drug abuse; these disorders include affective disorders, attention deficit disorder, generalized anxiety disorder, and panic disorder. Stimulant abusers evidence a higher frequency of affective disorders (particularly bipolar illness) than any other type of drug users. Among cocaine abusers, there is a higher rate of affective disorder than among non-stimulant users. Cocaine users also have a higher rate of positive family history of affective illness. Systemic imbalance theorists struggle with some of the same questions that plague other biological researchers. Which, for example, came first, the biochemical imbalance or the drug use?

Subtypes of Cocaine Users. Khantzian et al. (1984) found four subtypes of cocaine users who are at risk for cocaine abuse: "(a) pre-existent chronic depression (dysthymic disorder); (b) cocaine abstinence depression; (c) hyperactive/restless/emotional liability syndromes or attention deficit disorders (add); and (d) cyclothymic" (1984, 110). In more familiar terms, these subtypes were: (1) unipolar depression; (2) postcocaine depression due to a withdrawal abstinence syndrome; (3) problems with hyperactivity; and (4) manic-depressive illness. These clinical conditions all represent problems with mood regulation and affect. Khantzian explains that cocaine is an energizing drug that produces norepinephrine at specific receptor sites within the central nervous system. The production of norepinephrine elevates an individual's psychic and physical energy level. His psychoanalytically based premise is that depressed persons who are lacking the qualities cocaine produces might self-medicate with the drug in much the same way a pharmacologist prescribes antidepressants for the treatment of depression.

The recently abstinent cocaine user has a particular biological dilemma. It has been speculated that chronic cocaine use depletes neurotransmitters (see previous "chemical" section). Consequently, a chemical depression occurs that makes the ex-cocaine addict vulnerable to relapse in order to compensate for chemical deficits. Hyperactive individuals use cocaine, paradoxically, to calm themselves down, just as Ritalin (a stimulant) is used to treat hyperactive children. Finally, the manic-depressive person uses cocaine to change his or her biological poles; that is "reverse dysthymic cycles or improve rythmic mood states, and thus produce or maintain a functional hypomanic state which they consider normal" (Khantzian et al. 1984, 110).

Animal Studies and Addiction

There are a remarkably large number of animal studies in the addictions field. Some findings are important, if not essential, to an understanding of human addiction; most, however, are not relevant to natural recovery and cocaine quitting. We will review here one ingenious set of experiments called the "Rat Park Chronicle" (Alexander, Hadaway & Coambs 1980). This study integrates many of the findings and principles obtained from other animal research and illuminates some of the most basic assumptions about addiction and the interactive role of set, setting, and substance.

Alexander et al. (1980) compared opiate intake among two rat colonies. Each colony consisted of a radically different environment. The first rat environment was the typical laboratory setup of steel cages; each cage contained one rat that was physically isolated from the other rats. The second setting attempted to achieve a natural rat habitat: "Rat Park is open and spacious, with about 200 times the square footage of a standard cage. It is also scenic (with a peaceful, British Columbian forest painted on the plywood walls), comfortable (with empty tin cans and other desiderata strewn about the floor), and friendly (we ran coed groups of 16-20 rats)" (Alexander et al. 1980, 55).

The researchers conducted three experiments called the "easy access," the "seduction," and "kicking-the-habit" (p. 55). The "easy access" procedure involved two drinking solutions available to both rat colonies around the clock. These solutions consisted of narcotic morphine with sugar added, and sugar water.

The "seduction" procedure offered two liquids to the rats; one solution was morphine with an ever-increasing level of sugar (increases occurred every five days). Apparently, rats have a "sweet tooth" and the researchers sweetened the pot, or, in this case, the morphine. The second solution in the seduction experiment was plain, unsweetened water.

The third condition, "kicking-the-habit," provided the rats with only the morphine solution for a period (fifty-seven days) sufficient to produce physical dependence. The dependent rats were then given two solutions to choose from: morphine or water. The statistically significant results indicated the following: "No matter how much we induced, seduced, or tempted them, the Rat Park rats resisted drinking the narcotic solution. The caged rats drank plenty, however, ranging up to 16 times as much as the Rat Park residents in one experimental phase and measuring 10 times as much in some other phases" (Alexander et al. 1980, 56).

The researchers concluded that if rats are given a suitable environment in which to live, they will resist drug use. Alexander et al. (1980, 56) also state that the typical laboratory setting is extremely stressful for rats (and other animals) who are temperamentally "gregarious, active, curious animals." When put into "solitary confinement" with only a drug, "extreme forms of coping behavior" occur, such as drug intoxication. We believe these findings have important implications for humans and for the conventional belief that there are "addictive" drugs. It appears that drugs per se have little capacity for addiction and some capacity to produce physical dependence. The unique subjective effects or consequences of drug taking behavior has much more to do with the combination of substance, set, and setting.

Animal researchers, in their efforts to reduce extraneous variables, often contaminate the results of their own studies. Their research supposedly (1) eliminates "set" as a variable; (2) creates a world for the animal that exaggerates "setting" (and an artificial one at that) in which the animal exists in isolation and sensory deprivation; and then (3) draws conclusions based on the particular "substance" studied as if a drug could be observed in isolation.

Summary

Drug abuse and addiction have been considered the consequence of a complicated blend of biological, psychological, and sociological factors. In short, drug abuse and addiction reside neither in the drug nor in the personality of the user. Addictive behaviors are the result of many interactive factors that vary in prominence from individual to individual. It is essential to take a multidimensional view of drug use, abuse, and addiction: the psychological determinants of drug use, the developmental phase in which abuse occurs, the social and cultural contexts in which intoxicants are used and abused, and the pharmacological properties of the substance. Zinberg offered the tripartite model for understanding drug effects; that is, set, setting, and drug (substance). In this chapter, we reviewed a representative sample of models from each of these domains. In the next chapter, we will examine cocaine and the media.

4
Cocaine and the Media

Throughout history, drug use and abuse have been portrayed in vastly differing ways by the media. Substances now regularly consumed around the world were once depicted as poisonous. For example, Weil & Rosen (1983, 181–182) translated a portion of Johann Sebastian Bach's Coffee Cantata. This piece was written around 1732 when coffee drinking began to emerge from the male-dominated coffee houses and enter private homes where women began to drink it. In the cantata, the father is angry because his daughter is a coffee "addict." The following excerpt from the dialogue reveals how similar human attitudes have remained while the objects of those beliefs have changed.

Father: O wicked child! Ungrateful daughter, why will you not respect my wishes and cease this coffee drinking?

Daughter: Dear Father, be not so unkind; I love my cup of coffee at least three times a day, and if this pleasure you deny me, what else on earth is there to live for? [continuing in solo aria]: Far beyond all other pleasures, rarer than jewels or treasures, sweeter than grape from the vine. Yes! Yes! Greatest of pleasures! Coffee, coffee, how I love its flavor, and if you would win my favor, yes! Yes! let me have coffee, let me have my coffee strong.

Father: Well, pretty daughter, you must choose. If sense of duty you have none, then I must try another way. My patience is well nigh exhausted! Now listen! From your dress allowance I will take one half. Your next birthday should soon be here; no present will you get from me.

Daughter: ... How cruel! But I will forgive you and consolation find in coffee ...

Father: Now, hearken to my last word. If coffee you must have, then a husband you shall not have.

Daughter: O father! O horror! Not a husband?

Father: I swear it, and I mean it too.

Daughter: O harsh decree! O cruel choice, between a husband and my joy. I'll strive no more; my coffee and I surrender.

Father: At last you have regained your senses. [The daughter now sings a melancholy aria of resignation.]

Tenor: And now, behold the happy father as forth he goes in search of a husband, rich and handsome, for his daughter. But the crafty little maiden has quite made up her mind, that, ere she gives consent to marriage, her lover must make a solemn promise that she may have her coffee whenever and wherever she pleases.

The message of this cantata, with slightly different verse and focus, has been repeated throughout the years. Parents and governments have urged young people to change their ways and engage in different, more socially acceptable patterns of behavior. How many times have we heard, for example, individuals sigh with relief upon discovering that the intoxicant their child is involved with is alcohol rather than some other drug?

The Media and Drug Abuse Hype

At the turn of the twentieth century, medical textbooks referred to coffee and tea as poisons that were responsible for hallucinations and haggard appearances. Over the years, however, these substances have become accepted as mainstream. Coffee and tea are not considered as threats to the moral fiber of our contemporary youth.

In the United States, substance abuse hyperbole has been increasingly evident since the summer of 1986;[1] it now continues unabated. In this chapter, we will reexamine briefly the extent of drug abuse in this country and the trends evidenced by the past seven or eight years, as well as how this information has been exaggerated by the media. " 'The place of the drug issue among the problems of society has been exaggerated by the press,' says Ben H. Bagdikian, dean of the journalism school at the University of California at Berkeley. 'Trends in drug use have been misrepresented. The impression that has been given is that the problem is out of control and growing. That's simply not true' " (Gladwell 1986, 10).

Journalism. Weisman (1986), a noted journalist, "came clean" in his compelling article about the euphoria journalists experience when writing about drugs.

> Everything I read and everybody I talked to made drugs sound really bad, and I began to become intoxicated by the overwhelmingly negative reputation they have. What I didn't realize was that I was losing track of the facts

---

[1]The interested reader is encouraged to study the work of Trebach (1987) for the relevant and important account of the role that drug wars play in our society and the tendency for media and government to exaggerate drug use trends. His work was influential in the organization of this chapter.

and slipping into a journalistic dream world where the writer is free to write almost anything he chooses because nobody was going to defend drug abuse in America, least of all the people who use drugs every day. In a way, it was the perfect cover story: sensational, colorful, gruesome, alarmist, with a veneer of social responsibility. Unfortunately, it just wasn't true (p. 15).

For a reporter at a national news organization in 1986, the drug crisis in America is more than a story, it's an addiction—and a dangerous one. Some, but not all, of us feel mighty guilty for having tried to convince readers that practically everyone they know is addicted to crack, and that they too are likely to be addicted soon. We know the rush that comes from supporting these claims with a variety of questionable figures, graphs, and charts, and often we enjoy it. Blatant sensationalism is a high. . . . Let me say flat out that drug abuse in America is not a good thing, and that people who do drugs have become more messed up in recent years as drugs have become cheaper, more plentiful, and more potent. The problem is, the statistics do not show that more people are doing drugs. That doesn't mean drug abuse isn't a major problem. It is. But it is not, as Newsweek would have it, an epidemic "as pervasive and as dangerous in its way as the plagues of medieval times." Nor are drugs, as U.S. News and World Report puts it, "the nation's No. 1 menace." Not while we still have poverty, unemployment, illiteracy, malnutrition, murder, and the Soviet Union (Weisman 1986, 15[2]).

After explaining how he and other journalists duped the public about drug use levels in order to sell magazines, Weisman summarized the most recent drug use trends according to the National Institute on Drug Abuse, our government's most reliable source of information about drug abuse.

Based on NIDA's figures for 1985, 17 percent of all high school seniors have tried cocaine at least once in their life. That's a whopping increase of one percent from 1984. Between 1982 and 1984, the percentage held steady at 16. An upward trend? Sorry. In 1981, 17 percent said they had tried the white stuff. Yes, the percentage did go up in 1985, but it has been hovering around the 16 percent mark for almost seven years. Wouldn't it be more accurate to refer to the '84 to '85 increase as a fluctuation? If we were talking about the stock market, would a one percent increase four years after a one percent decrease and a three-year period of stability be cover-story material? Not on your life. . . . Here are some other drug abuse trends. According to NIDA, among 1985 high school seniors, one-time-minimum use of marijuana is down. So is the use of inhalants, hallucinogens, stimulants, sedatives, barbiturates, alcohol, and cigarettes. What's up, other than cocaine? Nothing. Several categories have held steady, including amyl and butyl nitrates, LSD, PCP, heroin, opiates other than heroin, and tranquilizers. . . . Are you alarmed by NIDA's statistics? Not particularly (Weisman 1986, 15).

[2]Excerpts by permission of *The New Republic*, 1986, The New Republic, Inc.

We can speculate that Weisman decided to "come clean" because he realized that journalistic hyperbole might lead to decreased credibility. Someone other than print media mavens might examine the data and come to very different conclusions about the extent of drug abuse. Other journalists, public policy makers (Kaplan 1983; Trebach 1987), and scientists corroborated Weisman's assessment of journalistic excess. For example, young adults ". . . age 18-25, those allegedly with too much money and few moral restraints, actually reduced current cocaine use from 9.3 percent in 1979 to 7.7 percent in 1985" (Trebach 1987, 13). "Hodding Carter, host of PBS's *Capitol Journal*, added his support to the growing number of individuals who identified the seduction of public acclaim. 'What the media have done is to throw the blood into the water and then look back and say, 'My, my, the sharks are feeding on this blood in Congress',' said Carter on the *MacNeil/Lehrer NewsHour* last week" (Henry 1986, 73).

Television. Television producers and news people have not been exempt from the "high" associated with exaggerating drug problems in the United States. Diamond, Accosta & Thornton (1987) asked whether TV news was hyping America's cocaine problem.[3] "Vietnam was the first living-room war, its scenes of death carried into American homes by the reach of network television. In the same way, cocaine . . . can be thought of as our first living room drug. Television brought crack home to us in the summer of 1986 with a frequency that was both furious and frightening. . . . A study of last summer's coverage of the 'crack epidemic' compared to the then available facts suggests that the network's alarums about a new nationwide plague of cocaine and crack addiction were exaggerated" (p. 5).

Diamond et al. (1987) conducted a study that sampled three time periods (baseline, surge of stories, reaction) and the corresponding extent of drug abuse and media coverage. The authors concluded, "there was no evidence that the level of drug abuse changed; rather, it was the level of media reporting of drug abuse—and, above all, of some dramatic cocaine cases—that soared and plummeted" (p. 6). Producers, lured by the high of high ratings, continued to exploit the public by presenting stories that they, like Weisman, knew were exaggerated. For example, '48 Hours on Crack Street'—a CBS documentary—reached 15 million viewers, the largest TV audience in the past five years. In the face of the mounting media attention to cocaine and crack related stories, on September 24, 1986 the Strategic Intelligence Section of the DEA released a report that said "attention to crack—as opposed to overall cocaine use—might have been 'excessive.' The drug, the agency suggested, was a 'secondary rather than primary problem in most areas.' That night, NBC's Tom Brokaw briefly mentioned the DEA story in his lead-in to

---

[3]The authors are members of the News Study Group at New York University.

a report on drug testing in the Boston police force. ABC's World News To-night skipped the DEA story, as did CBS Evening News" (Diamond et al. 1987, 10). The networks also questioned whether television programming should be used as a weapon in the war against drugs (Esterly 1987). Apparently, "good" news produces neither the rush nor the ratings.

Where is the "Good" News? Trebach (1987) also wondered why encouraging data about drug abuse seem to receive little attention. For example, although alcohol use has increased in some categories—alcohol use (during the past year) is up 1 percent since 1980 according to the NIDA findings reported earlier—we also know that deaths caused by driving drunk have decreased. Social efforts condemning driving drunk have worked—deaths caused by drunken driving peaked in 1970 at forty-seven per one hundred thousand and bottomed in 1983 at the lowest rate in history of thirty-five per one hundred thousand. All involved in this effort should be highly commended (Trebach 1987). It is interesting to note, however, that these lower rates (we recognize that we all still have even lower rates to strive for) actually preceded the media blitz of the late 1980s in which public service messages implored: "friends don't let friends drive drunk."

To suggest, as have some of our leading political figures, particularly during an election year, that substance abuse is the biggest issue that they have encountered in public life ignores totally the omnipresent threat of AIDS, nuclear annihilation, cardiovascular disease, cancer, poverty, domestic violence, and child abuse. Public life can be very isolating indeed.

In spite of the wealth of available evidence that suggests the media have provided uneven and sensationalistic treatment of drug related news, we are fully aware of the dangers associated with drug use. In the absence of a drug abuse "epidemic," the absolute level of drug use still remains a serious problem and very real concern. Every life touched by substance abuse risks tragic consequences. Nevertheless, people of all ages know someone who has tried an illicit drug and lived to tell about it. These individuals include Supreme Court nominees and presidential candidates. Like Trebach (1987), by calling for more calm and reason, we risk being misperceived as apologists or drug abusers. No thoughtful person would encourage drug abuse. We are not now nor ever have been in favor of psychoactive drug abuse. It is important to recognize—and this is why we decided to take the risk—that there is no situation so bad that we cannot make it worse (Kaplan 1985, personal communication). Exaggerated stories of drug abuse and tragedy may unwittingly sustain, or even increase, the current level of drug abuse.

Some Consequences of "Hyping" Drug Abuse

There are serious consequences of drug abuse hyperbole and misinformation. It is possible that media claims will lead to disenfranchisement among generations of youth, not to mention their parents. When greed encourages the media to mislead viewers with exaggerated information they readily understand as unrealistic and irrelevant, the media lose legitimacy. Hysteria and hyperbole only serve to reduce media credibility. We all know of the "boy who cried wolf" once too often; dramatic cries of spreading drug plagues have echoed more than once in the face of reliable evidence to the contrary. The primary benefactors of the 1986–87 drug abuse media blitz have been urine analysis laboratories and inpatient drug treatment programs. Many of these secure programs have diagnosed and admitted young people who did not have drug abuse problems (Trebach 1987); falsely imprisoned individuals have won lawsuits or received settlements as a result of overzealous clinicians who tried to fill treatment slots at the encouragement of parents who felt out of control.

One Small Town in America. The sense of lost control can be illustrated by the recent events in a small suburban town near Boston. The residents of Andover, Massachusetts were asked to rally in response to the conclusions offered in a new study of thirty Andover residents—identified for interview by the superintendent of schools and/or associated town officials—that "there is concern about how parents raise their kids." The alleged study, which attracted statewide media attention, suggested that Andover had a substance abuse problem. The implicit message of this study was that Andover had a drug problem that was worse than other communities because parents in Andover were apathetic and morally bankrupt.

The suggestion that more community involvement would solve this problem was overly simplistic. The history of intoxicant abuse is more than seven thousand years old; community participation has never succeeded in ending it. National prohibition did not end alcohol abuse. There have been situations in which well-intended social policies and programs actually increased social problems rather than reduced them. Several high school principals have requested us to come and talk about drug abuse with their students—after a so-called expert who employed scare tactics actually increased the problem! Similarly, patients in our practices regularly report, for example, that television advertisements intended to reduce or prevent cocaine use stimulate their desire for the drug. News stories about celebrity antidrug messages have corroborated this observation (Frisby 1987).

Under some conditions, interviews with thirty carefully selected sources could possibly (but not likely) reflect a cross-section of a small, fifty-thousand-person community. This sample, however, was selected without scientific care. These thirty sources offer little more than selected opinion; conclusions based on feelings should be considered little more than speculation and tender nothing more than food for thought. Presented in the face of conflicting evidence available to everyone, findings such as these do little more than diminish scientific credibility and increase public apathy. Indifference is an appropriate response to irrelevance. The solution to apathy is neither social blame nor political manipulation. Honesty still is the best social policy. Just ask the boy who cried wolf.

In his zest to confront a problem largely created by the media, the superintendent of the Andover schools was chastised publicly for undertaking and promulgating this bizarre study without informing the school committee to whom he directly reported. Remarkably, about eight weeks after Andover was disrupted by political and media hype, Andover High School was named as one of America's model drug prevention programs (Carras 1988).[4]

One American Family. The fear and anxiety stimulated by exaggerated claims about drug abuse have led many to employ dramatic methods. Consider the story of Deanna Young, the thirteen-year-old who turned in her parents to the police to stop their drug involvement. "Deanna Young had finally had enough. Her decision came as she listened to an anti-drug lecture at the Peace Lutheran Church in Orange County, Calif. She returned home and collected her evidence in a trash bag. Shortly before midnight she went to a police station—and turned in her parents for alleged drug abuse. . . . she had already tried less drastic ways to make her parents give up drugs. She confronted her mother with what she thought were telltale marijuana seeds and pleaded with her father to stop. She says when they didn't she flushed their dope down the toilet. After the drug lecture Deanna went home with new resolve. She collected drug-packaging equipment, pills and nearly an ounce of cocaine—with an estimated street value of $2,800. . . . Bob Theeming, director of a county foster-care facility, . . . called Deanna's action 'a genuine act of love.' Her mom and dad may find it hard to agree. Police arrested Judith Young, 37, . . . when she went down to the station to pick up Deanna. Officers were waiting for Bobby Young, 49, as he returned home. . . . Charged with possession of cocaine, Deanna's parents now face a possible sentence of three years in prison—and Deanna, who at a custody hearing pleaded that she be allowed to return home, was ordered for the time being to remain a ward of the state" (Turning in your parents 1986, 34).

Media Hype, Conventional Wisdom, and Epistemology

As we discussed in chapter 3, Understanding Addiction, empirical findings inconsistent with the prevailing wisdom tend to be suppressed, oppressed, and even censured. When research findings anomalous with conventional

---

[4]It is incredible to think that while the superintendent of schools was reporting the "study" findings that focused on Andover's drug and alcohol problems, the high school was concurrently submitting its claim as the "best drug-free program" (Carras 1988).

views are ignored or denied, the conventional ways of understanding a social problem are maintained and the conceptual (that is, epistemological) crisis is averted.

Conceptual crises are dilemmas in knowing; these emergencies challenge existing ways of knowing and, therefore, threaten epistemological structures. It is important to understand the nature of epistemological crises, or crises of knowing, and establish how and when these occur. In order to accomplish this, a brief diversion is necessary before we return to our discussion of media and conventional wisdom.

Epistemological Crises. Macintyre (1980) suggests that in order to understand epistemological crises most simply, we should consider the events of ordinary, day-to-day life. Consider, for example, someone who believes that he is highly valued by his employer and colleagues but is suddenly fired; consider someone who is proposed for membership in a club by members who are believed to be close friends and supporters, but who is then blackballed; or finally, consider someone who has fallen in love and wants to know how the loved one "really" feels, or alternatively, someone falls out of love and feels the need to know how he or she could have been so wrong in his or her earlier judgments. For each of these people, the relationship of what *is* to what *seems to be* becomes critical. These individuals encounter difficulties associated with inferring the presence of generalizable, "invisible" feelings, thoughts, motives, from the behaviors they have observed. This capacity to generalize is valuable, if not essential; this process helps sustain beliefs that enable us to predict reliably the future behavior of those around us. The sense that we know what is and what will happen around us provides a modicum of stability and the illusion of control.

In each of the examples above, what was taken as unequivocal evidence (that is, the inferred motives, feelings, etc.) that pointed in one particular direction turned out to be information that had meaningful alternative interpretations. The awareness of meaningful alternative explanations for the same evidence can be paralyzing. Given the seemingly infinite number of interpretations available to each of us during the course of our day-to-day social lives, we could barely act if every alternative interpretation required careful consideration. This problem is magnified even more by the existence of human error, deception, irony, ambivalence, self-deception, and so on. During the course of routine social activities, defense mechanisms (such as denial) operate to reduce the conflict associated with confusing environmental information. When denial mechanisms break down and alternative explanations of our existence become unavoidable, a crisis has occurred.

Scientific Crises and the Media. As we discussed earlier, in science, when anomalous data are ignored, denied, or suppressed, current ways of knowing are maintained and a crisis averted. There is a natural tendency among social systems to avert crises and, therefore, maintain the status quo. Print and electronic media are expressions of a culture's conventions and priorities: what news is important and what is not is a direct expression of a culture's value system.

Science, as a way of knowing, is as much an extension of the popular media as the media are an extension of science. The media maintain a culture's conventional wisdom by attending to those stories the society deems important and are blinded to the data that are inconsistent with that view. Thus, it should not surprise us to learn that interesting, if not essential, drug abuse prevalence data are ignored by the media when they do not conform with the audience's, sponsor's, or producer's invested point of view. Further, it is impossible for governments to wage war against a foe that is not, in fact, spreading like some plague.

Two competing world views cannot be held simultaneously. Either drug abuse is epidemic and war is warranted, or drug abuse is static and sustained levels of intervention are appropriate. Consequently, some data are censured to maintain an orderly world view. Since the summer of 1986, the American public has been led by the media to believe that drug abuse—cocaine and crack abuse in particular—has been increasing geometrically. In spite of all the best available data that suggest otherwise, politicians campaigned on an antidrug platform and local communities budgeted for drug abuse prevention. On January 25, 1988, in his last State of the Union address, President Reagan reported that drug abuse in the United States had diminished; quickly, he added that we must continue every effort in our "war" against drugs.

Conclusions

The question here is not whether Deanna Young's parents, the Andover school system, or the United States can use help to regain control over drug using behaviors; the essential issue is how our society understands and, therefore, suggests that we support loved ones who are troubled by drug involvement. Hyperbolic media claims maintain cultural convention and stimulate exaggerated interventions capable of waging destructive havoc on families and communities. At the very least, genuine honesty about drugs and their influence is required for social policy to be believed, accepted, and enforced. Media hype may be one of the essential factors, making an admittedly difficult situation worse.

5
Natural Recovery: Quitting Cocaine without Treatment

Natural Cocaine Recovery: Background

Individuals who recover from drug dependence without the intervention of professional drug treatment services or lay groups such as Cocaine Anonymous are given a variety of names, for example, "spontaneous," "natural," or "untreated" recoverers. Very little is known about these people. While the subject of natural recovery from psychoactive substances such as alcohol and opiates has received some attention in the professional literature, cocaine-specific natural recovery processes have not been examined.

One of the reasons for this scarcity of information is that most theorists, researchers, and clinicians in the addictions have not accepted the proposition that such people exist or even that the phenomenon of natural recovery is possible. For example, proponents of the disease model of addiction energetically assert a position similar to that proposed by Johnson (1986): "Unless the chemically dependent person gets help, he or she will die prematurely. . . . Unlike many other diseases, however, chemical dependency is also progressive. This means that it always gets worse if left untreated. . . . once a person becomes chemically dependent, he or she remains so forever" (Johnson 1986, 6–7).

Johnson's statement reflects an ignorance of the literature on spontaneous recovery as well as a belief in chemical fundamentalism. He believes that although there are many entrances to addictive life patterns, there are but two exits—death or intervention. Johnson may be right for some, or even perhaps most people. The clinical and research evidence, however, indicates that this model does not characterize everyone who has experienced chemical dependence. More specifically, Johnson, like other chemical fundamentalists, denies that people *have* and *do* recover naturally from narcotic, alcohol, or tobacco dependence—and, as this book posits, cocaine dependence.

Natural cocaine recoverers make compelling subjects for inquiry. They have descended to, and then ascended from, the depths of compulsive cocaine abuse, dependence, and addiction. Such individuals are well-versed in the "ups and downs," as it were, of cocaine abuse and successful recovery. The lessons we may learn from those who have gone to the brink and met the test have much to offer. They may guide us, in essence, toward paths to follow in treatment programs developed for others less able to direct their own recovery. It is our intention to let their voices be heard.

An Initial Look. When we interviewed spontaneous recoverers, they were often surprised at our interest; most thought they were the only ones who had recovered in this way, through their own efforts. Because of the media's coverage of drug abuse, cocaine and addiction, they universally believed that self-directed recovery was not possible. They further concluded that they should not talk about their experiences with others who would likely think them frauds. As we shall see, cocaine abusers are remarkable people who have remained, until now, an untapped resource. Their self-acquired techniques of recovery can, in general, enrich the field of the addictions. More specifically, these techniques can benefit drug treatment specialists by providing a variety of "tried and true" folk treatment approaches specific to cocaine abuse. We believe these recovery-oriented techniques can be applied, at times with modification, to other drugs of abuse and/or compulsive activities. The health and psychological relief associated with one's capacity to control excessive behaviors, be they chemical or psychological in nature, is of potential benefit to the individual sufferer and society as a whole.

Currently, cocaine interventions are based on alcohol and other drug treatment models which may not be effective for all cocaine abusers. Alternatively, treatment techniques can be selected prescriptively by asking which therapies work best for which patients with which therapist. By identifying effective techniques, a repertoire of effective treatment approaches can be established. We favor the development of prescriptive treatment interventions for cocaine abusers. These interventions can be made according to individual needs and situations rather than adopting the "one treatment fits all" philosophy.

Cocaine abuse has been identified as a major public health research priority by The National Institute of Drug Abuse (NIDA 1984). This exigency provides an opportunity to understand potentially new social/psychological treatment interventions in the field of the addictions. Cocaine abuse as a nationally recognized problem is a relatively recent phenomenon. Consequently, the theoretical, clinical, and social knowlege regarding its use have not as yet been studied in sufficient clinical detail. The oral histories included in this volume, therefore, provide a careful firsthand examination of issues previously ignored—in part because they were thought to be nonexistent—in an attempt to understand how people use and stop using cocaine compulsively.

Cocaine Quitting. Although they are few in number, some researchers and clinicians have been willing to consider the possibility of natural recovery from a variety of drug addictions.[1] By contrast, as mentioned earlier, cocaine-specific natural recovery has not yet received similar attention. In an extensive literature search in the fields of psychology, medicine, psychiatry, and the social sciences, not one book or article was located that focused on the topic of natural recovery from cocaine addiction.

In the remainder of this chapter, we will examine the characteristics of spontaneous quitters from compulsive opiate, alcohol, and tobacco use. We will also describe spontaneous cocaine quitters and some of the similarities between this group and other groups of natural quitters. Finally, some of our positions will be illustrated with clinical material obtained directly from our experiences with this very special group of people.

Spontaneous Recovery from Chemical Dependence

As was mentioned, the idea of spontaneous recovery is anathema to many who hold the concept of irreversible addictive disease as paradigmatic. Consequently, there are few empirical studies that focus on spontaneous recovery in general, and none that examine it as an exit route from cocaine dependency. In recent years, a small but meaningful amount of literature has emerged based on the notion of natural recovery from substance abuse. Natural recovery has been associated with "certain individuals [who] have been able to end careers of problematic substance use without formal or lay treatment" (Stall & Biernacki 1986, 2).

Because the notion of spontaneous recovery runs counter to the popular wisdom of our time, most available studies have focused largely on whether the process, in fact, has been demonstrated. The results of these studies are consistent with the conclusion that there does exist a subgroup of substance abusers that recover naturally and without outside clinical intervention (Stall & Biernacki 1986).

The abuse of and recovery from a variety of substances have been studied with respect to establishing spontaneous recovery: heroin and opiates (Vaillant 1966, 1973; Waldorf & Biernacki 1979, 1981; Waldorf 1983; Graeven & Graeven 1983; Jorquez 1983); alcohol (Smart 1975/76; Vaillant & Milofsky 1982; Ludwig 1985); and tobacco (Schachter 1982). All of these studies find some evidence for the existence of spontaneous recovery.[2] In the fol-

---

[1]It is interesting and curious to note that cigarette quitters have been accepted readily as natural recoverers by the general public.
[2]One of the best sources of information regarding spontaneous recovery was compiled by Stall and Biernacki (1986). These authors included a comprehensive review of the current research, published and unpublished. The prevalence of spontaneous recovery is difficult to determine because the available studies vary significantly in the methodology and criteria used to define "recovery." Nonetheless, the available literature indicates that spontaneous recovery is a phenomenon that has been observed repeatedly.

lowing sections, we will summarize briefly the findings of researchers who have established the baseline work regarding natural recovery for opiates, alcohol, and tobacco. This review will provide an empirical and theoretical context within which to consider the results of our interviews with spontaneous recoverers from cocaine abuse.

Opiates. Spontaneous recovery from heroin addiction has been studied more frequently than recovery from other substances. Evidence supporting this process has been gathered from a variety of sources: life history interviewing (Jorquez 1983); social surveys of large random samples (O'Donnell, Voss, Clayton, Slatin & Room 1976); and examination of government statistics (Winick 1964). Most of these studies examined their subjects at only one time (for example, Robins 1967; Waldorf 1983); however, a few applied longitudinal methodologies involving followup observations of up to twenty years (that is, Vaillant 1966, 1973). Different demographic populations were explored, such as New York City hospitalized addicts (Vaillant 1973), high school students (Graeven and Graeven 1983), and Vietnam veterans (Robins 1973). Numbers of subjects ranged from forty-five participants to 45,391 (Stall & Biernacki 1986). Spontaneous recovery was found to be a consistent and substantial factor in all the studies mentioned.

Alcohol. Researchers have determined that alcoholics also evidence spontaneous recovery (Smart 1975/76; Vaillant 1983; Vaillant & Milofsky 1982). Some natural recovery studies were short-term longitudinal projects that involved repeated interviews over a span of five years; others followed their subjects for eight to ten years (Goodwin, Crane & Guze 1971), and one for more than forty years (Vaillant 1983). Populations examined included people referred to hospitals for treatment (Kendall & Stanton 1966), patients waiting for outpatient clinic treatment (Kissin, Rosenblatt & Machover 1968), self-identified alcoholics in a health survey (Bailey & Stewart 1966), patients from a medical ward (Barcha, Stewart & Guze 1968), convicted felons (Goodwin et al. 1971), and first admissions to a detoxification program (Smart 1975/76). The recovery criteria ranged from avoidance of public drunkenness (Miller 1942) to abstinence and social competence or stability (Kissen et al. 1968).

Spontaneous alcohol recovery rates vary from 10 percent (Smart 1975/76) to 42 percent (Goodwin et al. 1971). The numbers are far less important than the observation that the phenomenon does, in fact, occur. The mere existence of this recuperative process challenges the current beliefs of our time (that is, addictive disease). In particular, instances of natural recovery confront many of the coercive treatment strategies currently employed to deal with chemical abuse. Many treatment providers consider these disorders to be evidence of a primary, progressive, and terminal disease that *always* leads to death in the absence of intervention (Johnson 1986).

Tobacco. Spontaneous recovery from nicotine addiction (generally applied by inhaling tobacco smoke) has received scant attention from researchers. Information about spontaneous tobacco quitting has been gathered predominantly through interviews (Schachter 1982). Most studies have used time-limited and cross-sectional research designs. A few researchers observed their subjects over short time periods (for example, DiClemente & Prochaska [1979] did a five month followup of ex-smokers). Subject populations have included: the public at a large university and a small resort town (Schachter 1982); older male health professionals (Hecht 1978, cited in Stall & Biernacki, 1986); college students (Perri, Richards & Schultheis 1977); and television viewers (Baer, Foreyt & Wright 1977). The reported prevalence of spontaneous tobacco recovery ranged from 33 percent (DiClemente & Prochaska 1979) to 63.6 percent (Schachter 1982).

Spontaneous recovery research is in its infancy. The domain of spontaneous recovery has remained unexplored for a variety of reasons. One set of factors is associated with the dissonance experienced by "disease" model proponents with the very concept of natural recovery. The existence of spontaneous recovery from addictive patterns of behavior directly challenges the viability of the disease model. Most observers whose disease model orthodoxy is penultimate require that chemical dependency and recovery be explained from this particular position; the existence of spontaneous recovery still remains to be verified in their opinion. For those who subscribe to the disease model as the ultimate orthodoxy, there are no data or research findings that can convince them of the reality of spontaneous recovery or its importance.

Toward a Theory of Natural Recovery

Some prominent theorists have speculated that users self-select a "drug of choice" (Khantzian 1985) as a consequence of their specific, individual needs. This model, then, implies that the process of recovery from drug addiction also may vary according to the distinctions among the various drug categories. In other words, each category of substance may require a treatment approach tailored to the unique properties and experiences associated with its use and abuse. Drug treatment programs have been based upon several well-studied drugs, such as alcohol. These programs are then generalized to the treatment of other substances without regard for an individual's drug of choice or abuse.

It is informative to compare the natural recovery findings cited above with those events experienced by cocaine self-quitters. The following section, therefore, will compare the existing research on self-quitting with our observations of cocaine quitters. As before, our attempt is not meant to be definitive. Rather, it is our goal to identify some of the similarities and differences among various drugs and the ways in which people have stopped using them.

Recovering from Chemical Addiction: Common Threads

Self-Quitting

Marlatt, Baer, Donovan & Kivlahan (1988) noted, "Many individuals choose not to seek treatment because they perceive themselves as having been responsible for the development of their problem and assume that they are capable of overcoming it on their own; others have negative attitudes toward treatment and also wish to avoid the labeling process (for example, alcoholic, addict) and its related stigmatization. . . . self-change does not appear to be spontaneous, for a number of factors have been found to be related to the initiation of change efforts. . . These factors include a personal illness or accident, hitting a personal 'bottom' (involving real or perceived humiliation, shame, despair, or loss), some meaningful religious experience, direct support from or intervention by families or friends, financial and/or legal problems related to substance use, or the alcohol-related death or illness of another person. The common feature of these factors is that the apparent internal psychological commitment appears to be mediated by external events or aspects of the individual's social environment" (pp. 237–238).

It is important to understand that spontaneous recovery is not actually spontaneous. In fact, it is the result of interaction among a variety of identifiable factors. By understanding these factors and how they interact, it may be possible to simulate the development of these events in order to stimulate recovery processes among those who have attempted unsuccessfully to abstain or control their drug use. We will review briefly the available research on the factors—intrapersonal, biological, and social—associated with people who stop using drugs and compare these data with our observations of natural cocaine quitters.

Intrapersonal Reasons. Researchers have found that opiate and alcohol abusers report a variety of reasons for their cessation of drug use. Opiate users describe humiliating experiences (Waldorf & Biernacki 1981; Waldorf 1983), moving cognitive or emotional incidents (Jorquez 1983), or shifts in the source(s) of gratification previously associated with their drug use (Vaillant 1966, 1973). Similarly, alcoholics have reported that they hit a personal "bottom" (Ludwig 1985), experienced a sense that they had lost control over their life (Ludwig 1985), had a spiritual experience (Ludwig 1985), or developed a stable source of increased hope and self-esteem (Vaillant 1966; Vaillant & Milofsky 1982).

During our work with compulsive cocaine users who managed to stop using without the aid of treatment, we observed individuals who evidenced intrapersonal processes remarkably similar to those described above. These people reported "self-loathing" and extreme levels of low self-esteem, a sense that they had hit "rock bottom." They recounted that their behavior had become intolerable and their thinking was "reckless." These cocaine quitters sensed they could no longer pursue their careers, aspirations, or dreams. Even before—sometimes long before—these more extreme subjective feelings were experienced, individuals recalled that their cocaine use euphoria had become dysphoric: "It was never as good as the first time."[3] Further, there were noticeable changes in their cocaine use behaviors. For example, people often noticed that they had started to use the drug alone. They hoarded what they had and no longer shared it socially. Also, they noticed the tendency to obsess about cocaine rather than think about it only during those social occasions to which it had previously been restricted.

These observations are consistent with the intrapersonal findings reported earlier by people who managed to quit other drugs. This correspondence suggests that the intrapersonal reasons associated with the natural recovery from cocaine, opiates, and alcohol may lie on some common pathway.

Physical Reasons. Health reasons have been reported by researchers in every area of natural recovery. Research from opiate quitters (Waldorf & Biernacki 1981; Waldorf 1983) and alcohol quitters (Stall & Biernacki 1986; Smart 1975/76) reveals that self-quitters are motivated consistently by physical concerns. The problems range from a general concern about health to more specific allergic or physical distress on the one hand (Waldorf & Biernacki 1981) and an acute threat to life on the other (Ludwig 1985).

Cocaine quitters reported they often felt overstimulated or "too high." They noticed that the crash took too long to pass or that they had a "hangover." One of the most common factors reported among cocaine quitters was that their noses knew; they had developed irritations, ulcerations, or perforations of the nasal passages. Cocaine abusers often reported cardiac-related fears as well: "My heart was pounding so hard that I thought my chest was going to explode." They also complained of frightening paranoid, psychotic episodes associated with cocaine "runs." Cocaine abusers feared for their hearts and their minds.

Social Reasons. A growing sense of commitment to a loved one or a fear of losing an important relationship (Waldorf 1981, 1983) are the two most common reasons cited in the opiate literature as precursors to natural recovery. Among alcoholics, the evidence is similar. Vaillant (1966, 1982) noted the importance of acquiring a new, close relationship to self-quitting. Stall & Biernacki (1986) reported that pressure from one's family, mate, or colleagues provided impetus to some self-quitters.

---

[3]Depending upon perspective, these characteristics can be considered warning signs of an addiction cycle soon to follow, or alternatively, notice that recovery and self-change be contemplated.

Once again, our observations of cocaine self-quitters revealed similar findings, when: (a) social attachments became more important than cocaine use; (b) the fear of losing these relationships was associated with cocaine use; or (c) remorse grew in regard to the effects of one's cocaine use on important social relationships, the process of self-recovery was motivated. Other social reasons for quitting have been described consistently by cocaine quitters. These included geographic changes, legal troubles, and financial hardship.

Uncommon Threads: Cocaine as an Illicit Drug

Because cocaine is an illicit drug, some aspects of the quitting and recovery experience were dissimilar to recovery from licit drug abuse. Cocaine quitting, for example, often involved fear of legal ramifications and financial hardships that were not observed with tobacco and alcohol abusers. The availability of cocaine also illustrates another difference between licit and illicit drug use and abuse. Cocaine is an unauthorized commodity; unlike tobacco or alcohol, cocaine supplies can dry up temporarily. Occasionally, quitters referred to this dry spell as a time when they began to speculate and consider terminating their use. Given this evidence, "dry spells" can be an important aspect of recovery. Furthermore, because cocaine abuse often involves the illegal selling or "dealing" of the drug, quitters often experienced dissonance between their personal values and their observed lack of standards while dependent on cocaine.

Coping Strategies for Maintaining Abstinence

The scientific literature, though scanty, is consistent about the strategies reported by natural recoverers for maintaining their newly achieved sobriety. These approaches include avoidance, self-reinforcement, social support, structure building, and substitutions. Each of these areas will be reviewed briefly.

Avoidance. The most common strategy for maintaining abstinence and avoiding relapse is to remove oneself from the drug-using environment (Waldorf 1981, 1983; Jorquez 1983) and break off social relationships with those friends who continue to use drugs (Jorquez 1983; Stall & Biernacki 1986). Jorquez (1983) also noted that many quitters attempt to avoid emotional crises and, therefore, have to pay attention to their affective states in a way quite different from when they were using drugs.

Cocaine quitters often recalled how they tried to avoid cocaine and those situations, places, and things that reminded them of it. Several people remarked that television cocaine-abuse prevention messages present one of the most difficult-to-avoid cues. These individuals noted that when they see cocaine prevention messages they think about "just how much people are willing to give up for cocaine." One individual remarked, "I had forgotten just how terrific it was!"

Self-Reinforcement. Alcohol research has demonstrated that physical aversion and negative associations to drinking help ex-drinkers maintain their sobriety (Ludwig 1985). Opiate users have found it helpful to activate both fears of relapse and positive reasons for abstaining to maintain sobriety (Jorquez 1983). Tobacco quitters provided evidence that if they carry on an internal dialogue regarding the negative aspects of tobacco use (Stall & Biernacki 1986), they are more effective in maintaining their status as exsmokers. Similarly, ex-cocaine abusers report the strategy of telling themselves, "I am a better person without cocaine."

Social Support. Stall and Biernacki (1986) identified that social support from friends and family is very important in maintaining abstinence among exsmokers. Cocaine quitters, too, report that they often practice a form of self-initiated social control by asking their friends to assist them in avoiding cocaine-use settings, provide recovery-oriented "sponsorship," and hold them (that is, the quitter) accountable for his or her behavior.

Structure Building. Opiate quitters change a multiplicity of social structures to help them maintain drug abstinence. These changes include attempts to create new, more positive interests and develop new friends and social identities (Waldorf 1981, 1983). Consequently, these new identities help to develop new activity patterns that promote assimilation into the drug-free social environment (Jorquez 1983). Similarly, cocaine quitters also report a tendency to build new life structures. Our clinical experience has demonstrated that these structures include a wide range of activities: emphasizing relationships, careers, and social responsibilities; cultivating new forms of intellectual stimulation; emphasizing self-development (such as learning new skills, entering psychotherapy); transforming the tendency to abuse health into health-promoting activities (such as jogging, bicycling, eating health foods); and, finally, developing a spiritual relationship.

Substitutions. Both opiate and alcohol quitters have reported substituting religious involvement for their drug-using behaviors (Vaillant 1966, 1982; Stall & Biernacki 1986; Waldorf 1981, 1983). Attending Alcoholics Anonymous has been substituted for drinking (Vaillant 1966, 1982) and actively supporting social causes has been substituted for opiate dependence (Waldorf 1981, 1983). Chemical substitutions (food for tobacco, coffee for alcohol, and alcohol for heroin) have been reported by tobacco (Stall & Biernacki 1986), alcohol (Vaillant 1966, 1982), and opiate quitters (Waldorf 1981,

1983). This chemical substitution itself can become excessive and lead to abuse (Vaillant & Milofsky 1982), thereby threatening the process of recovery.

Cocaine quitters report similar substitutions. They tend to experience religious conversions, develop new patterns of exercise (occasionally compulsive), encounter patterns of over- and/or undereating, experience excessive sexual activity, and confront drug substitution (such as alcohol, marijuana, and caffeine). One of the most interesting substitutions can be considered self-serving in character: some cocaine quitters report new interest in acquiring enormous power, wealth, and influence.

Summary and Conclusions

The findings regarding cocaine self-recovery are remarkably consistent with the results cited by researchers in other drug areas. The chief reasons for terminating the use of various substances are similar; these motivations can be grouped conveniently into physical, social, and psychological categories. The process of self-recovery is also similar for alcohol, opiates, cocaine, and, to a lesser extent, tobacco. Some quitters hit "rock bottom," a point at which the structure of their lives has turned to chaos and loss, and experience critical moments or turning points ("naked lunch") in which they "see the light" and decide to quit (Jorquez 1983, 343). Other cocaine quitters do not "hit bottom." They recover by building satisfying new life structures. Shifts in social and vocational activities (love and work) correspond to what we have considered "structure building." Vaillant suggested that these life structures include some combination of the following: (a) the development of a new close relationship; (b) alternative sources of gratification (other than addiction); (c) an elevated sense of hope and self-esteem. Quitters find more gratification (internal and external) as a result of their new structures and, therefore, express less need for cocaine.

Various coping strategies that have been employed to maintain cocaine abstinence were also reviewed in this chapter. This area of investigation is more scarce than the "reasons for termination" literature, but is essential if we are to assist individuals to quit and remain abstinent. These abstinence-sustaining strategies incorporate avoiding the abused substance, applying self-reinforcement, developing social support, building new social structures, and substituting new, more constructive activities for cocaine abuse.

The available research and clinical data suggest that there are three major phases of change (for example, DiClemente & Porchaska 1982; Prochaska & DiClemente 1986) associated with recovery from addiction: (1) precontemplation, (2) active change, and (3) relapse prevention or change maintenance. In this scheme, the first (precontemplation) phase is a time when individuals ". . . do not perceive themselves as having significant problems" (Marlatt et al. 1988, 237). The second phase (active change phase) is associated with the avoidance of drugs and related social activities (such as avoiding the drug, drug users, and drug-related activities). The third phase (abstinence maintenance or relapse prevention) contains the implementation of a variety of coping mechanisms designed to sustain the new behavior patterns obtained during the actual quitting or active change phase. All available evidence suggests that drug quitters employ a range of identifiable techniques to cope with drug cravings. In addition, numerous findings report the phenomenon of compulsive drug or behavioral activity substitution during the active change and change maintenance phases of recovery. These substitutions occur predominately in the change maintenance phase of recovery and also confirm the observation that former drug users build social structures into their lives as a means of staying drug-free.

In the next section of this book, we will expand upon the three-phase change model. We will suggest that successful cocaine quitters actually pass through a two-stage, six-phase process.[4] The first stage describes the emergence of addiction; the second stage depicts the evolution of quitting. Within each stage, there are three different phases. During stage 1, the emergence of addiction, successful quitters experience (a) the beginning of the activity, (b) the positive consequences produced by the activity, and (c) remain *unaware* of the adverse consequences that the activity is causing. During stage 2, the evolution of quitting, successful quitters (a) *experience* the adverse consequences of the behavior so that a "turning point" is weathered, (b) actively separate or quit the activity, and (c) change their lifestyle behaviors to prevent relapse. A more detailed discussion of this model will be presented later; however, we are introducing the structure of this model now so that it can serve as an organizing point for the oral histories that follow in Part 2.

Part 2 of this book will describe cocaine abusers who became cocaine quitters. In addition, we will examine some of the principles associated with quitting and maintaining abstinence from cocaine. This material will be illustrated with oral histories taken directly from successful cocaine quitters. As you will soon see, these oral histories provide direct evidence that an array of cocaine coping styles exist and that specific phases of quitting can be identified. The similarity of self-quitting styles across different drugs was established earlier in this chapter. Consequently, many of the quitting methods distinguished by researchers who studied drugs other than cocaine will be in evidence among spontaneous cocaine quitters as well.

---

[4]It is possible that individuals who successfully "quit" other addictive behaviors also pass through these stages and phases.

Part II

A little learning is a dang'rous thing; Drink deep, or taste not the Pierian spring: There shallow draughts intoxicate the brain, And drinking largely sobers us again.

—Alexander Pope, 1711

6
Initiation:
Beginning Cocaine Use and Abuse

How Cocaine Users Become Abusers

This chapter will describe how cocaine quitters initiate, escalate, and abuse cocaine. Among cocaine abusers, a variety of user types emerge. These types provide a feeling for those individuals whose oral histories illustrate this book. In addition, distinct types of users represent different categories of quitters. We will begin with several illustrations of cocaine initiation. In these examples, the individuals began to use cocaine during a major life transition (from college to adulthood). These periods are often associated with drug use and abuse.

A friend of mine in college was doing cocaine, a fellow student, and we also worked in the same place. And I had a lot of admiration for the guy. He turned me on to some (cocaine) and I liked it. I wanted more. It made me feel like a superman of sorts. And basically I was just doing cocaine fairly frequently. Then I graduated from college. I just turned twenty-two when I graduated. I studied art and had a teaching certificate at the time. But in 1979, the economy wasn't looking too good for teachers or the arts or anything like that. So I was fairly discouraged about the whole thing. And I really had no idea of what I wanted to do. A women I fell in love with had to go back to California. I was here feeling very lonely. I wound up meeting somebody (another girl friend) at work. Meanwhile I was doing more and more cocaine. So I started to deal cocaine. Because I figured since I was doing so much of it, I might as well buy it wholesale for myself, sell some, and hope to make a profit. Which I was able to do. That's when I really started full blast. The girl (friend from work) wasn't thrilled. She was already seeing someone else even though she was basically living with me. I felt rejected and I was feeling sorry for myself. The cocaine had sort of taken her place already.

As I look back I can see that I was a nervous wreck by my junior year in college. I definitely had insomnia. I didn't sleep a lot at that time. I would just get very fidgety. I just couldn't sit still. I had to get out . . . I had to get up and run or ride my bike or do something but just get out and move. I guess it was a form of escape. I was out all night long, as opposed to being home. No one could touch me . . . no one could come near me . . . no one could hassle me. I was on my bike, it was just like that's it! You have to catch me first. At night a lot of times things broke loose at home and you didn't know what was going to happen at night. You know, if (a friend) came home drunk or something like that. So I was just very on edge. I had some stomach problems around that time, a nervous stomach. Part of me wanted to run away from (a friend who offered cocaine) and part of me wanted to say, Yeah, I want some coke. . . . I know that I wanted coke all the time. I just wanted to feel good a lot. I just wasn't feeling good about things. The closest I've come to a cocaine high was through (a sport) and maybe the running. Definitely the (sport), if I played well then I felt really good. You'd get the feeling of accomplishment and achievement, a very good overall feeling. The cocaine didn't give me a feeling of achieving but rather a very good euphoric feeling. I got more emotional at times on it. I definitely was more bubbly, more open, much more talkative. I just felt on top of the world, very bubbly, very open, it was easy to talk, I would just have a big smile on my face. I didn't feel pressures, I didn't feel tensions.

High school was easy for me, I really didn't have to pick up a book. And all of a sudden in college I really had to study. It was the first year. I took economics and sociology with five hundred other people and I was like, Oh, no. And I ended up dropping most of my classes. And the ones I didn't drop, I failed. And I was just very, very unhappy. . . . I was just like gliding along at that point. Just kind of going to work, earning money, going out and having a good time. I wasn't really accomplishing much of anything and I didn't want to. Whenever I did coke it was usually fun and it got out of hand and I let myself down. Once, after a cocaine run, I was exhausted and I had to leave work early that day. I felt depressed because I wasn't being responsible and I had let my friends and co-workers down and they had to do an extra shift.

Each of these examples illustrates the positive or beneficial effects co-caine has during the beginning phase of use. In addition, the last oral history reveals that some individuals experience adverse consequences very early in the sequence of events that ultimately leads to quitting cocaine. For most, however, the early phases of cocaine use are associated with positive consequences; any adverse effects tend to remain out of the user's awareness. Cocaine users who experienced a positive effect and/or relief from their psychic distress are more likely to continue using the drug then those people who were not in need before their first cocaine use (Marlatt, Baer, Donovan & Kivlehan 1988). Therefore, persons whose use continues on to abuse might represent individuals who have a greater "need" for the sought-after (positive) effects of cocaine. In addition to these intrapersonal factors that facilitate cocaine use, there are important social or relationship events that contribute to the development of cocaine abuse. Both of these influences will be considered in the following sections of this chapter.

Cocaine-use Catalysts

Cocaine-use catalysts are the external or internal events that quitters believed precipitated their first use of the drug. The catalysts usually represent vulnerable areas in a person's life. An extensive review of the literature (Marlatt et al. 1988, 231) reveals that drug abusers have "a high level of depression and/ or low self-esteem." These conditions are associated with difficulties in relationships and career. In this section, we will examine the social and intrapersonal catalysts that stimulate beginning cocaine use.

Relationship Catalysts (Loss or Threat of Loss)

Difficulties with interpersonal relationships can catalyze cocaine use. The loss or threat of loss of a relationship can stimulate the use of cocaine (for example, separation from home for the first time, losing best friends, parental divorce, being disowned by parents).

Among quitters, cocaine use contributed psychological support to individuals who were confronted with a range of relationship concerns. It served to bolster people against loss or threat of loss. Cocaine acted as a chemical substitute for relationships or it provided enough self-esteem to promote the formation and development of romantic relatonships. Paradoxically, cocaine allowed one to relate to others while needing them less. For cocaine quitters, relationships were intertwined with cocaine use in a number of complex ways. For example, cocaine use often begins after relationship instability or loss. Conversely, when stability develops within important relationships, cocaine abusers often decrease or terminate their drug use. Cocaine seems to have the capacity to foster intimacy among users, reduce social anxiety, create a sort of "instant" affiliation or sense of belonging, both through the "high" state that it produced and the social setting that surrounds the drug use.

> My boyfriend picked up a sleazy bit of stuff one night and flaunted her in front of me and everything just sort of caved in on me. I've always been against cocaine. Whenever I've seen people use it . . . and when I was a kid, I instantly didn't like them. I sensed something was wrong, and I always stayed away from it. I've been in countless situations up until last year where someone says, "Do you want some?" And I say no thanks. And I did it, because I had this destructive part of me when I'm feeling bad, I'm just one of those people who take it out on myself. So I used cocaine to abuse myself

deliberately. Cocaine completely distracted me, made me feel good. Made this new social life happen, with the dealings.

Career Catalysts

Entering the adult world involves defining a career or work-related identity. Some cocaine quitters mentioned not having a career aim or purpose, "not knowing what to do." They often experienced this chaos as a personal crisis. Some people especially prone to a career crisis are college dropouts who suddenly became aimless. Other individuals know what they want to do, but are psychically or situationally derailed from their aspirations. Lastly, some people know what they want to do but are forced to find an alternative career.

> It made me feel like I could conquer the world. I felt brilliant when I did coke. Well, it got to the point real quick that I couldn't get on a stage without coke, if I hadn't done a couple lines there was no way that I could get out on a stage. I was incomplete, I couldn't be the brilliant performer that everybody expected me to be, I thought everybody expected me to be, the coke that made me that way. I didn't have any pizazz, none at all, and I'd get the feed from the audience for that too, you know, I would get . . . especially because we played mostly in the (Northeast) circuit, and people knew us, and if I got up there and I hadn't done any (cocaine) during the break I'd get a lot of shit from people—"What's the matter with you? I don't know why we paid money to come here tonight." There was a real strong personality change that went on with me. So without it I was kind of shy and introverted and insecure, very insecure on stage, and with it, I was the best that ever lived, watch out world.

Self-Esteem Catalysts

Another general category of cocaine catalysts involved emotional reactions to events, particularly when these feelings relate to self-esteem. Some ex-abusers were generally sensitive to self-esteem assaults because their sense of self-worth already was at a low level. Cocaine use is cited frequently by ex-abusers as an anodyne to their depressed sense of self-esteem. Cocaine's stimulant properties help to recover (chemically) from blows to self-esteem.

> I was a jock in college but then I had knee surgery and had to stop. It was a big blow and the first time I ever quit sports. And I literally quit when my record was ten and zero. My coach was furious. I guess that was a major change in my life at that point. I forgot about it. That preceded the coke. I did kind of feel as if that was a failure of mine. And that tied along with me dropping the math degree. Another failure and this time an intellectual failure.

I would say that it was my lack of self-esteem that I got involved with drugs around. Drugs loosened me up and I felt less inhibited about who I was and socially going out with girls or whatever. I didn't worry about my thinking. And then it just became self-perpetuating.

I had a mother who said, "Go out and do, the world is a very safe place," or "maybe you shouldn't take any chances," "don't do anything that you're going to risk yourself," "don't go skiing because you might break a leg," "don't run track because you might hurt your knee or sprain your ankle," "don't do anything," "but really you should be doing something." I think that there was an increase in cocaine around my leaving home. The notion that you grow up with at a certain age, is that you have to leave home. You have to gain access to dealing with yourself in relation to authority, in relation to your breadwinnership, or your career, or whatever you're going to do. You have to do all that. And for me it seemed like an unreachable task. So I avoided myself. I didn't feel good about myself.

Individuals who lose the customary means of feeling good about themselves often find alternatives. Sports, for example, often help maintain self-esteem. However, if a sports injury forces an athlete to stop playing, not only can he or she suffer from the loss of a fulfilling activity, but self-esteem can also be in peril. People who were required to stop their athletic lifestyle occasionally initiated cocaine; often they compared the perceived positive effects of cocaine with an experience similar to a sports "high."

The Continuum of Cocaine Abusers: From "Brief Encounters" to "Dealers"

In this section, two groups of cocaine abusers will be described. The "Brief Encounters" and the "Dealers" represent end points on the continuum of cocaine abuse.[1]

Brief Encounters

"Brief Encounters" derive their name from their brief and relatively discrete cocaine using period. Members of this group have a quick brush with cocaine dependency. They tend to go through the phases of the cocaine experience more quickly and with less intensity than the dealers. They manage to curtail their abuse before it escalates and consumes their lifestyle. In fact, the cocaine

---

[1]Brief encounters and dealers both used the self-esteem and relationship-enhancing functions of cocaine. Dealers tended to experience more self-esteem difficulties; the brief encounter group expressed more social vulnerability.

abuse period is more of an anomaly than a predictable event in the brief encounters' lives. Their cocaine use in terms of amount is the "lightest" among cocaine quitters and their "heaviest cocaine period" is comparatively brief and without major adverse consequences. Primarily female, this group has no prior history of abusing drugs and cocaine termination occurs without the substitution of other drugs.

Composite Picture of a "Brief Encounter." The brief encounter is a female who comes from an impaired family with alcoholic parents. She is not raised in a nuclear family situation, but rather an older relative "looks after" the child and fills in for the parents as a caretaker. The relationship with the older caretaker always seems to be better than the alternative, the biological parents, but is nevertheless characterized by ambivalence and conflicts of loyalty. By the time the brief encounter becomes an adolescent (approximately age thirteen) she has experienced at least one major traumatic event, such as the death of a caretaker. Grief occurs alone. For the most part, the family is emotionally unavailable, and feelings are not discussed, but the family does provide rules and limits for the child. Verbal or physical abuse is the exception rather than the rule.

Her adolescent drug experiences before cocaine involve recreational (non-abusive) use of alcohol, marijuana, and perhaps LSD. College represents a difficult transition from high school. The brief encounter has to struggle academically with course work and often makes the difficult decision to drop out. This decision is seen as a failure by the young woman herself and by her highly educated father. Now a woman in her early twenties, entering adulthood and leaving behind her childhood and adolescent world, she no longer has four years in college to make a slow transition into an adult role. After leaving college, she moves away from home, starts working at her first job, and supports herself for the first time. The previous plans of her next stage in life (college and pursuit of a specified career) have vanished, and the psychological comfort of structure, plans, and procedures are now gone. Furthermore, her self-esteem suffers a blow from which it will take years to recover. Although she has had opportunities to try cocaine before, it is not until this point that she decides to take up an offer by a good friend to do so. The initial cocaine experience is a positive one and cocaine helps the woman to socialize and develop a new set of friends (the need for this arising from having left both the high school and college environments). Cocaine helps relieve some of the emotional tension of this transitional period—the situational depression, social self-consciousness, and vulnerable self-esteem. She feels that both she and others open up emotionally, which promotes a more intimate level of communication but also protects her from previous losses (death) and emotional abandonment during childhood.

Cocaine initiation leads relatively quickly (within a year), into her heaviest cocaine involvement period. The duration of "heavy" cocaine use lasts approximately three to four months. The amount or intensity of cocaine use, in terms of dosage, is among the "lightest" in our sample, probably amounting to two hundred dollars or two-plus grams of cocaine a week. Her initial use is mostly on the weekends, becomes extended to three or four days, and eventually turns to daily "light" use, relative to the "dealer." The abusive cocaine pattern represents the first drug problem for the brief encounter. She works continuously throughout her heaviest cocaine involvement and buys her weekly supply of cocaine from her small income. She never buys the cocaine directly from a dealer but has a "go-between" pick the cocaine up for her. Usually this accomplice is a male friend and "illicit partner in crime," or a cocaine-using buddy. The buddy is frequently a married friend hiding his use from a disapproving wife. The cocaine buddy has a heavier habit and is the person who introduced the women to cocaine. They see each other daily at work as a friend and/or boss. The frequency of her cocaine use increases and is accompanied by an increase in alcohol consumption to modulate the side effects of the cocaine high or crash. The eurphoric stage is short-lived. The side effects and other warning signals of cocaine abuse are recognized and experienced with dysphoria. The woman knows without a doubt what she wants for herself, in terms of a career. However, the plans for realizing her aspirations were derailed when college did not work out. The major revision of her career dreams brought her to a temporary standstill. She elects consciously or unconsciously to take a "time out" period (facilitated by cocaine) to recoup from the gap in her life structure. Eventually this "time out" is perceived as "wasted time" and becomes as intolerable as the cocaine side effects. Her psychological "sabbatical" begins to interfere with moving out of limbo and progressing with her life goals. This delay in forward motion or progression brings with it self-disgust once she is psychologically ready to move on. Cocaine becomes an obstacle preventing her progress.

In response to the urge to move on, she becomes more active in career pursuits. She purposely lets cocaine use taper, giving herself permission to use it only at times when it does not interfere with her daily functioning. She experiences only negative consequences of cocaine during the last phase. Her turning point consists of interpreting the warning signs, which occur early, as a danger signal. The brush with cocaine abuse initiates a therapeutic consult or contact on a nonregular basis with a professional in human services. As she becomes more engaged in career and health activities she has less desire and opportunity to use cocaine. The cocaine phases out as she adds more to her life that is on target with her goals. Some time passes in this fashion, and the brief encounter realizes it has been a while since she last used cocaine and decided not to use it again. Her alcohol consumption decreases effortlessly back to its precocaine pattern of occasional use once termination of cocaine occurs.

The acute phase of quitting cocaine is short. However, this phase of cocaine quitting does require thought and caution. The longer relapse prevention phase ushers forth a sense of relief and progression associated with cocaine abstinence. The brief encounter develops a healthy respect for her "addictive" potential, which previously had not been a concern, even though she is an adult child of an alcoholic parent. During the first year of cocaine recovery the brief encounter slips at a party where cocaine is readily available. Once she sees the cocaine she is unable to resist, and instead rationalizes that she stopped her drug abuse pattern long enough to start using cocaine recreationally again. However, she contains the misstep to one event, which actually helps reinforce the negative effects of cocaine use. The entire cocaine experience lasts approximately one year. Her postcocaine drug use is minimal and drug use of any kind is not a part of her day-to-day lifestyle.

"Dealers"

Cocaine dealers tend to have more extreme cocaine involvement than brief encounters. Their drug abuse is more intense; and side effects of cocaine are more harsh; the drug abuse lifestyle more threatening; and the overall effect on their lives more destructive. Cocaine dealers tend not to develop satisfying life "structures" for themselves. During the end point of their heavy involvement with cocaine, these individuals perceive themselves at "rock bottom" or their "personal worst." Dealers quit cocaine more abruptly and intensely than brief encounters, that is, they go cold turkey. The initial phase of cocaine quitting is consuming and the relapse prevention phase of maintaining cocaine abstinence emotionally painful. Cocaine dealers tend to be predominately male.

> **Composite Picture of a "Dealer."** He comes from drug-impaired parents. His family is distant, emotionally unresponsive, and feelings are denied. He experiences trauma (death of a significant caretaker) and is emotionally abandoned by his father, who favors his older brother. He, unlike the brief encounter, lives in a family that is occasionally explosive and marked with physical violence and verbal abuse in the form of criticism, ridicule, and humiliation. The abusive parent is unpredictable; the son never knows what to expect. He tries cocaine for the first time in high school. The initial experience with cocaine does not progress immediately to abuse but takes a period of four years, until he is in his early twenties, before an abusive pattern becomes established (in this way similar to the brief encounters, who also abuse cocaine in their early twenties). In early adolescence he becomes involved with other drugs and develops two drug abuse problems before his heavy involvement with cocaine takes place. The introduction to cocaine and its effects lies dormant for a few years while other drugs such as alcohol, marijuana, LSD, and amphetamines are used/abused. Cocaine use is reintroduced to the "dealer" at age twenty-one while he is involved with other drugs. However, this time, his cocaine use turns to abuse, as do most of his other drug relationships. His period of heaviest cocaine involvement is the "heaviest" amount used by our clinical cases. His cocaine habit will amount to well over a gram a day, a state of constant intoxication. The route of administration is intranasal, and during the last phase of cocaine abuse changes to freebasing. Freebasing requires larger cocaine amounts and fre-

quency of use. His heaviest period (freebasing) lasts one year. As his habit grows larger he starts dealing to pay his cocaine expenses. Once dealing, the problem of cocaine availability and money as a limiting factor to abuse is removed. Dealing starts off small, to friends, and grows to dealing with larger and unknown populations. His dealer's habit grows, and additional drugs are used to counteract or enhance the cocaine high. He develops secondary addictions with alcohol, and frequently uses sedative-hypnotic drugs. Cigarettes and marijuana are staple drugs used throughout the day. However, marijuana use remains constant even with the introduction of cocaine, with daily use before and during the cocaine experience amounting to nearly a decade of abuse. He tries to maintain a job but is fired because of absenteeism and irritability at work. He becomes a full time dealer.

All his friends consist of users/abusers, and "hang out" at his apartment. He carries out business transactions and answers "business" calls at night, sleeping during the day. People come to him, and he has little need to leave his apartment anymore. Eventually his "friends" become an annoyance because they call him up at all hours, and he stops wanting to share or sell his cocaine supply. As he uses more and more cocaine intranasally, his nasal passages can no longer absorb such large amounts, so he starts freebasing.

Once he begins to freebase he can not stop using cocaine. His supply runs out. Financial difficulties begin and he decides to get more business. He has an answer to all the warning signals: if you lose your job because of cocaine abuse, deal; if you're overstimulated by cocaine, use other drugs to modify the "high" state; if your nose is starting to go, freebase; if you're financially stretched, deal more; if the high is not "fun" anymore, then try, try, again and get it right.

The turning point arrives after living through a year of his "heaviest" involvement period. It takes a great deal of accumulated negative experiences before he arrives at a realization of the need to terminate use. First the dealer recognizes that his sense of integrity has declined and he realizes with shock that he does not really know who he is anymore. He begins to hate the person he has become but no longer is able to recall what he was like before cocaine. His use is so extreme and the consequences of such use so pronounced that he comes to believe his life is in danger from cocaine abuse. Each time he wakes up with a cocaine hangover he resolves that this is the day to quit, but he can never go without cocaine for more than a day. After months and months of trying to quit he begins to feel hopeless about ever stopping. His original group of friends has given up on him, and his "new friends" only use him for his cocaine. He has a few terrifying psychotic episodes from cocaine toxicity and constantly worries the police are after him. He hits rock bottom: no job, no money; friends and family have given up on him. The alternative to not stopping cocaine, he decides is death.

By his mid-twenties he has been involved with cocaine and/or other drugs of abuse for nearly a decade. However, he finally quits cold turkey. It is a miserable time. He gives up his drug, friends, and lifestyle; all his attention is focused on avoiding cocaine and distracting cocaine cravings through activity. He has insomnia and lies in bed without physical or mental relief. Each day he has to avoid all associations to cocaine, such as his friends, apartment, etc. He takes a part-time job to help him stay busy, and sleeps or hibernates the rest of the time. This acute phase of cocaine recovery lasts about three months.

The phase of maintaining his abstinence poses a different sort of challenge. In contrast to the activity and avoidance of the quitting phase, relapse prevention requires affect tolerance. His painful feelings, which the cocaine initially helped to ameliorate, come back in full force. His childhood history of family denial of feelings, coupled with a long period of drug abuse during adolescence and young adulthood, have not equipped him to learn about his inner life, but rather how to avoid the pain associated with his feelings. Therefore, the flood of feelings overwhelms him and he turns to alcohol for relief. Within a year he has a drinking problem.

What "Brief Encounters" and "Dealers" Reveal about Human Development.[2] The brief encounter group may shed some light on the events associated with cocaine use as an instrument of self-care. This model suggests, for example, that cocaine may be used to compensate for a personality deficiency or as a defense against overwhelming emotional states. As children of impaired parents, brief encounters often are sent to other family members for childrearing. They regularly experience abandonment and loyalty conflicts. They also experience more death at a younger age and more incest than the general population. It is not surprising that a chief area of concern for them would be the entire realm of relationships.

Dealers, as children, experience verbal and sometimes physical assault by ridicule, criticism, and humiliation from parental figures. They are emotionally abandoned rather than passed on to others to be cared for. This chronic degradation of self-esteem in childhood may lead to long-standing self-esteem deficits in adult life that will cause them to seek external solutions for an internal deficit.

Consider the analogy between brief encounters and dealers and two different physical environments. One environment has the necessary conditions to sustain an underground water table (or in this case, a supply of self-esteem). The other environment, a desert, does not have the prerequisites to form internal water supplies (or self-esteem). The desert's living residents are, therefore, forced to rely solely on external sources for life maintenance. By way of this comparison, the brief encounter group lives in the more clement self-environment, where internal resources and esteem are available. For this group, however, there are times when the water table falls; these periods are associated with specific situations such as relationship losses and the developmental demands of transitional periods. At such trigger points, self-esteem

---

[2]This discussion is speculative and based solely on the clinical evidence obtained during the course of our work with cocaine quitters and others devastated by drug abuse. We hope that this brief discussion will encourage and stimulate new research.

can become depleted and cocaine may function, temporarily, to artificially raise self-esteem.

Dealers are not provided with alternative caretakers to their dysfunctional parents. They reside in a harsher environment. Perhaps this emotional abandonment prevents them from internalizing a sense of self-esteem, personal identity, and the self-care skills that are modeled by a caretaker. The dealers' long standing problem with drug abuse may represent an internal deficit of self-care and self-worth. Cocaine may function for this group as a type of "chemical mothering" (Gombosi, Personal Communication, August 1987). In contrast to the forsaken desert conditions of the dealer, the brief encounter group receives more caretaking, usually from less dysfunctional custodians than their parents; perhaps this experience empowers them (in varying degrees) to internalize nurturance and the ability to care for themselves from the inside out.

Turning Points: The Beginning of Quitting

The Beginning of the End

Until now, we have examined the beginning phases of cocaine careers: the initial conditions that can precipitate the first use of cocaine and the catalysts that facilitate various patterns of cocaine abuse. "Brief Encounters" and "Dealers" were featured as end points of the cocaine abuse continuum. This section will describe the more advanced phases of the cocaine experience, the beginning of the end. This is a time when cocaine users become aware of the warning signs associated with their cocaine abuse. As the warnings of cocaine abuse begin to enter awareness, cocaine quitters become ambivalent about their use. They begin to *want* to want to stop. To nourish this desire for motivation, while avoiding personal responsibility, they may ask friends or family to help them control their drug abuse. The wish to want to stop abusing cocaine eventually is strengthened by the awareness that drug abuse is no longer fulfilling. Cocaine, once the source of joy, competence, or psychic pain relief, now becomes identified as the cause of a growing number of concerns and difficulties.

"The Thrill is Gone" (Song Title by B. B. King)

When "The Thrill is Gone" the cocaine use honeymoon is over. The initial euphoric response is replaced by the opposite effect, dysphoria. This is a time when quitters say "coke turns on you" and "is a big lie." A number of symptoms or "warning signals" alert abusers that cocaine is not without its problems. Different levels or thresholds of recognition (or denial) are associated with cocaine warning signals. Some cocaine quitters quickly see the warning signals; others experience a host of symptoms but respond only when the more severe warning signals increase their doubts about cocaine.

> I think that what rings the alarm for me is that I can't deny the evidence. I come from a family in which there are a lot of medical people and engineers. I was kind of brought up to examine the facts and if there's a difference between the facts and your perception then your perception is probably wrong, and that's kind of what you go on. So I think that's what happened, that at some point, especially in this case, it was obvious to me that I couldn't deny any longer that I was doing bad things to myself and that I wasn't particularly happy and that the course that I was on was not helping. I don't like being dependent on something.

> The cocaine high is no longer fun . . . I no longer liked the high . . . The high times are shorter and the crashes are longer . . . I hate the feeling. Even when we were doing it, I really didn't like the feeling any more.

Warning Signs

The warning signs that follow the initial and euphoric phase of cocaine use are presented here exactly as cocaine quitters have described them. As was mentioned, some abusers experience only a few signs while others weather an unabridged register of symptoms. Warning signs are often experienced in concert, rather than as a singular event. These patterns tend to demonstrate maximally that the cocaine thrill is indeed going or gone.

"Never as Good as the First Time" (Song title by Sade & Mattheman 1985)

> Initially it was great fun. But it doesn't last. You lost that. And you never get it back. Even if years go by and you don't do any and you try it again. It's not fun. You never get that feeling at first when it was really fun.

> The whole thing is so insidious, the whole thing is like building up. You just keep doing it to try to get that rush, it's never quite right. I mean the first hit is the best anyway. After that whatever you do all night long is just like shit, it's like . . . that's not IT . . . that's not what I wanted. Let's try it again and get it right this time. And again, No, that's not it either, and on and on it goes.

"The More I Get, The More I Want" (song title by Whitehead, McFadden & Carstarphen, 1977)

> I can't refrain from doing it once engaged.

Instead of you walking the dog it becomes the dog walking you.

The least that I would buy was twenty-eight grams. I was the type of snorter that when I started snorting, first of all when I did start snorting, I mean I couldn't put anything down. I just went for days. Even at three o'clock in the morning and at that time like instead of going back to bed I couldn't. You see I was never happy when I snorted because there was no such thing as enough. In other words when I did coke, I had to fall asleep with the coke beside me. That's the only way I would be happy, if I woke up the next day and found it next to me. In other words, there was no night even if I did a thousand dollars I would say, Oh, well this was a good night and bye bye. It wasn't like that, it was always more, more, more, when I enter the high.

The whole time I am talking to myself while freebasing. I mean I'd be writing things down and talking to myself and telling myself . . . No, don't do this anymore. You'll kill yourself. And I'd answer right back to myself . . . That's right. Yes, I am.

I started getting the cravings. I couldn't avoid noticing them, let's put it that way. While you're doing it, there's always the craving, clearly. I'd wake up semi-straight and real tired. I craved coke and that was a new thing.

Starting when it came in on Friday and then the coke was gone Monday or Tuesday. The weekends were getting longer and longer and I was staying up three to four nights . . . staying up for four days at a time.

Don't Leave Home without It. Cocaine quitters notice a change in their co-caine use when they start carrying the cocaine supply wherever they go. Their cocaine intake progresses to daily use; they begin to use in different settings other than home, such as work.

I would have a little (cocaine) before work. Just a little to give me a little buzz. Then I'd go off to work. Sometimes I would take it with me and sometimes I wouldn't. So let's say I did, because toward the end I was carrying it with me all the time.

Solo Use. What once was a sociable drug eventually becomes a drug most of the quitters do in isolation. This change is notable.

That's when I knew I was getting in trouble. It had gotten to the point where I didn't want to do it with anybody else, I didn't want to share it, I felt like this was mine, and I got to the point where I didn't want anyone to know that I was doing it by myself.

Hoarding Behavior. The example above mentions the experience of selfishness. The user noticed his behavior with cocaine changing from social to antisocial. He noticed diminished cocaine generosity and increased cocaine hoarding. "I started getting very selfish with my coke." Dealers, for example, become reluctant to sell their cocaine. Furthermore, some nondealing quitters start "hassling people for cocaine" or "hanging around people who use cocaine, even if you don't like them, in order to do free cocaine."

Obsessiveness or Being Led by the Nose. The concept of dependency implies a narrowing of previously enjoyed activities; behavior becomes more restrictive and cocaine abusers become obsessed with "hunting and gathering."

> I just got very obsessed about it, thinking about it all the time, thinking about where I was going to get the money, being with people I really didn't want to be with because I knew that they were going to get high.

> I stopped buying it, which was interesting because then I began to realize that I would go to parties and associate with people. But at parties it used to be that people would get together and have a good time and talk to one another, had sort of degenerated into everybody hanging around wondering who had the drugs and when they were going to get some or how they would get some or how they could get close to so-and-so who had the drugs.

Physical Side Effects. Initially, during the "honeymoon," or euphoric, phase of cocaine use, quitters rarely mention the annoying side effects of cocaine. However, after chronic use develops, the side effects are frequently reported as problems and interpreted as warning signals. The physical side effects most frequently mentioned by quitters include: overstimulation, cocaine hangover, irritability, insomnia, nose problems, the "crash," and change in cognitive functioning.

"Too High" (From a song title by S. Wonder, 1973)

Being "too high" from cocaine is described as "a gnashing, grinding high" or "a high-strung, nervous, teeth-grinding" state. After a cocaine-using period, the abuser's teeth started to grind involuntarily as if in a form of tension reduction. When cocaine is used all night long (often solo use), quitters become increasingly out of "sync" with the normal time table of sleeping at night. So in the middle of the night, the abuser is "too high" and wishes to get out and socialize. This phenomenon is described by one quitter as being "All dressed up and nowhere to go (at five in the morning)."

I do a line (cocaine dose), then another maybe, then he'd (cocaine supplier) leave it with me. So I'm sitting there, completely wild. The same thing, no one to talk to and the more you take the worse it gets. You're twitching, you walk around, your head is just pounding, your eyes are aching. I saw someone on TV the other day at one of those anticocaine things, the one about the rats or mouse which is fed cocaine and they actually show it on TV how it always goes back to the cocaine and it keeps going back and back and back. And they show it in about three minutes and then it just sweats and sweats and slides around the cage and then falls down dead. And seeing that, it's so close. No one can tell you what it feels like, but watching that rat makes you feel it. It's like drowning, there's nothing you can do. You're just swallowing more and more. And you know it's not helping. It's hell. You may lie there 'til daylight. And you just keep thinking, I want to go to sleep. I'll go to sleep in three minutes if I just close my eyes. And you can't wait for three minutes, you're heart's pounding. Your eyes keep opening. You've got pictures in your mind. And it feels like pressure on the brain. Not like you had a headache, but something physically going on in there. It's just the worst feeling, that trying to go to sleep. But if you were out somewhere in a club, you'd get tired naturally with people who were doing the same thing. That's OK.

The initial hour or two I liked the uplift in it. I liked being able to think things out, meaning plan goals. I would just think about, one of my goals was to be a millionaire through my hobby, which is investing in real estate, how can I do this, what can I sell. I used to just plan. After the high would wear off it was like who cared about what you thought. After the first couple hours then it's women. There's when the sexual part comes into play. From that point on basically to the next, it would be to go to strip-tease clubs, just be with women. My sexual drive was just, I think it is probably with most, although I've seen a program on TV that explained about cocaine and alcohol how it deals with humans in that particular area of their brain, where it begins and how it affects that particular area. But that would basically be it, just be with a woman. I was no longer (me). The cocaine would just overwhelm me, it would just overwhelm my being, my everything. I just wasn't . . . well, I was human naturally but I was wired for sound, I couldn't think properly, I couldn't clearly keep myself in one place, I would bounce from place to place to place. It was the chase from one bar room and bang on to the next. You might be in one house, on to the next. You couldn't keep yourself contained. I wasn't (me). The drug was controlling me.

The Crash: A Long Time Passing. During the euphoric phase of cocaine use, the cocaine crash, or withdrawal from cocaine, is often reported as mild enough to pass without difficulty. Prolonged cocaine exposure gradually changes this experience and eventually the crash gets worse, lasts longer and provides a new set of regular problems. "I couldn't get up in the A.M. . . . I was late for work."

The Hangover. One prominent side effect of cocaine abuse is the headache.

> The hangover was unbelievable. I would feel like there was a vise on my head and I couldn't remove it and it was getting tighter and tighter.

The Nose Knows, or It's as Plain as the Nose on Your Face. The first notable physical symptoms are often nose problems. These difficulties include chronic runny nose, red nose, and sinus or breathing difficulties.

Career or Job Decline. The career warning signs typically include a decline in performance, frequent sick days ("crashing days"), morning lateness, a decrease in work functioning, and being fired because of cocaine abuse. In the case of one full-time cocaine abusing dealer, he started tampering with his stock, depleting his assets, and getting "taken" by other dealers—for example, buying a pound of powdered aspirin for a small fortune.

> I was still at (names place of employment) and at that particular time I started noticing what was happening, meaning my awareness of what I was doing to people. I always loved my athletic world, and I'd seen that falling apart. My production level, my bank account dramatically going down from black ink, and it went from pretty serious amounts in black ink to a point where, I remember one time where I actually, I had no more money in the bank, I actually used my credit card to buy coke. That's when I realized . . . at one time you were making serious money in sales, you were making more than you could afford to spend realistically, and the things that you were spending it on investment-wise were fairly good. Now you don't have any more money in the bank, your production at work has gone dramatically downhill, you're not really making that much more money, you're not making as much money as you used to, your work is not really effective, and you're still dealing with this drug, you're still in a cocaine world . . . these were signs.

> I was working for a year or two and I guess the next traumatic thing that happened was I wanted a raise. I was getting shit for money, only like seven dollars an hour. And I was really working hard, yeah. Well, I thought they were calling me in to talk to me about a raise and they called me in and told me that I had to go. And the reason being is that I was too fucked up on cocaine. "It's affecting your work," I was told, you're too high and irrational. I'm sure they were right, too. I was sabotaging my own job. Unwittingly, but I was. I was trying to get out. I was unhappy there. I was bored. I wanted more money, I wanted more responsibility, there was nothing challenging about it for me. I mean, that's what it was, it was a rut. And I was in a rut in the job and I was in a rut with the cocaine and my whole life was a fucking rut. So I get the ax and it was very emotional. I mean because I'd been there

for a while, it was probably the longest job I'd ever had, except for going to college, and I did that for four years.

I was not being a responsible human being. I had this business I was trying to work on and I had to be available to that and I wasn't and it made me feel terrible. I was drinking too much and was always waking up with a hangover or . . . I felt lousy.

Financial Squeeze. The experience of financial pressure varies among quitters. One felt the pressure in spite of an income that ranged between fifty thousand and one hundred thousand dollars a year. Others notice money is tight when they spend half their income on cocaine, never having any spending money, not able to afford going out on the weekends, spending grocery money for cocaine.

This is Crazy. A frequent theme that emerges when the thrill is gone involves a pattern of consistent statements. Quitters say to themselves for the first time, "This is crazy!" Often, the quitters report their sense of "ah ha!" recognition and many of them use the word "crazy."

I guess just one day it hit me and it really scared me because I was at home. The person I usually get high with didn't know that I was doing cocaine on my own. I was in my room and I was getting ready to do some and he came in the house. I heard him. I just freaked out. I was cutting it at the time and I was like, oh my God! He's going to see and he's going to find out and I didn't want him to know and I didn't want to give him any. And I had to do it. I went out and it just hit me, this is crazy. I knew I was getting wicked selfish and hung-up. That's when I knew I was in trouble, on that day. I was going to just stop which of course didn't happen but eventually I cut down. It just scared me more than anything. This is just nuts.

A Case Illustration of the Warning Signs: A Summary

Cocaine completely distracted me, made me feel good. . . . But then you're hooked . . . And the way you know you are hooked is the feeling—when you have done it for four hours straight and it may be seven or eight at night. And you are sitting there wired. Your eyes are twitching, you're tapping your feet, you can't sit still, you can't eat, you don't want to drink. Well, you drink a lot of beer. I drank a hell of a lot of beer. It makes you very thirsty. You don't want to go out, but you do want to go out. You want some life, you want something to happen. If you go out no one's in the state you're in, so that doesn't help. You can't read, you can't watch TV, you can't do this, you can't do that. Everything you do, you can't . . . , so I would write. And I would write trash. I've read it. I was going to bring you some today, I forgot about it. You can't. . . . So then you might go to bed later on after you speed past four or five hours just sitting there. And you lie in bed and your mind is going wild. And you can't sleep, your eyes are wide open. You close your eyes and you're thinking, you're thinking, you're thinking. And there's nothing you're thinking about. But you try to give yourself something to think about. You try and give yourself something dreadful to worry about which would really be worth your while that would be worth staying awake for. But there's nothing that you can care about. You simply do not care. Nothing matters. So I try and tell myself dreadful things, and it didn't work . . . And that feeling is the worst feeling in the world. . . . Just the feeling of being awake and your mind is working like that. And even your first hit of the day, you'll be revived, you'll feel good about yourself again. In fact you're over the moon about yourself. You're happy. Real pleased with yourself. Then you just go down and down. By the end of the evening you feel so small and there's nothing you can do. So when you wake up the next morning, after maybe three or four hours' sleep, you're still in the . . . pretty much in the same state, except your body is exhausted. You're very depressed, you're very irritable. And you know, your body tells you . . . it's not like I think I better have a hit of cocaine so I feel better . . . it's not like that. Your body just does it. And you instinctively, like you would take a glass of water if you were thirsty. You instinctively need it. And then you feel fine again and it goes on day after day.

The Turning Point: When Costs Begin to Exceed Benefits

The warning signs inform quitters that a change in their cocaine experience has occurred. No longer does cocaine simply produce euphoria; cocaine use is beginning to generate concomitant dysphoria. The discomforts associated with this experience sometimes give rise to questions about the use of cocaine. Cocaine use has not yet become intolerable, nor do the quitters necessarily tell themselves it is time to stop using cocaine. Brief encounters, however, often are sufficiently "warned" by the signs that they stop using cocaine.

A turning point[3] represents the transition between unencumbered cocaine use and the realization that cocaine abuse is responsible for meaningful adverse life situations. The thought of quitting or controlling cocaine first appears before the actual point of transition. Users *want* to want to quit. Self-observation is involved. The users realize, as if in an epiphany, that the costs exceed the benefits. Cocaine has become a destructive agent in their lives. Their ambivalent feelings surface and are more fully experienced. It is now

---

[3]Turning points represent the first phase of the quitting stage of addiction as represented by the model introduced briefly in the last chapter and discussed in more detail in the final chapter.

that quitters often ask friends and loved ones to help them stop. The burden of self-control is delegated more to others than oneself. The acceptance of personal responsibility represents the actual turning point.

A turning point, then, is actually an end point in the thought process about cocaine, even though abstinence and recovery might be months or years away. The experience of a turning point does not produce instant results. Dealers with large habits have the greatest tolerance for warning signs and negative cocaine consequences. Some even come close to death several times before the turning point arrives

> So over a period of time, it wasn't so much that I woke up one day and said that's it, I'm quitting, this is the end. It was more of a matter of I kind of stopped buying it, I stopped associating with the people who had it, and sort of withdrew from contact with it.

> Something about hitting rock bottom really does it to you. Sometimes you don't even have to be there very long, I mean it's just, sometimes you get an epiphany, it's like the last straw, you know, whether shitting your pants or you know, watching a pet die from neglect, or having a convulsion, or any of those things might be enough to trigger something in you that says it's not right and not necessary.

Discrepancy between Ego-Ideal and Current Self-Concept

Cocaine quitters frequently recognized that their personal values had been compromised.

> Well, at that point it was kind of . . . I had been a heroin addict for a number of years and than I was getting into coke and I realized one day that . . . it came to me—an accumulation of incidences where I was exposed with the threat of my life, going to jail, getting arrested, smacked around for ripping people off. I had degenerated into breaking and entering into houses and, you know, big-time dealing where people were around me carrying guns. And I said, "This is crazy. What's a nice Jewish kid from a nice Jewish family doing in a place like this? I could have a brilliant career. I've got to get out of this."

Self-Loathing. Initially, cocaine often is used to regulate a vulnerable self-esteem; cocaine "made me feel good about myself." Once cocaine use progresses to a pattern of chronic abuse, quitters begin to feel much worse about themselves. "It backfired."

> I mean I couldn't believe it . . . you know, you stop bathing. I mean, I looked in the mirror, all I saw was a real animal. No, not even that, I mean animals

take better care of themselves. I hit rock bottom, I figured I was the lowly of the low. I was definitely the kind of scum you'd scrape off your shoes. That was how I felt. My self-esteem was down to zero. I didn't even know what myself was anymore.

(This case illustrates two aspects of turning points, both "self-loathing" and the "discrepancy between ego ideal and current self-image.")

> You know, you suddenly have no self-worth and you're not doing anything that makes you feel good about yourself. Because you feel good about yourself only while you're doing cocaine. When you're not doing it you feel worthless . . . that you're wasting away.

"You Can't Hide from Yourself" (From a song title by T. Pendergrass)

Unplanned reductions in their cocaine supply sometimes force a decrease in a quitter's usual cocaine intake. This unplanned decrease occasionally triggers thoughts of terminating cocaine use.

> It registered in bits and pieces by reflecting, basically. You know, suddenly I'd be . . . I wouldn't have money to have coke for a couple of days and things would start to sink in, and suddenly I would be sitting there thinking, well, gee, it was nine times last year that I OD'd and I didn't die. That's how it began to sink in, it wasn't that one time I overdid and I got scared. It was that in reflection I realized that I was using it up (life), and if I didn't do something about it, it was going to be too late.

> Looking at it from now, it was hell, and in the middle of it I remember every once in a while coming up for air and realizing that probably the rest of the world didn't live this way, but I didn't have a whole lot of comparison. Everybody that I knew did it. I had myself set up in a real nice circle of people who were as bad as I, if not worse, and my whole entire lifestyle was centered around it (cocaine). It was frantic, disorganized, moody.

When the Defense Becomes the Conflict. When cocaine is used as a defense against psychological conflicts, it can become more of a conflict than the problem that it was intended to defend against.

> I was sick of the conflict that was ever-present as long as I was doing things (cocaine) that were getting in the way of my furthering myself and my abilities, my self-esteem, my awareness, my pursuit of the world.

> I got a chance to really clearheadedly see the process that I put myself through when I attempt to quit something, the psyching process. I had myself so disgusted with cigarettes by the time I was ready to quit that it was

very difficult for me not to quit. I have to get good and disgusted with my-self, a chronic nagging feeling. Eventually, quitting becomes easier than not quitting.

Relationships. Relationships often served as turning points.

What happened at that point I guess is that I got involved in a group of people that I cared enough about that I didn't want to do an environment change, and you can rip off your friends for only so long before they're on to you. So I didn't have that option then to, to steal, because I wanted the friendships more.

It got in the way of my relationship with a woman who is now my wife. Because I would do things like say I'd be someplace and not be there. That kind of thing. It was a relationship that I felt I wanted to remain committed to, that I wanted to continue. So when my drug habit started to get in the way of that, I knew something was up. That's when I started saying, "OK, I've really got to seriously plan how I'm going to get off this habit."

I guess I wasn't totally aware until people brought it to my attention, that I was hurting myself or killing myself . . . I was self-destructing.

Adverse/Noxious Physical Feedback. Some abusers say their physical reactions (other than the common side effects mentioned under the "warning signs") to cocaine made them too sick to want to continue the abuse. For example, one person became immediately nauseated after ingesting cocaine and another individual developed an asthmatic reaction of difficulty breathing after administering cocaine.

Do and Die. This turning point is almost exclusively associated with the heaviest cocaine abusers. The notion of "do and die" develops when a cocaine quitter recognizes that continued abuse of cocaine directly threatens his or her life. Death is experienced by heavy cocaine abusers as inevitable, either through cocaine overdose and medical complications such as heart attacks or by the dangerous activities of dealing with the cocaine underworld. The recognition of mortality is experienced as a kind of revelation.

I started to look at the way the rest of the world lived and realized what I was doing. I got to the point where I realized that I was either to stop or to die, that was my choice, and I had pushed death so many times and gotten away with it. There were many times when I would do an ounce of coke in a night, no problem, and then do eighteen "ludes" (Quaaludes). And you know one time I did fifteen "ludes" and woke up three days later, I was black and blue from having convulsions and my head was swollen and that was just normal for me to do things like that. I didn't even think twice about it. Gee, I had a rough couple of days, what's next? I realized I was using up life, I had nine overdoses in one year and either I quit or I die.

See, you keep building up and building up to a crescendo, I knew something would have to give. It was either going to be my life, or I was going to stop, or I don't know what. It was like I said, I was trying to reach this ultimate rush which wasn't ever there. You just try again the next night with a bigger bag of coke.

A friend would come up to visit. . . . he had a stroke at thirty-two from an overdose (of cocaine). That was actually the real beginning stages of me thinking that there may be something wrong with what I'm doing here.

Cocaine Psychosis. A toxic dose of cocaine can produce psychosis in which hallucinations and paranoia occur. For some quitters, hallucinations represented experiences upsetting enough to become a turning point. This type of turning point, like "do and die," was limited to heavier cocaine abusers.

I had reptilian hallucinations . . . Really, I mean real, like horror movie schlock . . . They were intellectualized about . . . hey, that's not there. Oh, it was awful. And they'd crawl up to me and they'd crawl over me and I could feel them and I didn't like it. This was a horrible feeling. It like . . . made my skin crawl 'cuz it wouldn't stop no matter what I did. I'd close my eyes, I'd see them. Open my eyes, I'd see them. And then I'm going, I know I'm hallucinating. Started talking . . . I know I'm hallucinating, it's OK. They're not really there.

We'd get this rock coke imported. And then I started getting very paranoid reactions with it. A funny story—I was with a friend of mine and we had been doing coke all day after we got off on methadone. And he used to get extremely paranoid to the point where he was checking doors. And he had two beautiful white German shepherds. And he had them surrounding the perimeter of the house. And he was always afraid the police were going to come—and they never did. And finally it started to get me paranoid, if I wasn't already. So finally I said to my friend, I can't handle this, I'm leaving. As I walked out of the house—and he lived with his mother. As I'm walking out the door a police car rolls up with his probation officer and his mother pulls up right behind him . . . and I walk out the door and say, see you later. And he just stood there with his mouth hanging down to his feet. That time his suspicions were confirmed. Just because you're paranoid, doesn't mean they're not out to get you.

Financial Hardship. Most cocaine quitters we talked with started out with the principle, "don't spend more money than you have" on cocaine. Most abusers compromise this maxim as their cocaine use shifts to abuse. However, the degree of financial hardship because of cocaine costs and indebtedness is relative and varies greatly with different types of abusers, for example, the two extreme groups of "dealers" and "brief encounters." A few dealers change their initial rules of conducting business (dealing) as their abuse worsens. First the rules are "only deal cocaine to maintain your own habit" and then "only deal to friends." After their abuse progresses, dealers sell cocaine for a profit or start dealing "dirty." For example, "I started to rip people off" and dealt with the "big-time dealers in sleazy neighborhoods who carried guns and stuff."

> In two years you're talking probably thirty, forty thousand dollars. I don't know how much I spent there. It was quite a bit of money and then the lack of sleep, trying to hide it from my job, the fears, the hallucinations, the paranoia, the wondering sometimes at nights if I was going to live.

Fear of Legal Consequences. The continuous fear of "getting busted," experiences with "close calls" with the law, and learning about friends going to prison also serve as turning points.

> I got tired of staying up all night. I got tired of the sick feeling. Got tired of the anxiety of worrying who was going to be the next informant to squeal, or to go to the police officers. I got tired of worrying about crime stoppers, 'cuz anybody could call them up anonymously.

Summary

Cocaine users represent a diversity of people. There are many types and methods of cocaine use. This chapter described the extent of cocaine entrances, the variety of using patterns and the range of user types. In addition, this chapter considered the factors that facilitated and helped sustain cocaine use and abuse among those who ultimately knew how to quit. Finally, we described the "turning points" experienced by cocaine quitters. These events and experiences are instrumental in helping them realize their cocaine use is destructive.

The next chapter focuses on the active change, or stopping, phase of cocaine quitting. As was mentioned earlier, active quitting represents the second of three phases that comprise the second stage of stopping addictive behavior. Next, we consider the strategies and tactics cocaine quitters use to help them successfully separate from their drug of choice.

7
Actively Quitting Cocaine

There is little systematic evidence that describes the strategies and tactics employed by those who have recovered naturally from problematic substance abuse. However, the available evidence does indicate that various quitting strategies are regularly employed across the range of abused substances. As with other addictive behavior patterns, there are identifiable phases associated with cocaine quitting. These phases can be grouped conveniently into three categories: (1) turning point(s), when the addict begins to consciously experience the adverse consequences of his or her behavior, (2) active quitting or stopping drug abuse, and (3) relapse prevention or maintaining abstinence. Until recently, research has focused more on the active phase of quitting drugs than on the abstinence maintenance stage.

In this chapter, oral stories will demonstrate that cocaine quitters often experience an assortment of life circumstances before they actually stop using the drug. For example, some quitters reach their "personal worst," or "rock bottom" before stopping. On the other hand, others manage to build and secure a satisfying life structure during their cocaine abuse.

This chapter is organized into three sections. The first part presents first-hand accounts of the "rock bottom" quitters and the "structure building" quitters. The second describes exactly how these drug abusers quit cocaine. Two basic categories of quitting styles are evident: "tapered quitting" and "cold turkey quitting." Last, we consider the most operative approaches associated with active change and offer additional oral stories as case illustrations. These methods for quitting cocaine include avoidance, social support, and self-development. Each of these areas will be examined briefly.

"Rock Bottom" Quitters

> So in a year and a half I blew all my inheritance, all the money that I had made, about seventy thousand dollars. I decided that I needed to quit, and the only way for me to quit was to do an environmental change. So I decided to go back to (a city in the Northeast). There were an awful lot of emotional

factors at that point that made the difference, like the age of my son, realizing, finally beginning to realize, that I am physically and emotionally responsible for somebody else, that my body was falling apart, my life was completely falling apart, I was beginning to go through the process of feeling remorse, which up until that point I hadn't felt any, and I looked at the fact that I had blown probably a hundred fifty thousand dollars in two and a half years and I was living destitute.

Something about hitting rock bottom really does it to you. Sometimes you don't even have to be there very long, I mean it's just. Sometimes you get an epiphany, it's like the last straw, you know, whether shitting in your pants or you know, watching a pet die from neglect or having a convulsion, or any of those things might be enough to trigger something in you that says it's not right. And not necessary.

I don't know how much money I spent on cocaine. In two years you're talking probably thirty, forty thousand dollars. It was quite a bit of money and then the lack of sleep, trying to hide it from my job, the fears, the hallucinations, the paranoia, the wondering sometimes nights if I was going to live. These were the signs that I was going downhill.

It's just really not feeling any progressing in life. It's kind of like a stagnant state, a lull, always wondering am I going to be like this for the rest of my life, how am I going to quit, I've tried and failed, gee, maybe I can slow the situation down, maybe I can't. I never really had any real, probably being in the darkness I just didn't see a light at the end of the tunnel. I didn't see a lot of hope. I'd seen some and tried to keep pushing myself towards, it is going to end, it is going to end, and then the negative would come in. God would tell me it's going to end, Satan would say it isn't going to end, you're going to be like this all your life, don't believe the truth, let me tell you about the lies.

I was just sick and tired of going through the physical and emotional pain. I was totally fed up with it. I just hated it, hated myself for doing it.

Structure Building Quitters

It is always easier to give up something when something else more gratifying fills in its place.

I had started taking a class in the spring semester. I had really decided I wanted to go back full time in September. I had been thinking about it for a long time and I was looking at music school catalogs. I knew again I would be thrown into a situation with people that had a lot more theory background. So I thought more stability in music theory would provide me with a good foundation. And this particular theory teacher was very good. It was very important for me to do well because all of a sudden I didn't have sixteen other classes going on and I could really concentrate. And I understood everything. And it wasn't like a foreign language to me anymore. So I wanted to do well. The cocaine really tapered off and became more of a drag than anything else. At the time I just had other things to do. I was concentrating on that class, and I just wasn't interested in cocaine. I didn't want to be exhausted by using cocaine because I knew I had to work the next day and go to school. I didn't want it to interfere with school. It was just too much of a hassle, more than it was worth. Things were really beginning to fall into place. And cocaine just didn't have the magic that it did before.

My primary reason for quitting had to do with what I saw happening in my life, what I wanted to do with my life. I don't know if that was quite psychological, but it was kind of "I don't have time for it anymore. It's not a high priority anymore."

The end of my coke was when I got out of college (dropped out) and involved myself with work for someone else and working on my own dream . . . building up my own company.

My whole lifestyle was changing anyway. You know, I went from being a student to working. I mean it's just around the time we were getting married. And now it's got to the point where I don't even live in the same city anymore. I don't run into these people anymore. I just don't run into them.

Quitting Styles

There are two primary cocaine "quitting" styles. One method is called "tapering"; this involves a gradual decrease in cocaine intake over a period of time. This style of cocaine recovery requires time. In this case, "quitting" cocaine is more descriptive of the gradual process than abstinence.

The second cocaine recovery method is designated "cold turkey." Terminating cocaine is an appropriate description for this strategy. The term "cold turkey" originally was used by heroin addicts detoxifying from their narcotic addiction. One of the detoxification side effects is goose bumps (or turkey bumps) and clammy skin. "Cold turkey" has been used as a shortcut to mean an abrupt termination of the drug of abuse. The cold turkey method differs from the gradual, more tapered approach because it is abrupt and dramatic.

I wondered if I was going to be able to quit. I would have this kind of dialogue in your mind; I can do this, I know I can do this. I am the supreme being of willpower and on the other side, Oh, come off it! You're stuck. You know better than anybody else, you're not going to get out of this. The thought of not being able to get out of it was not a pleasant one. That losing control of something I had so proudly been able to control my whole life. But then again there's got to be something . . . I mean, self-doubt was nothing new to me, it's something I kind of live with.

Tapered Quitting

Some quitters who tapered would consciously control and reduce their cocaine consumption and frequency of cocaine intake. For example, instead of daily use, the abusers tried to control or limit their use to certain times such as weekends or Saturdays only.

Other styles of tapering involved using the permissive style of "Never Say No." These people were initially unable to say to themselves, "I will never use cocaine again." Such a statement made them feel "rebellious" and/or "overwhelmed," which produced the opposite effect of intended decrease. They instead said to themselves, "I am just cutting down" and gave themselves permission to still use cocaine but at lower levels. "This is just for today and tomorrow you can use it."

> I said to myself, "you've really got to cool it," but I didn't say, "you've really got to stop completely." I'd say "You can have it tomorrow" . . . or "You can't do it today because you have to do this and tomorrow you have to do that and so the next day you can do it." I never told myself that I couldn't do it. If I had said I could never do it again then I would have done it tomorrow, I would have done it tonight, so I never tell myself that. I just keep myself out of situations that will make cocaine easy to get.

> It was kind of . . . gaining a little bit of distance gave me a little perspective on what was going on. I've always been somewhat of a loner and the idea of kind of being involved in the pack and doing something like that was not something that I liked to think of as being the way I was. So over a period of time, it wasn't so much that I woke up one day and said, 'that's it, I'm quitting, this is the end.' It was more of a matter of I kind of stopped buying it, I stopped associating with the people who had it and sort of withdrew from contact with it. . . . It was definitely something that tapered off. I would say that within a year of that time I would have felt that I was controlling it more because I was staying away from it. As I say, I suspected that if it was around, if I had free access to coke I would probably use it . . .

> It was pretty tough because I wasn't doing much. I was doing it a little bit, you know. Maybe a quarter of a gram at a time. And that just fed the craving.

"Cold Turkey." The tapered style of quitting is in direct opposition to the "cold turkey" style of cocaine termination. In the latter style people say, "No! . . . Never again . . . This is it!"

I essentially did my last batch (of cocaine) that I had stashed. And I had stashed away more than one ounce. And I spent the last three weeks of school, high. Twisted out of my mind. And it was wonderful. And it was that point that I came closest to overdosing. (This individual then quit cocaine, cold turkey). Cocaine, that was all I wanted. Simply put, I would think about it. I would wake up thinking about it. I was pretty ornery. All the way around. Not very active, couldn't sleep very well.

I would say, I could literally say to myself, "No, you can't do that. You don't do that anymore. And you don't do cocaine. Cocaine is your enemy." And so that was happening. It wouldn't make me happy. It'd keep me from doing it. And I'd remind myself to stop cigarettes, this is harder, I'm not going to do it. Reminding myself that I needed a challenge. It was definitely a challenge.

Avoidance

The time period required to quit cocaine varies. More specifically, this phase is a time when individuals vacillate between old and new behaviors. This quitting phase may range from one to six months; three months is about the average time frame for this phase. The initial period of quitting cocaine requires psychic and behavioral avoidance of situations where ex-cocaine users are at risk of relapsing. This period, therefore, is marked by avoidance of any exposure to cocaine and cocaine-related activities.

I stopped keeping it around the house. In situations where people were doing it I would sort of avoid, because everybody, you could tell when somebody in the party's going to do coke. All of a sudden all these people disappear into a room. If you see a mixed couple going into the bathroom, they're going in there to do coke, because if they were going to have sex they would go in their car. If you do coke you know the signs. And the first thing to do is to stay away from that; I mean, if you see all these people going into the bedroom you go to the other end of the house. The same thing with quitting cigarettes. You sort of have to do it one shot at a time.

I had the idea that when it came time to quit, I would be able to quit cocaine 'cuz I could give up cigarettes. I said, "I can give up cigarettes, I hope to hell I can give up cocaine." I was an addict of nicotine. Life was planned around cigarettes. When I was broke, my money went to cigarettes over food. I said, "Dammed if I'm going to let cigarettes control my life," and quit. The cigarette quitting sensitized me to the issue of addiction.

I guess to involve yourself in something totally different, something you believe 110 percent in. And if need be, totally disassociate yourself with the lifestyle and the people that, I guess, you tend to be around with whenever you're doing cocaine. I think you need to disassociate yourself with *anybody* doing the drug. Be involved in something to take away your mind and to instill new, not new beliefs, but new desires.

Out of Sight and Out of Mind. Avoidance of cocaine and cocaine-related people, places, and things are typically the first steps taken immediately following the decision to quit cocaine. Many quitters report their fear that, if exposed to cocaine, they would be unable to refrain from doing it. Therefore, quitters spend much time and energy ensuring that they will not be caught in a position where they might not be able to "just say no."

> To this day I don't know what would happen if I were in a room where a bunch of people were doing (cocaine) lines. I haven't been in that situation recently.

> I avoided parties as soon as cocaine came on. As soon as I saw cocaine it was a signal that the party was over for me. It was time to just leave. I was a big avoider of that kind of situation.

> Leave town when you feel you will slip, go where you know no one and have no cocaine contacts.

Avoiding Cocaine Cues. To avoid temptation, cocaine quitters tried to avoid things associated emotionally with cocaine and cocaine use. "I hide my money so that cash isn't around." Alcohol, which tends to disinhibit personal resolve, should be avoided. Alcohol is often associated with cocaine intake; sometimes alcohol is used to take the edge off the cocaine high, sometimes it simply lubricates judgment so that cocaine use becomes an option. Cocaine "lookalikes," such as sugar or powder, trigger a craving response and stimulate a desire to use. The special cocaine stories that appear on television or newspapers are difficult to look at for the ex-cocaine abuser because they stimulate craving. Similarly, cocaine paraphernalia (for example, cocaine preparation equipment such as the dealer's scale) should be avoided so that external cues will not stimulate internal longings. Cigarette smokers who recently quit their habit have employed similar safeguards against inadvertently becoming stimulated by cues. Smokers, for example, hide ashtrays, avoid places where they used to smoke or temporarily give up their morning cup of coffee that was paired with the first (and often favorite) cigarette of the day.

> Right, but I would say drinking was the first and then coke. Right now I think I would even have more of a heart attack because right now every time I would go for a drink and you start getting buzzed, I can't get buzzed drinking because I used to do the coke and then I used to drink. But right now I know if I ever went drinking and I got drunk right away in the back of my

mind I would say, right now a couple of lines will pick you right up, you know.

New Lifestyle Patterns: Acquiring Social Suport and Beginning to Build Life Structures

Active cocaine quitters modify their daily routines. "You start joining the living." Quitters learn reluctantly that successful abstention requires some sort of lifestyle modification.

> The other thing that is very, very strong since stopping all substances is that it's very painful, very, very painful. I have not learned in my life anything that didn't assist me in getting high—I don't know how to vacuum, I don't know how to wash dishes, I don't know how to make a relationship work, or, well, I don't know anything.

Many ambivalent quitters try to continue living their same cocaine lifestyles (such as dealing cocaine and socializing with cocaine) while trying to stop. Eventually most of the quitters have to "stop dealing," "stop handling cocaine," and avoid "vicarious cocaine use" (keeping cocaine around for friends and watching them do it) or risk slipping back into abuse.

Career. Cocaine abuse can conflict with career aspirations.

> I'm very committed to this (career), I have been committed to this since I was in high school, for a long time. It's a field, and it's the kind of work that brings me to life. It sounds kind of corny to hear myself say this, but one of the things about our wonderful modern age and the twentieth century, is kind of these ridiculous tendencies that reduce everything to technology or technocratic ideology kind of stuff. And to me it engenders a lot of mean-inglessness. So I've been able to find something that I find a lot of meaning in. And the political work I do and that kind of stuff. And that carries on in my personal life as well. The relationship with my wife is a very equal relationship. And that's important to me.

> I had a full-time job as a kind of therapist. . . . And it (cocaine use) was running into conflict with what I was thinking and trying to do on my job. And not that I got high during work, but just . . . I'm saying one thing and doing something else.

> I was not being a responsible human being (while on cocaine). I had this business I was trying to work on and I had to be available to that and I wasn't and it made me feel terrible.

Friend as "Sponsor." Quitters often elicit the help of a good friend or friends upon whom they learn to rely. Often these friends help the quitter when she or he feels "vulnerable" to relapse. Sometimes this friend or partner actually sets limits.

> We decided to get married and we had to save money to get married, to be able to move out from my mother's apartment, have a honeymoon and everything. So we saved and we weren't doing it as much.

> He was more support because I was always like, I wish we could have some, I wish we could have some, and he was like no we can't, the wedding's coming, this is coming, that's coming. Life was doing pretty good there because we were making all the plans and arrangements for the wedding and I did have a lot on my mind about that, but there was always in the back of my mind, I wish I could have a gram, I wish we could just get some.

> I've also been able to set up a whole really powerful network of great friends, really great people, strong, self-aware people.

> It is a hard one. I mean financial reasons of course are a big one, but if I didn't have the money I'd steal something, you know. What happened at that point I guess is that I got involved in a group of people that I cared enough about that I didn't want to do an environment change, and you can rip off your friends for only so long before they're on to you. So I didn't have that option then to, to steal, because I wanted the friendships more.

Reversing the Nocturnal Cycle of the "Vampire Life." Often cocaine-abusing lifestyles take on a nocturnal schedule. Cocaine abusers use drugs at night and sleep ("crash") during the day. "We were high and scared of the daylight. When daylight came out we used to hide under the bed. It was scary." Recent cocaine quitters train themselves to return to the world of "the living." "Go to bed early, get up in the A.M. and go outside in the sunlight."

Change Daily Routine. Cocaine quitters arrange their daily activities to discourage drug use.

> Plan events for the following day so you can't afford to crash. . . . Start jogging in the early morning or to go to work early in the mornings.

> Develop hobbies, something concrete which you look forward to doing daily . . . model building, gardening.

> If unemployed get a job which has a fast-paced work activity where you don't have time to miss coke. Keep active and fill up the hours and stay on the go.

Self-Development

> It's an exciting time for you because you have the opportunity to get to know yourself for the first time and your feelings, and there is joy in recovery and learning how to relate to people and having good friends who care about you. Another big piece of it is knowing what the emotions are, that I feel for somebody and that my feelings are real, and that they're going to be the same tomorrow morning. When I wake up they won't disappear like they did when the drugs wore off.

Education. Many cocaine quitters mention that their minds felt "asleep" during the early stages of cocaine recovery. Some use the time that had been associated with cocaine use to educate themselves about different interests (such as classes in physics, sign language). Others eventually return to formal education.

> That would be my one other thing that I would suggest to anybody who's trying to quit, is education—learning, and not just learning about your addiction, just learning, just learn something every day, because you stop learning when you're an addict, and it can be really exciting to start again.

Service to Others. Some of our quitters described a need to become more socially responsible on an individual level. Some ex-abusers volunteered time to help others who had experienced similar problems with substance abuse. Some worked in social areas independent of the field of substance abuse. One of the subjects volunteered her time at a suicide hotline as well as holding down two jobs.

> If I can help somebody, that helps me a lot, because I am just going out of my way. And it's not even going out of my way, but just to hold a door open for a few seconds for somebody or to sit out a light for a few seconds longer for someone to walk across. Being able to help people is probably my greatest love at this time, meaning not being selfish but when I help other people, putting other people first and putting God first. That's in the word of God also, putting other people before yourself, their cares, their considerations before yours, take that extra step even if you have to go out of your way for others.

> Keeps you honest and accountable.

Emphasizing Physical Health and Exercise. Quitters who exercised after terminating cocaine often felt that physical exercise helped to reduce the effects of cocaine withdrawal. Exercise seems to counteract many of the negative results from prolonged cocaine abuse. These people reported that their self-esteem returned, that they had reduced cocaine cravings, gained a health consciousness, energy, and a sense of well-being similar to that which cocaine had initially produced.

> And later on that summer I started to run everyday and that was a major factor. I turned down so much cocaine because of it. No, I have to get up and run tomorrow. I have to get up and run tomorrow. Running was very important to me because I felt better and I wasn't as tired. You know, I didn't want to jeopardize my running routine because it wasn't easy and I was afraid if I missed a day I would stop running, period. I felt good, like even if I had the worst day ever—I had always run that morning—at least I ran my mile. I can't afford cocaine in a lot of ways. I can't afford it monetarily, I can't afford it time-wise, and there's too much I want to do and I don't want the cocaine to get in the way. And in a way I think if I were to try it again it would be fun and I'd like it and I might want more, but I know better. But I'm still wondering whether I can control it. And I really don't want to find out. Does that make sense?

> When I was in high school, junior high I should say, I was seriously into drugs to the point where in tenth grade I quit totally. Wait a minute, this is too much, I got to get out. So I dry myself off it for about a year. I played jock, this kind of stuff, became very active in student government kinds of stuff as well as music and sports. But it was not very often at all. I thought I was a fairly good athlete and I took it seriously and I had a good time doing it, so I realized I didn't want to have a hangover the next day.

Some cocaine quitters rely heavily on their previous experiences as serious athletes during their attempts to quit. Ex-athletes try to recall a state of physical and mental well-being they remember as possible without drug abuse.

> Whenever I was away from drugs or went a couple nights without doing any drugs at all I was athletically centered. I woke up motivated; I would wake up early in the morning, I would run, do my ten-mile run and then look forward to going in at nine o'clock to work. I was happy-go-lucky. Every ingredient that was needed to make me successful (at work) was injected into me through my athletics other than just my basic training and knowledge. I felt drugs pulling me one way and my athletics pulling me another way because I felt in my life the lousy feelings, or the bottoms, and I also felt on top of the world in my athletics. Athletics added value to my life instead of taking it away.

> I think the reason I could do it (quit cocaine) is because I had this huge ego that says I can do anything. I don't really believe that anymore, but when I need to rely on this kind of faith in myself, I can do it. A lot of that faith

was developed in athletics. It's amazing how much you can come to believe in yourself when you realize that your body will improve with work.

It was a period of stability. I got rid of my wife. And that was the sword of Damocles waiting for something to happen. And I was in school or had a direction and I got into exercise. And I have a friend of mine who . . . I've been on and off as a runner and doing calisthenics and I really got into it at that point. Doing calisthenics on a regular basis. And running pretty much five or six times a week for five to ten miles a day. I was feeling good about myself. I think that if endorphins have anything to do with your self-image, it wasn't so much the high from the actual event, it was the overall outcome of it. Coke didn't offer me anything anymore. I thought it would just get me nowhere. And I could see most definitely that drugs were conflictual with anything that I wanted to do with myself. I had a better image of myself, I didn't need it to get socially anywhere. I didn't feel like it offered me any-thing, any of the drugs offered me anything in terms of being less inhibited or being cool or whatever they offered me when I was a very young kid. They had lost all meaning in terms of representing anything in a healthy way. And I realized that I needed to have a future and I wasn't going to get it that way, for certain. I mean, I've been realizing more and more pieces of that as time went on. And my overall theory is that I continued to elaborate on the theme that I was a nice kid from a pretty good family and I could do better for myself.

Trying on a New Identity. New quitters often have to remind themselves why they chose to discontinue their cocaine abuse.

I don't know if I have any great truths about trying to quit cocaine. I think they're my truths and everybody is an individual when it comes to that, but I would say that one great truth is that life is a lot nicer without it. And people . . . I find I enjoy myself and feel good about myself and that's nice. And I have an affinity for exploring the world and seeking out new adven-tures and you can't do that if you're going to be strung out on some drug. You live in a really narrow shell. You can't grow. And I've never, myself included, seen anyone self-destruct from growing. I think people think they might, and, once again, offer themselves lots of distractions to how come they can't grow.

My primary reason for quitting had to do with what I saw happening in my life, what I wanted to do with my life. I don't know if that was quite psy-chological, but it was kind of, "I don't have time for it anymore. It's not a high priority anymore." Being, as I said before, being able to put something together for myself and then pursue it and not just plan it and not do it.

I think it was more of a need to get away from what I had been into (co-caine). To get away from the life and the town and the situation and the people. As soon as I moved up to (another city) I met just as many if not more coke users than I knew at college, but I just didn't have that desire anymore to participate in that type of atmosphere. When I started working and saw the money that was coming in, to me it wasn't worth putting it into something (cocaine) that's just short-lived.

Cocaine is still a low-grade and constant thought. Life without coke? Well I definitely don't have those highs. It stinks, it's the pits [laughs]. It's not as daring, I don't know if daring is the word. I don't think it has to be, but I think there has to be a replacement. If I thought it was going to be this boring, this mellow all the time, there would be no reason to stop. I tell myself things will get better, things will get more thrilling, exciting, whatever. The sneaking around was exciting in itself. Any good news? Well, you're not totally crazy. You don't get the crashes. You're not as broke all the time. You're just in more control, you're not just running around all the time figuring out where you're going to get the money, and if you're going to get the coke, and if the coke's going to be good. So you're just not as crazy, high-strung all the time. And not so much guilt. I would feel so guilty because I would get myself into certain situations via certain people. And now I don't have to deal with that so much. So I guess there's a lot of good things. There isn't the self-hatred. You just get totally . . . you feel worthless.

I didn't think it was healthy for me to just continue to do it. I knew I was going to continue to get into trouble and not progress in my life. And at that time I had, I was working as an outreach worker at first and then it was a full-time job as a kind of therapist, outreach worker for kids in an alternative education high school. And it (doing cocaine) was running into conflict with what I was thinking and trying to do on my job. . . . I'm saying one thing and doing something else.

Once stopped, cocaine quitters find ways to remain abstinent. The final phase of stopping addictive behavior, the relapse prevention or abstinence maintainance phase, is associated with identifiable strategies and tactics that are essential to maintaining a nonaddicted lifestyle. These issues will be examined in the next chapter. In addition, we will consider some of the problems and challenges that are encountered during attempts to maintain abstinence.

8
Staying Quit: Maintaining Cocaine Abstinence

Relapse Prevention

Until recently, very little research and treatment attention has focused on staying off the problematic drug. In response to high relapse rates among addicts, the development of addiction aftercare and relapse prevention programs have started to emerge (for example, Marlatt & Gordon 1985; McAuliffe & Ch'ien 1986).

Many cocaine quitters find that maintaining abstinence is more difficult and challenging than getting off cocaine during the active phase.

> I was real aware of a sense the minute after making the decision to stop. From that moment on there's been a sort of exuberance and joy at finally getting my shit together. And that lasts for a couple of months and then, after that, the doldrums set in and that's when it gets difficult.

Perhaps because relapse maintenance is for the "long haul," many quitters experience overwhelming negative feelings during this phase of recovery. These affective states were not as powerful during the active quitting phase.

> I didn't do any drugs at all for about six months after I first quit (cocaine). Just all of those years of emotion that I never dealt with at all since the age of twelve, I never dealt with them. And it was all coming back in just these huge gushes of emotion. At that point I was beginning to realize what I had done to my body, what I had done to my self, my sex life, you know, all of the abuses that I put myself through physically and emotionally, for the sake of a drug. And included in that of course is my son, who was born an addict, born four pounds and had just terrible, terrible complications at birth and had spinal meningitis, the whole works. And nobody knew that he was an addict, I didn't tell anybody and they never figured it out.

Marlatt (1985), a pioneer in the area of relapse prevention, demonstrated that *intra*personal negative affective states present the greatest risk to prolonged abstinence. Dysphoric, uncomfortable feelings such as rage and depression place the quitter at great risk for substituting one compulsive behavior pattern with another. Similarly, the problems associated with the management of negative physical states present an increased risk of relapse. Marlatt noted that relapse episodes can be classified according to a variety of other intrapersonal events: for example, enhancement of positive emotional states, testing personal control (to see if the substance can be used in moderation), giving in to cravings. There are also an assortment of *inter*personal determinants of relapse. These factors include coping with interpersonal conflict, managing social pressure and enhancing positive affect within the context of social events. Ultimately, each of these risk factors must be confronted to maintain abstinence. In the next section, we will discuss the pharmacological and behavioral substitutions that commonly are associated with attempts to maintain abstinence from one (such as cocaine or alcohol) or a group of substances (narcotics).

Substitutions during Relapse Prevention

Pharmacological and Behavioral Substitutions

There are different types of cocaine abstinence: cocaine termination with or without the substitution of another compulsive activity. With substitution, cocaine quitters replace their drug of abuse with either another drug of abuse or a compulsive activity, such as excessive over- or undereating, sexual or religious activities. The next two sections consider pharmacological and behavioral substitutions, respectively.

> **Pharmacological Substitution: Out of the Frying Pan, into the Fire.** This (maintenance of abstinence phase) is when you come to terms with the damage you did. After I quit I felt enormous depression. I started to drink like a fish, although gradually. Two years later I am now coming to terms with alcoholism. I was numb when I was on coke and didn't have my emotions. When I quit, I started feeling a disappointment in myself. The wasted time and wondering how I was going to get it back. I started drinking more. It strengthened me against the coke. I learned to be alone. One to two years without a relationship. Now I'm ready to avoid another addiction.

> I drank sometimes when I did coke just to get a grip on reality, a little grip because I would do so much coke, and then I'd just be crazy, so I'd use alcohol to bring me down a little bit but I never considered myself a drinker, and I didn't do any drugs at all for about six months after I first quit (cocaine). And then I just gradually ended up. . . . I had a lot of guilt, I started to flood from all of the years of coke . . . you know, and all of it started to hit me after I quit doing it, and that's when I started drinking. And when I

started it was night drinking, where I'd drink myself to sleep. There was a lot of guilt, there was a lot of guilt about ripping people off. My drinking got worse, I got to be as heavy a drinker as I was a coke user. I got to the point of blackouts, and constant drinking, and losing days and days at a time.

Marijuana. Marijuana use often increases dramatically as quitters attempt to maintain their cocaine abstinence.

One of my connections owed me a fair amount of money. He didn't have the money, but had lots of pot. So, I took lots of pot from him instead, and we went and we smoked our brains out for a month. That was fun. And wrote and read, that's all we did. That's essentially when the cocaine came to an end. In many ways, I guess, you'd have to look at the period of that month as a detox period . . . as a transition point.

Stimulant Surrogates. Some quitters use caffeine excessively during their efforts to maintain cocaine abstinence. Caffeine mimics the sought-after stimulation that cocaine once provided them.

I've always liked stimulants as opposed to downers. The idea of chemically inducing stupidity isn't a subject that's been big with me. I think coffee is necessary to sustain life. I think Pepsi is a reasonable substitute if no other caffeine source is available. For me to some extent coffee is the substitute for all these other things. At this point physiologically I probably am slightly addicted to caffeine. I drink enough of it and a day without any coffee is a day in a coma.

Behavioral Substitutes for Cocaine Use

During the relapse prevention phase of cocaine recovery, quitters sometimes engage in other excessive behaviors—for example, excessive exercise, food, and sex.

Excessive Exercise. One of our quitters, a triathelete, had a childhood illness that previously prohibited endurance exercise. However, this quitter continued running dozens of marathons a year in addition to participating in triathelon events.

When I had my athletics I could be without money that day and without anything and everything. That fits because running releases endorphins which are natural-based opiates. When I got my run in my body was cleansed, I was happy, I was relieved, I was pleasantly fatigued. I know that the high is from the run, it's a natural high. So basically I was always striving to go back to where I was when I was a real jogger and when I was happy-go-lucky and people looked at me with respect as being a superior athlete. There's something unique about an endurance athlete, there's a uniqueness that people sense within another human being about that phenomenon of running a great distance, the marathon. They look at you as more of a supernatural human being, like someone out of the ordinary, and then when you combine triathalons they look at you as being very supernatural, very disciplined, as high caliber. The growth begins, the accomplishment, the achievement, when you start going after goals and putting the body to degrees that most people don't think the body can go to. It's unique. If I take the miles that I've logged in my years of running on these two legs, I've actually gone around the world.

Changes in Eating Patterns. Female cocaine quitters who used the stimulant to control their diet may have difficulty with weight control during the relapse prevention phase of cocaine recovery. For example, two of our female quitters gained thirty-five and eighty pounds, respectively, while another developed an anorectic eating disorder.

I drank a lot of coffee. I drank probably, I don't know, I drank coffee all day long, constant cup of coffee. I did a lot of physical exertion, which I had never really done before. I gained weight immediately. I gained a total of eighty pounds altogether.

Compulsive Sexual Behavior.

I wanted to kill myself because of that girl, after that, I straightened out (my drug abuse) until I ran into cocaine. Now, no problem with them, they love me. I thought there was no love after that girl. I think I still hold a grudge. I call the shots now. I sometimes think I am cruel to women. But I am all right now, I don't fall in love. With coke they were under my thumb and under my control. We could manipulate people, we owned them. It's unbelievable how you can manipulate women who want coke or who are on coke and I like (sexually) a lot of different women. . . . I'd walk into a party and everyone would flock over knowing I had coke. . . . We could make nuns strip for us. . . . My all-time record was nine different girls in one week. The average is three different girls a week.

Narcissistic Replacement. One of our quitters was motivated to stay clear of his previous cocaine abuse because he had new ambitions to become the president of the United States. At the time of our interview, this person was living hand-to-mouth, was forced to use his car as temporary lodging, failed college, and separated from his fiancee.

What really encourages me to keep my life straight and my act straight is the fact that I want to be able to talk to people about my past. I really do, I would like to run for political office and, if what I'm telling you is not too off the wall, I would like to run for president of the United States someday.

One of our cases replaced his cocaine abuse and the powerful position of dealing with the new ambition of making "macho (sic) money. I am money hungry. I want to concentrate on making money. I want a money addiction."

Religion or Religious Conversion. Some quitters experience a flight into religion just before or after they quit abusing drugs. For example, one cocaine quitter had a religious conversion a few months after terminating his cocaine abuse. He became a "born-again Christian." For this man, his religion became a substitute for cocaine.

> I've been cured. I mean I think of it (cocaine) once in a while but not in the manner to really do it. But then again, see, Satan deals with people in many ways. He deals with people in feelings, he deals with people through situations and circumstances, through their thought life. But the power of God teaches you and gives you the supernatural ability, once again, in the beginning when I told you he dwells in me, God is much greater than in the world, when I get that thought or when I get a thought that is unGodlike I have the ability and power and wisdom and understanding and knowledge to take it captive before it goes any further. Right now you could have a pound of cocaine and put it on the table. It would have no effect on me at all whatsoever. It just wouldn't matter because it's not really the hows or how I quit cocaine. It is the relationship that I have with God and the things that He wants to do with my life.

Religious conversion is like many of the other ingredients often identified as important aspects of recovery. Frequent and intense religious activities provide the opportunity for individuals to change their behavior patterns and consequently their identity. Furthermore, the formal structure of religious traditions and rituals permit new quitters to integrate these regulatory social supports into their day-to-day lifestyle. When this integration produces a subjective sense of well-being and control, individuals can experience an immediate and total conversion or change of belief (an epistemological shift) rather than an integrated religious experience formulated through personal reflection. Recovery and relapse prevention through religion is more common among alcohol and heroin quitters than those who quit cocaine.

Quitting Problems: Slips

Abstinence and Sobriety

The concepts "abstinence" and "sobriety" have been used interchangeably throughout this book. Abstinence refers to the absence of any use of a certain substance, in this case, cocaine. Heated debate exists in the field of substance treatment regarding exactly what abstinence includes. Some believe that abstinence can be achieved only when *all* psychoactive substances are eliminated. Anyone who has gone to an Alcoholics Anonymous or Narcotics Anonymous meeting[1] knows that abstinence does not include abstinence from cigarette smoking and coffee drinking. Further, some believe that if an abstainer should "slip" and ingest a forbidden substance, his or her accumulated sobriety starts over again ("day one"). In other words, for some people there is no such thing as a little bit abstinent. It is akin to "a little bit pregnant" (Weil 1972).

Slips. There are many things that can go wrong during prolonged attempts to remain abstinent. In fact, few quitters remain completely abstinent after they "stop" using their drug of choice. The vast majority of quitters have one or many slips. Marlatt & Gordon (1980) emphasize that slips are very likely occurrences. It is essential to understand the role of slips in the recovery process and how important they can be for long-term relapse prevention.

The following poem, "Autobiography in Five Short Chapters," nicely illustrates the role of slips in recovery. This poem by Portia Nelson was read at an Alcoholics Anonymous meeting.

I
I walk, down the street.
There is a deep hole in the sidewalk.
I fall in
I am lost. . . . I am helpless
It isn't my fault.
It takes forever to find a way out.
II
I walk down the same street.
There is a deep hole in the sidewalk.
I pretend I don't see it.
I fall in again.
I can't believe I am in the same place.
but, it isn't my fault.
It still takes a long time to get out.
III
I walk down the same street
There is a deep hole in the sidewalk.
I see it is there.

---

[1] We encourage anyone interested in the area of addictions to attend an open meeting of Alcoholics Anonymous, Cocaine Anonymous, or Narcotics Anonymous. These groups are valuable resources, both educationally and clinically, to those who are confronted with the issues of chemical dependence.

I still fall in. . . . it's a habit.
   my eyes are open.
   I know where I am.
It is my fault.
I get out immediately.
                    IV
I walk down the same street.
   There is a deep hole in the sidewalk.
   I walk around it.
                    V
I walk down another street.

Slips and relapses are a reality of recovery. Marlatt & Gordon (1980, 417-419) developed a detailed scale for classification of relapse episodes (Marlatt 1983; Marlatt & Gordon 1985). They recognize the importance of intrapsychic, interpersonal, and environmental determinants of relapse. For example, as was mentioned earlier, they consider the most common triggers for relapse situations to be "intrapersonal" difficulties in the management of negative feelings such as frustration or anger. Interpersonal situations that commonly cause relapse include difficulties with relationship conflict. Marlatt & Gordon say, based on studies of relapse episodes with alcoholics, heroin addicts, and smokers, that most relapses occur as a consequence of "intrapersonal" difficulties. There also appear to be differences in relapse among different substance users.

Consider the following illustration of an intrapsychic risk situation. Sherlock Holmes, who recently became cocaine abstinent, is described by his companion, Dr. Watson: "Things had indeed been very slow with us, and I had learned to dread such periods of inaction, for I knew by experience that my companion's brain was so abnormally active that it was dangerous to leave it without material upon which to work. For years I had gradually weaned him from that drug mania (cocainism) which had threatened once to check his remarkable career. Now I knew that under ordinary conditions he no longer craved for artificial stimulus, but I was well aware that the fiend was not dead, but sleeping; and I have known that the sleep was a light one and the waking near when in periods of idleness I have seen the drawn look upon Holmes's ascetic face, and the brooding of his deep-set and inscrutable eyes" (Doyle 1984, 483).

"Blowing" It; Ingredients for "Slipping." Our clinical experience with ex-cocaine abusers indicates that cocaine quitters are at the greatest risk for slips immediately after their abstinence is established. This high-risk period can continue for up to one year. Shortly thereafter, the intensity of the risk to abstinence seems to diminish, but it does not disappear. Cocaine quitters have their own, unique, drug-related risk slip situations. These occasions differ slightly from those determinants discussed previously by Marlatt (1985) and Marlatt & Gordon (1980). For example, most ex-cocaine abusers said that "seeing cocaine meant doing it." Exposure to cocaine, cocaine parties, and cocaine buddies were the most common ways to slip.

> I definitely felt beaten a couple of times that I took a little out (cocaine) and did it. I knew, I wasn't going to kid myself and say a little bit is OK. I know too many people who smoke cigarettes who say, well, it's just a drag (puff). And three weeks later you see them smoking a pack and a half again. It's like, uh huh. So I knew that's what would come of it. So I didn't give in to myself but continued to use cocaine. I told myself right off; "Well what you're doing is wrong." There's no way to rationalize it as being OK. It was wrong, I knew it was wrong, I did it anyhow. I beat myself over the head for a couple of hours about it and tried not to make myself feel too bad, because I figured that would make me more likely to go and get some for myself and sit down and blow a whole gram.

Slippers and Sliders. Those people with the highest rate of cocaine slips are individuals who cannot give up their cocaine friendship networks and continue to place themselves in "slippery" situations, such as attending cocaine parties and drinking alcohol to excess. Alcohol intoxication is often paired with cocaine use for abusers. They often continue to expose themselves to high risk situations even though they are aware that they will not be able to turn down cocaine once they see it, especially in a drunken state.

> I didn't understand the concept behind it so that the first slip, and then I would probably say the second one too, sort of experimenting, sort of well . . . I quit and now I've got it under control and I'll do one line and I'll walk away and I'll feel great and everything will be fine. And that's not how it worked out the first time and so I tried it again. I'm definitely an experimental person, I have to really do it until it's dead.

The Abstinence Violation Effect

During any discussion of slips and relapse it is essential to understand how individuals deal with cocaine slips without completely going "off the wagon" into a full-blown relapse. Gordon & Marlatt (1980) consider slips and relapses in the context of the "abstinence violation effect." "The requirement of abstinence is an absolute concept. Once someone has crossed the line, there is no going back. Only one drink or one cigarette is enough to break the rule of abstinence: The deed cannot be undone" (Marlatt & Gordon 1980, 427). The authors postulate that when the rule of abstinence has been violated, the recently abstinent person reacts with lowered self-esteem because his or her behavior is in direct opposition to the ideal self-image of an abstainer. Secondly, the slip or relapse is explained by the ex-drug abuser as an "internal weakness or personal failure," thus undermining both the self-esteem and the self-efficacy of the ex-user (Marlatt & Gordon 1980, 428). It becomes a challenge for the defeated and demoralized ex-cocaine abuser (who slipped or relapsed) to get herself or himself back into the abstinence saddle before a full-blown relapse occurs.

Dealing with Slips and the Abstinence Violation Effect. Some ex-abusers are able to use slips to their advantage. For example, they feel the slip serves as a useful reminder of the negative effects of cocaine intoxication. "I think it reinforced my decision to stay out of it. In all sincerity, I just don't see any desire to go back into it." Still others experience slips as a disadvantage in that it rekindles the original desire to use cocaine.

These examples illustrate how some cocaine quitters overcome the "abstinence violation effect."

> Slips? After a year and three months, doing some wouldn't be the end of the world, but it would also be the end of my streak. And I think I'm doing pretty well. I've held down two jobs and I do volunteer work within the caring profession and it's not worth jeopardizing all that.

> I would say that I had temporary setbacks in my process towards quitting. I learned from smoking that when you set yourself up so that one incident is pass/fail, then you're going to fail. That's where I really derived the idea that you have to treat each incident as a separate entity, a separate step on the path to the goal. Each time the urge comes along and I say no, I've taken another step. After you practice something for a while, you start to get good at it . . . and I'm good at turning down coke now. I can turn a slip around to be positive because it pisses me off. It really forces me to be angry at being dependent, that I'm not in control. . . . I'm definitely attempting to channel that so that the negative energy from the failure gets reversed into positive energy. It's attempting to make use out of anger and frustration. What I would tell people who are trying to quit is don't be too hard on yourself but keep trying. Pamper yourself. Go do good things that don't involve the behavior you're trying to get away from, and if you slip up, pick yourself up and keep going.

> It's not for me. If I can justify one then I'll justify every one. In some ways it's the same as—it's the reverse order of quitting; if you have one then you can use that same argument for each one, and if you can say no to this one and that's a separated instance, it's like beads on a string. When the next one comes along you say no to that.

> **Cravings.** I would just acknowledge them and let them go. I have a craving, but I'm not going to do it. Think about the outcome. I cued myself differ-

ently . . . different lines of thinking about the whole nature of doing it. Well, before I just wouldn't do anything, I would just use. I wouldn't put any thought into it. Here, I inserted thought between the wish and the action.

I still every now and then get that passing urge to have a cigarette and a lot of it's not so much the cigarette itself but the ritual. I can still feel the cigarette between my fingers, and if I see somebody that will just trigger off the association. There's a whole ritual with coke, there's chopping it up on the mirror, but I know it's just going to go, it'll just be a brief peak and then that urge will be gone.

Summary

In this chapter, we reviewed a variety of issues that influence an individual's chances of relapse. Intra- and interpersonal factors weigh heavily on those attempting to maintain sobriety. In addition, we presented clinical evidence that portrayed some of the risks, experiences, and solutions practiced by those who were faced directly with challenges to their abstinence. In the afterword, we will consider a somewhat different perspective from that adopted up to this point. We will explore an interactive pharmacological and sociocultural view of drug use and abuse, as well as the regulatory lessons that can be obtained from this vantage point.

9
Lessons in Quitting: Learning from Natural Cocaine Quitters

We began this book by proclaiming it an account of human resilience and spirit: a collection of valuable information and insights gained from special people who confronted and conquered their impulses. Quitting cocaine cannot be considered spontaneous. Rather, it is the result of a sequence of events that tend to be associated with the recovery of self-control. Natural cocaine quitters were found to recover their independence through a series of identifiable activities. The major events associated with quitting are observable and can be made explicit.

It appears that all successful quitters pass through these phases, though at different rates. It does not follow, however, that if one goes through these phases, one will be assured of breaking the habit. Systematic research will be necessary to confirm that conclusion or the circumstances under which the sequence of quitting phases proves to be insufficient for recovery. At present, we suggest that identification of these phases, and recognition that they are an integral part of the quitting process, holds great promise for those who desire more effective behavior change skills.

Cocaine quitters—those who have descended to the depths of despair and then ascended back from dependence—have a great deal to teach us about addiction. Perhaps most importantly, cocaine quitters reveal that addiction does not reside in drugs. It resides in human experience. A substantial number of cases of natural recovery from cocaine, alcohol, opiates, and tobacco *all* serve to remind us that, in spite of the physiological dependence that may be one consequence of drug use, addiction is not inevitable. Furthermore, neither physiological dependence nor behavioral addiction imply that death is inevitable. It is possible to recover and regain one's independence. To recover from addiction, however, a sequence of well-defined events must occur. The intensity and duration of each milestone will vary from person to person, but the basic sequence will be common to all.

The Process of Addiction and Recovery

In this section, we will introduce briefly an overview of a six-phase model of addiction onset and recovery. A more detailed discussion of each phase of this model will follow in a later section.

During the first phase of addiction, one *begins* to use a drug or engage in an activity that can eventually culminate in purposeful quitting. These patterns of activity have come to be identified as addictive behaviors. There are a host of biological, psychological, and social factors associated with the etiology of addiction. The premise upon which our recovery model rests postulates that any pattern of human behavior can become excessive. Therefore, although this model stresses cocaine addiction and recovery, the full range of excessive human behaviors can be considered within the parameters of this approach to quitting and recovery.

Second phase: The activity or drug use must yield direct or indirect positive consequences. For example, the direct *positive consequences* of drug use may include alleviating discomfort, producing euphoria, or both. Indirectly, drug use may alleviate social discomfort or improve one's standing within personal relationships, the community, or work. With nonchemical addictions the activity must involve the equivalent of euphoria; for example, with gambling, the activity would include an episode of "winning." For drug users, the behavior must lead to the counterpart of winning; for example, euphoria or the cessation of dysphoria.

Third phase: The behavior pattern escalates to the point that it begins to produce more frequent *adverse consequences*. These negative events remain out of conscious awareness at this point in the developmental sequence of an addictive disorder. As a result, the activity continues to escalate without any corrective regulation.

Fourth phase: The adverse consequences are consciously experienced. This set of experiences typically is associated with a period of hopelessness and helplessness. Some individuals have described this experience as hitting bottom; others have called it a disintegration of their value system. This system of events represents a *turning point* in the experience of addiction.

Fifth phase: The turning point must become associated with strategies and tactics that permit, encourage, and require behavior changes, shifts in daily living that are directly associated with *active efforts to stop* the addictive behavior(s). For example, cocaine quitters often change their social relationships, recreational activities, and telephone number to avoid the drug scene.

Sixth phase: The individual who is quitting must employ longer-term strategies and tactics to *maintain the newly developed abstinence* from the addictive behavior pattern. This phase requires that the social and personal changes initiated during the fifth phase be permanently integrated into one's lifestyle.

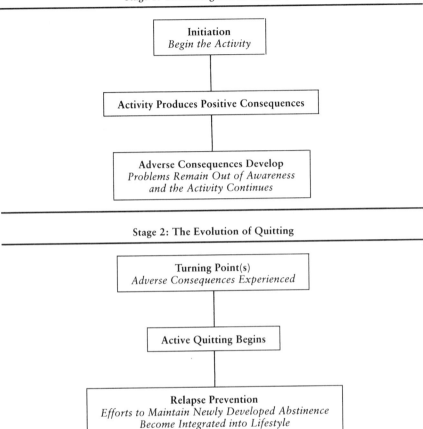

Figure 9–1. The Phases of Cocaine Addiction: From Start to Finish

Each phase of quitting represents distinct activities. The first three phases are associated with the emergence of addictive behavior. The latter three characterize the process of quitting. Figure 9–1 summarizes the developmental sequence of stages and phases that characterize addiction and recovery.

Although we have presented strong clinical evidence that the quitting phases can be achieved by some in the absence of a treatment program, it is our position that for many potential quitters, structure, such as that provided in formal treatment, is necessary. We recommend that addiction treatment programs employ activities that develop and exercise the skills and experiences associated with phases three through six. In the absence of these endeavors, sustained quitting is unlikely. In the sections that follow, we discuss each of these areas in more detail. Our emphasis will be, of course, on the quitting phases of recovery.

Stage 1: The Emergence of Addiction

Initiation: Beginning Cocaine. It is obvious that to become a successful quitter from any activity, one must participate in it at some point. Everyone who uses cocaine, however, does not become a cocaine abuser or addict. In fact, as we discussed in the chapter on understanding cocaine, most of those who try the drug do not become addicted to it. Earlier in this book, we examined factors that influence the use of cocaine; these catalysts explain why beginning users become abusers. In addition, these catalysts explain some of the reasons why quitters may remain abusers once initiated to drug use. An exhaustive explanation of the initiation phase is beyond the scope of this book; we are interested primarily in quitting. It logically follows, however, that there are no successful cocaine quitters who did not start to use the drug.

The Activity Produces Positive Consequences. If the activity—cocaine use, for example—is not associated with some positive consequences, it will not be continued. Positive effects can be a direct result of the pharmacological properties of the drug or the psychological reinforcement (such as relief of depression or sexual inhibition) obtained by its use. The consequences also can be positive in a more indirect manner. For example, some cocaine users experience more social rewards, are held in higher esteem, and have more to do when they are using cocaine. Without some positive consequences, any activity or drug use would not be continued to the point that addiction could emerge.

Adverse Consequences Develop but Remain out of Awareness. Cocaine use or any other activity must be, by definition, associated with adverse consequences if it is to be considered an addictive behavior. The essence of addiction is that it continues to provide some of the positive consequences described above while simultaneously producing adverse consequences that begin to weigh more heavily. Addictive behaviors serve while they destroy. The reason they can be so very destructive is because the addict is not fully aware that the adverse effects of their cocaine use (or other addictive behavior) is, in fact, the result of that behavior.

An epicycle of this nature can escalate without regulation because the cybernetic or feedback channels are impaired.[1] Addicts perceive others as the source of their problems while their behavior is perceived or experienced as having little to do with their suffering. The urging of friends and family to reduce or stop the addictive behavior is of little consequence; in fact, their pleading can become fuel that energizes the addictive behavior so that the pattern intensifies further. Bean-Bayog (1988) has called this type of denial a focused delusional system. At this level, addicts are capable of making sense of their world, with one exception: they cannot make the association between their addictive behavior and the life problems they have had to endure. In order to minimize the discomfort associated with these problems, addicts persist in engaging in those behaviors that previously produced positive consequences; that is, the addictive behavior—and the cycle—continues. Prevailing beliefs suggest that there is no escape from this epicycle unless it is interrupted from the outside. Often this is true. The natural recovery from addictive behavior, however, stands as a scintillating contradiction.

When this pattern of behavior continues, the adverse consequences mount, with little or no conscious causal association between the addictive behavior and the negative effects these produce. A sense of despair and hopelessness develops as a consequence of the sheer number of problems that emerge. This experience has been described as loss of control. Life becomes unmanageable. The feeling that one has little capacity to regulate the events and behaviors of one's life can lead to interminable addiction. Drug abuse, for example, can lead to despair, which, in turn, can precipitate more drug abuse.

For some—our quitters, for example—the adverse consequences enter awareness and their life takes a turn. This moment of awareness, or insight, has often been considered the end of denial. More accurately, it is a reclaiming of the projections that characterized phase three. No longer are one's problems the result of external events; no longer can one continue to claim victimization. The adverse consequences associated with addictive behavior now are experienced as one's own. This is the beginning of an epistemological shift. The addict is confronted by his or her own recognition of the causal connection between his or her drug-using behaviors and such problems as poor health, financial difficulty, and/or family disintegration. The addict now realizes that his or her behaviors are not anomalous and not without adverse effect. Often experienced as a life crisis, the addict recognizes that his or her lifestyle must now change if he or she is to regain control. The addict begins to recognize the necessity of giving up the positive consequences while gain-

---

[1]This circumstance is similar, in effect, to a furnace that continues to heat an excessively warm house because the thermostat is malfunctioning and cannot send a message back to the furnace indicating that it should stop.

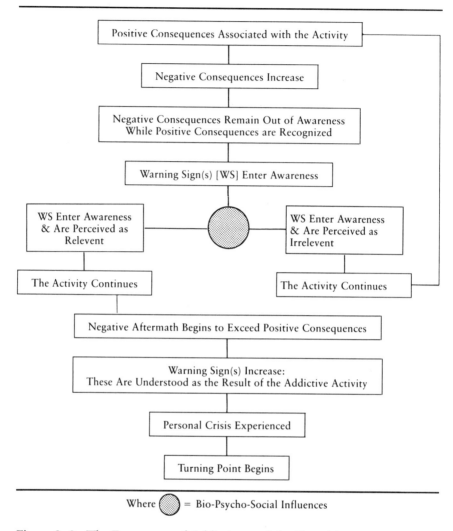

Figure 9–2. The Emergence of Addiction and the Transition to Turning Points (Phases Three and Four)

ing access to the negative outcomes that are connected with the addictive behavior pattern. The event or events associated with turning point experiences mark the beginning of stage two, the evolution of quitting. The events associated with the emergence of addiction and the transition that leads to quitting are summarized in figure 9–2. This figure also depicts the influential role that biological, psychological, and social factors play in determining whether warning signs enter awareness.

Stage 2: The Evolution of Quitting

Turning Points. The discomforts associated with the adverse consequences that enter awareness, as described in the last phase of stage 1 of the addiction model (figures 9–1 and 9–2), eventually give rise to questions about the use of cocaine or other addictive activity. Cocaine use becomes increasingly intolerable. As we discussed before, a turning point represents the shift between unencumbered cocaine use and the realization that cocaine abuse is responsible for the presence of profoundly negative life circumstances. The thought of quitting or controlling cocaine first appears before the actual turning point. Drug abusers begin to express a wish that they want to quit. Increasing levels of self-observation are involved. The abusers now begin to realize that the costs of their addictive behavior exceed the benefits. Cocaine is explicitly identified as the major destructive agent in their lives.[2] The full scope of their ambivalent feelings toward cocaine surface and are more fully experienced. It is at this point that a quitter often asks friends and significant others to help him or her stop. Before a turning point, the burden of self-control had been delegated more to others than oneself; the acceptance of personal responsibility represents the actual turning point.

A turning point is not simply a transition. It is actually the end of a complex thought process about cocaine (or other addictive behavior). We consider it an end point even though abstinence and recovery might be months or years away. Needless to say, the experience of a turning point does not produce instantaneous results. Commonly experienced turning points were described as periods of dissonance associated with feelings of self-loathing or a deterioration of personal values. Other turning point perceptions include the recognition that cocaine abuse begins to exacerbate rather than diminish intra- and interpersonal conflict. An extremely important yet commonly reported turning point centers around the recognition that one's deteriorating physical condition is related to cocaine abuse. This is experienced as a do-or-die situation: if cocaine is used, the user believes that death may be imminent. Other turning points, less extreme but no less important, involve the recognition that one may lose what is important, for example, a job, because of cocaine involvement.

Active Quitting Begins. Once a turning point is experienced, the process and task associated with active quitting can begin. Two basic approaches to quitting were described in the earlier chapter on active quitting: "tapered quitting" and "cold turkey quitting." It is possible that a successful quitter will mix these approaches to find a method that works. Most quitters, however,

---

[2]They may be addictively involved with other substances or activities.

fall predominantly or entirely into one style or the other. Few successful quitters mix their stopping strategies.

The notion of *active* quitting is important. Successful quitters make observable changes during this second phase of the stopping stage of addiction. The methods for quitting cocaine include energetic attempts to avoid the drug, gain social support for personal change, and engage in some form of self-development. Thus, this phase is characterized neither by thoughtfulness nor ambivalence. It is identified by important and marked behavioral change and lifestyle reorganization. New activities are elevated to a position of prominence; they gain intra- and interpersonal value. Old behaviors become devalued.

Relapse Prevention. Very few individuals who stop their drug use remain totally abstinent from that moment. Marlatt & Gordon (1985) examine how slips—that is, single episodes of drug use—can lead to full-blown relapse. Biological, psychological, and sociological factors interact to influence the risk of relapse for any individual. The final phase of quitting involves the development of skills and lifestyle patterns that promote positive, independent patterns of behavior. The integration of these cognitive and behavioral competencies into regular day-to-day behavior is the essence of relapse prevention. Alcoholics Anonymous, for example, promotes the integration of new behavior patterns for the recently sober by suggesting "ninety meetings in ninety days." The relapse prevention phase, unlike the other phases and activities of quitting, entails the development of a lifelong pattern of behavior that is designed to cope with the many situations and experiences known to lead to relapse among those who have yet to enter the final stage.

Once a user has experienced addiction, it is not reasonable to suggest he or she will never be reminded of those experiences associated with the excessive circumstance. More likely, as time passes, the intensity of the drug associations diminish and new patterns take their place. The older patterns do not disappear; instead the intensity of the response—for example, craving—is diminished.

It has been demonstrated that negative affective states such as anger present the greatest risk to individuals who are newly abstinent (Marlatt & Gordon 1985). Other negative interpersonal situations also are important risk factors during the development of relapse prevention and abstinence maintenance strategies. Stress and anger are often associated with craving; this experience may stimulate a slip. Since abstinence is viewed as an absolutely rigid concept that does *not* reside on a continuum; once someone has crossed the line and slipped, he has violated his abstention. One drink, one cigarette, or one line of cocaine is sufficient to violate abstinence. Alcoholics Anonymous, for example, maintains that if one were to have a drink after ten years of complete abstinence, the starting date for sobriety must begin anew.

Marlatt & Gordon (1980) noted that when the rule of abstinence has been violated, the recently abstinent person can react with lowered self-esteem and a diminished sense of personal control. This belief is the consequence of behavior that appears in direct opposition to the individual's newly derived self-image as an abstainer. If the slip or relapse is explained by the ex-drug abuser as the result of "internal weakness or personal failure," the slip can undermine both the quitter's self-esteem and the belief that he or she has the skills and motivation to maintain the new status as an ex-user. In fact, drugs may then be used to ameliorate the negative feelings associated with the slip. Among natural cocaine quitters, it is a challenge for those who feel defeated and demoralized momentarily by their slip to get back into the abstinence saddle before a full-blown relapse occurs.

Our quitters' experiences suggest that having a number of strategies and tactics to draw upon is essential to maintaining abstinence from cocaine. Successful quitters substituted a variety of behavior patterns for their old drug-using lifestyle. For example, they became regularly involved in physical exercise, eating, and sexual behavior. At times these substitute patterns also became excessive; this risk is most probable when (a) excessive behavior patterns serve as anodynes to uncomfortable affective states, and/or (b) self-observation skills are weak and poorly developed. Spiritual or religious conversions also helped many individuals sustain their abstinence. In addition, they occasionally substituted other drugs that they considered less troublesome. The use of pharmacological substitution is extremely risky and often backfires. The results of drug substitution can be as devastating and destructive as the original cocaine abuse.

In sum, there are six phases to quitting or stopping an addictive pattern of behavior. The first three phases comprise the addiction stage, while the last three are associated with quitting. The first stage is groundwork for the second stage (see figure 9-1) The three phases of quitting serve as the focal point of the second part of this book. In the sections that follow, we consider some of the implications of these phases for clinical practice, drug prevention, and education.

Quitting Lessons from the People Who Knew
How to Stop

Contrary to treatment perspectives such as those espoused by the disease model of addiction and drug abuse—which does not recognize the existence of self-quitters because drug abuse is a disease that can only worsen without outside intervention—the clinical data reveal significant evidence of individuals who have managed to terminate their abuse of cocaine without formal drug treatment. These individuals teach us the fallacy in maintaining a rigid adherence to a single theory and treatment perspective: we blind ourselves to

158 • *Quitting Cocaine*

the need for exploring diverse and effective forms of treatment. If one can believe in the existence of self-quitters, one can learn ways to advance treatment technologies by asking the "experts" (that is, the self-recoverers) how they quit. Our review suggests the possibility that what cocaine quitters tell us may be more useful clinically than what the prevailing wisdom has to offer.

Generalizations to Clinical Practice

Prescriptive Treatment. Our clinical observations of cocaine quitters lead us to recommend a shift in the current treatment of cocaine abusers (a recommendation that generalizes to substance abusers in general). We have demonstrated that cocaine abusers do, in fact, recover without the aid of formal drug treatment and that these individuals apply a variety of techniques to terminate from the drug and the lifestyle. Our evidence suggests that individuals often find their own special way of quitting. This observation reinforces the importance of prescriptive or personalized treatment based on thorough and detailed individual clinical evaluations. Nevertheless, prescriptive treatment for substance abusers is not the prevailing norm. Typical inpatient programs designed specifically to care for addiction remain the only hospital wards where one can find the same treatment plan in place for all patients.

> In treatment, people should not be wedded to any one idea. I think if there's anything I gained from my experience, . . . it was an accumulation of experiences. It wasn't going to this therapist or that therapist. But it was all of that stuff and putting it together over a period of time. Therapists need to think about custom-tailoring treatment for the substance abuser. If the patient is not responding to treatment perhaps the treatment is not appropriate. This approach might avoid "blaming" substance abusers in general for being difficult patients to treat.

Individual Psychotherapy. Nearly half the cocaine quitters we interviewed entered some form of individual therapy (non–drug-related) *after* they quit cocaine. Many individuals found psychotherapy helpful. For instance, some dealers who did not substitute chemicals as an active quitting strategy entered individual psychotherapy as a alternative. Therapy in these cases seemed useful and may have led to a more thorough recovery.

Therapy Directed at Structure Building. Our work indicates that cocaine quitters who were structure building during recovery fared well and tended not to replace cocaine with problematic substitutes. It is far easier to give something up when there is a positive alternative. Therapeutic programs, therefore, might include meaningful components that help patients discover what they are interested in pursuing during their lives. "Abstinence can best be induced by giving the addict something he did not have before, rather than by depriving him of what little he already has" (Vaillant 1966, 466). Therefore, a therapeutic endeavor might be to help the ex-addict replace the lost drug with something positive rather than substituting another compulsive drug or activity. This approach is different from current drug treatments that focus almost exclusively on giving up the drug, without providing significant alternatives.

Secondary Drug Use/Abuse. When a patient enters treatment to terminate cocaine, the clinician must learn what other drugs the patient uses. If our quitters are representative, we know that cocaine is not a drug that is abused alone. All our cocaine quitters used alcohol and most admitted they had alcohol problems during their heaviest period of cocaine involvement. It is crucial that the clinician pay close attention to the other drugs in the patient's life for two reasons. First, if the patient is planning to terminate cocaine, any secondary drug abuse with alcohol or sedative-hypnotics requires medical attention for detoxification and cannot be terminated safely without medical intervention. Some of our quitters tried to stop all drugs at the same time as they ceased the use of cocaine, to "cold turkey" totally, a strategy that might be life-threatening. Second, as we discussed earlier in this chapter, there are the potential problems often associated with the use of a substitute for cocaine. As cocaine use decreases, or after cocaine use stops entirely, therapists must not forget to assess other drug use. Clinicians must be prepared to help the quitter attend to any possible adverse consequences of replacements for cocaine use.

Risk Periods. Long-term efforts to maintain abstinence are the most difficult periods for the ex-addict. Relapse, drug replacement, and other compulsive activities are common. Clinicians should prepare patients for this period; they can anticipate and rehearse alternatives to their patient's old patterns of coping. Support during this phase can make the difference between relapse and recovery.

Affect Tolerance. The substance abuser has limited means of understanding and tolerating subjectively painful feelings. Our quitters reported the overwhelming experience of being flooded with feelings and depression during recovery. The therapist must help the patient learn to manage these feelings. We would recommend adoption of a much more active role than one generally would in psychotherapy. Such involvement by the psychotherapist may be critical, because during this period of emotional turmoil, the ex-cocaine patient is at greatest risk to slip, relapse, or substitute other compulsive behaviors for cocaine use.

The question remains as to *when* the therapist should try to help the patient understand the origins of painful feelings from such traumas as abandonment, verbal and physical abuse from dysfunctional parents, and/or a family history of drug abuse. There is much debate over this question because therapy, at times, is seen as stirring up material and conflict, which can lead to anxiety and renewed use of drugs. The first priority with substance abusers must be to maintain safety. Therapy, in the beginning, should be actively supportive to the patient by providing a source of security, hope, self-esteem, respect, and value to themselves and others (for example, career, volunteering themselves to organizations). Because the patient is likely to be overwhelmed by affect, uncovering should be done with timing and great caution. We suggest that psychotherapy can be a fruitful activity for the substance-involved patient; however, the therapy must attend to the addictive behavior pattern. Addicted patients must be greeted at their own level. This tired phrase offers new meaning to psychotherapists who have considered previously that therapy was impossible. It suggests that addiction is like trauma and that patients should be supported and directed to experience recovery-enhancing activities before they are exposed to the discomforts associated with uncovering painful information that might explain how, why, and when cocaine provided an adaptive environment for them.

The reasons a patient initially found cocaine beneficial are useful information for the clinician nevertheless. This material should alert clinicians as to where and when the therapeutic effort should begin. In the case of patients who suffered from self-esteem difficulties, for example, therapy might begin by providing secure, external support to the patient, allowing the cocaine function to be performed by the therapist. This transition represents a productive rather than destructive substitute. In addition, the therapeutic relationship itself can be helpful for those subjects who used the drug primarily for relationship protection.

Special attention must be paid to patients when they try to socialize without cocaine, in terms of where they go and with whom they associate. These situations place them at great risk and should be discussed in therapy. Often, separation is a prominent issue for the substance abuser. The therapist must, therefore, attend to the needs and desires of the patient in his or her attempts to avoid loss through separation by continuing to socialize with cocaine abusers during recovery.

Special User Types. The special needs of women who use cocaine must be addressed. Females who report, for example, that they use cocaine for weight control may have a history of eating disorder or food management difficulties. While not restricted to women, these issues are more prevalent among women and can complicate the clinical picture. They may be fearful of quitting cocaine for many of the same reasons women worry about giving up cigarettes. An obvious parallel is the fear of weight gain when weight loss is or has been the desired goal. Most clinical evidence concerning substance abuse has been obtained from male patients and women's issues tend to be overlooked. Therapists *must* remain cognizant of the special needs of the female patient.

Another special type of user may be the injured athlete who no longer can participate in sports. We have encountered a number of athletes who started using, or increased their cocaine use, after sports were no longer a viable option for them. A serious athlete (daily participation) who abruptly stops physical activity suffers an endorphin depletion in much the same way as does the ex-cocaine addict. This leaves the ex-athlete vulnerable to a chemical depression and, more specifically, to the use of stimulants as a source of affective nourishment.

Sports or vigorous physical activities offer quitters an advantage. Many of our quitters, for example, found exercise a helpful replacement to cocaine abuse because it provided energy and a feeling of enhanced self-esteem. In effect, exercise acts as an antidepressant. The antidepressant effects of exercise are very important for the ex-cocaine abuser who has depleted certain neurotransmitter actions resulting in a postcocaine depression. This depletion increases the recent quitter's vulnerability to relapse.

In short, a more holistic attitude should be considered by clinicians who work in the addictions. The *entire* life structure of the cocaine user should be of therapeutic interest as an object of treatment. Within this perspective, special clinical attention paid to feelings about the drug and the role it played in their lives, a watchful eye on current substance involvement and behavioral activities, and help regarding the identification, exploration, and pursuit of meaningful structure in the patients' lives can all be of therapeutic value.

Educational Efforts

Our quitters often mentioned that they did not use heroin, or some other drugs, because they had learned in high school drug programs about its addictive properties. We learn from them, however, that a serious educational gap exists about cocaine. Drug programs should educate young adults about the effects of cocaine. The Reagan administration campaign of "just say no" does not help people who may be unable to say no. Further, the notion of "*just* say no" implies that just saying no is sufficient. It is not. New behaviors and skills associated with avoiding and escaping peer pressure are essential to any drug prevention effort. Unfortunately, the teaching of these skills is currently lacking in many educational programs on drug and alcohol abuse that instead focus on pharmacology.

Our experience also reveals that people do not just say "no" without sound reason. Educational efforts might be more helpful if directed at the experience of addiction rather than the drugs that are often associated with dependence. As we discussed earlier, addiction does not reside in chemistry. Rather, addiction is a human experience. By creating more information about drugs and their different effects without emphasizing the human emotions and experiences associated with drug use, prevention specialists may be sustaining drug experimentation and abuse. Drug education efforts might stress the warning signs discussed earlier in this book. These programs might increase the self-observation skills that are essential to quitting; these same skills are essential factors needed to limit the emergence of addictive behavior. Strong and active observational skills help a person recognize when drug use (or any other behavior) no longer is adaptive.

Educational programs could inform people who are abusing drugs concurrently by including information about the ways other individuals quit that drug. Such information could prepare them for some of the pitfalls or risk situations and times for relapse, and also alert them to the tendency for another compulsive activity to take over. The dangers associated with relapse prevention should be anticipated and rehearsed. Generating ideas for dealing with difficult feelings have already been demonstrated to help to avoid relapse (Marlatt et al. 1988). We encourage educators to use what we have learned from our quitters. We suggest they make a special appeal to those students currently abusing drugs; educational prevention programs should be directed toward those whose behavior has yet to reach the first phase of our model (that is, primary prevention) or those who are in the second or third phases of the model.

Caveats

The six-phase model was offered primarily for its organizational and heuristic value. Although successful quitters pass through these stages and phases, there is no guarantee that a user will become a successful quitter if he or she experiences this sequence of events. However, we do expect that systematic research will find significant correlation between those who do experience these phases and those who successfully stop their addiction. To illustrate: although one can copy the movements of a professional golfer, that does not secure a place among the world's great touring professionals. More likely it simply will improve one's golfing skills.

Advances in personal performance should not be taken lightly. The capacity to develop new skills, whether golfing or quitting, and then translate this new learning into performance, has been an age-old challenge. The three phases of quitting an addiction can serve to guide this sequence of activities. It can also guide the development of self-help and professional treatment programs that are better matched to the problems of addictive behaviors.

Afterword

"Pharmecology": Sociocultural Lessons about Stopping Addiction

T hroughout this book, we have stressed the lessons learned from individuals who managed to stop their cocaine addiction. In this afterword, we will review a different perspective, one that requires us to
step back from individual drug-using patterns and observe social and ecological trends. These trends reveal a great deal about the natural history of drug
use and abuse. Furthermore, examinations of ecological trends illuminate a
variety of sociocultural lessons about natural processes that promote, prevent, and stop addiction. We will review a sampling of these lessons by first
examining pharmacological issues and, second, considering the social and
ecological factors that influence drug using patterns.

The purpose of this afterword is to endorse and encourage a more realistic approach toward drug abuse treatment and research than those perspectives that now dominate the field. Instead of taking a unidimensional, categorical approach toward the understanding of drug use and misuse, it is
essential to examine and appreciate the entire psychopharmacological menu
from which drug users select their substances of use and abuse. The chemical
ecology of the individual or, in other words, their "pharmecology," is a critical but often neglected aspect of drug use and abuse treatment and research.

Another essential factor that influences drug use and abuse patterns is
the social context within which drugs are used (for example, Shaffer 1983;
Shaffer & Zinberg 1985; Zinberg 1984; Zinberg & Shaffer 1985). This
evolving relationship between the cultural environment and the intoxicant
use pattern(s) in vogue will be referred to as social ecology. In the sections
that follow both the concepts of "pharmecology" and social ecology will be
examined in more detail.

Using cocaine, alcohol, and marijuana as the primary illustrations, we
will consider the lessons obtained from an interactive or ecological approach
to drug use and abuse. For example, how do occasional cocaine users, or
"chippers," manage to control their intake and guard against the compulsive
use of cocaine; how do various patterns of drug use interact with other regulatory or self-control mechanisms?

Finally, this afterword will examine the interaction between social and personality factors within the context of an evolving social milieu. We suggest that social ecology has not been sufficiently emphasized when considering intoxicant use and abuse.

Metascientific Thinking: Aristotle to Galileo

Kurt Lewin (1931) described two types of scientific thinking: Aristotelian and Galilean. The first approach defines and organizes our explanations of the world by sorting information descriptively and categorically, much like the index to an introductory psychology textbook. The latter organizes information interactively. Ecology is the dynamic, interactive relationship between organisms and their environment. Bateson (1979) noted that there is an ecology of both "mind" and "nature." Drug abuse research tends to rely primarily on Aristotelian investigations. Researchers, guided by Aristotelian principles, fail to consider the ecologically interactive processes that develop, for example, between the drug user, the chosen drug, and the social setting within which such use occurs.

Guided by a Galilean perspective, drug use behaviors should be studied systematically by examining an individual's pharmecology as well as his or her social ecology. The interaction between the social ecology or cultural milieu, that is, the surrounding environment, and the pharmecology or individual drug use patterns, can have a powerful influence on drug use choices. Recent patterns of cigarette and marijuana smoking provide a powerful example of interactive megapharmecological trends. According to the surgeon general (1979; 1982), the prevalence of regular cigarette smoking among the adult population has declined from an estimated 42 percent to 45 percent twenty-five years ago to approximately 25 percent today. Conversely, the prevalence of marijuana smoking has increased multifold since the 1920s: an estimated 32 million Americans now smoke marijuana. The social stigma once associated with pot has decreased while the social acceptability of cigarette smoking has greatly diminished—it is no longer fashionable to smoke cigarettes. Perhaps if the present ecological influences continue to reduce the prevalence of cigarette smoking, many years from now the few remaining cigarette smokers will represent a pathological population within our culture. Society's attitude toward these deviants will not be gracious. The result of this trend may be the age of "nicotine madness" instead of "reefer madness"!

Pharmecology

An individual's pharmecology (polydrug use) can be illustrated by the current pattern of collateral sedative/hypnotic drug use and abuse (such as alcohol and/or valium) by cocaine users to medicate the stimulating effects of co-caine; for example, a "down comforter." Preliminary evidence (Burglass 1985; Kozel & Adams 1985) suggests that there is an important relationship between the use of cocaine and sedatives. Often the sedating effects of alco-hol, for example, are sought to "take the edge off" the stimulating effects of cocaine.

Historically, drugs or other substances have often become paired: caf-feine and nicotine, the "speedball" effects of heroin and stimulants, or pret-zels and beer. The interactive, cybernetic characteristics of drug use "ecosys-tems" can serve to stimulate secondary drug use patterns and/or encourage users to seek drugs that they do not prefer (for example, Hartford 1978). It is not unusual for a disequilibrium to develop within the pharmecology of an individual user such that other drug-seeking behavior is stimulated. The use of phenothiazines as antipsychotic medications, for example, precipitated the concurrent use of antiparkinsonian drugs to minimize the effects of tar-dive dyskensia—a nervous system disorder caused by the effects of the phenothiazines.

Similarly, pollutants in one part of the environment can affect the entire ecosystem by producing effects that ripple throughout the system thereby al-tering the delicate balance of nature (consider the destructive effects of acid rain). Likewise, when pesticides are used to depopulate a geographic area of a particular insect, its prey—without a natural enemy—multiply without reg-ulation and overpopulate the same region, eventually suffering the same fate (that is, excessive population growth) as their predators. Therefore, another insecticide is often developed or implemented to limit the side effects of the first pesticide application. If the reader detects any similarity between the problem-solving strategy of substituting one chemical agent for another and the approaches offered by contemporary drug treatment programs, it is in-tentionally coincidental!

Similarities and coincidences such as these reflect the breadth of phar-mecological phenomena. Bar owners understand pharmecology; they serve pretzels, peanuts, and other salted foods to customers as well as supply cig-arette machines for unlimited smoking. The salt and smoke make patrons more thirsty and, therefore, increase their drinking levels.

Pharmecology and Subjective Experience: Drug, Set, and Setting

To better understand the subjective experiences that can be produced by an individual's pharmecology, it is necessary to consider drug, set, and setting as an ecological whole. As was discussed in chapter 3 (Understanding Cocaine), "set" refers to the personality structure of the drug user, including one's at-titudes toward the experience and any values that might be associated with the activity. "Setting" is considered to be the influence of the physical and social environment within which the drug use takes place. "To understand an individual's decision to use a drug and his response to the experience at any effective dose below toxic levels, one must consider . . . the drug-set-setting interaction, because these factors affect the drug experience directly" (Zinberg 1974; 1981, 242). Drugs, for example, can serve to alter one's experience when ingested, a biological reaction, or can serve as an object in the environment that affects goal-directed behavior patterns. Similarly, expectations can influence behavior patterns, which, in turn, can provide a changing milieu that affects the behavior of others. The drug, set, and setting schema can clarify the interactive relationship between history, culture, and subjective experience.

Zinberg (1974, 1984)[1] noted that the dynamic relationships among drug, personality, and social structure, or drug, set, and setting, seem straightforward initially. He recognized that most observers of social behavior, for example, know that psychic states vary greatly, are influenced by the environment and, of course, that drugs affect these states. These relationships are easy to grasp in the abstract; surprisingly, however, these issues are very difficult to understand and accept in practice.

As individuals, we are encouraged to accept simple explanations of drug effects. Zinberg (1974, 1984), for example, recognized that most of us are so accustomed to thinking of drugs in a medical context—medicines used for the treatment of specific conditions—we assume the effect of a drug to (1) be the same for everyone and (2) remain relatively constant for anyone. Physicians are not eager to dispel this belief. To maximize the therapeutic effect of the prescribed drug, physicians avoid reminding the patient that it may have different effects on different patients with the same condition, and, furthermore, that its effects on the same patient may vary over time. In spite of the medical/medicinal aura surrounding drugs, most drug experts have accepted the important influence of set and setting in determining drug effects. For those not experienced or accepting of the drug-set-setting interaction, Zinberg (1974; 1984) described the effects of alcohol.

The Interactive Effects of Drug, Set, and Setting: The Subjective Experience of Alcohol. Almost everyone must be aware, either from observing his or her own behavior or the behavior of others, that the effects of alcohol vary from person to person and over time. We all have seen happy drinkers, morose drinkers, belligerent drinkers, and flirtatious drinkers. Sometimes alcohol can be a relaxant (the martini after a hard day at the office), and sometimes it can act as a stimulant (the first drink at a party). At times, alcohol releases

---

[1]We are indebted to Dr. Zinberg for his assistance with the following material that examines drug, set, and setting. This discussion is based primarily upon his work (Zinberg 1974, 1984; Zinberg & Shaffer 1985; Shaffer & Zinberg 1985).

inhibitions, and at other times, those who have already put aside their inhibitions will take a drink or two to provide themselves with a socially acceptable alibi. Often, alcohol is a mood accelerator, deepening depression or heightening elation, depending upon preexisting conditions. From the pharmacological perspective, alcohol suppresses the action of certain inhibiting centers in the brain and can have no result inconsistent with this action. Yet the range of actual effects observed—both behavioral and psychic state changes—is extremely wide. It may be precisely this wide range of possibilities that makes alcohol such a popular drug. The multidimensional effects of alcohol serve to illustrate the importance of the interaction between an individual's pharmecology and the surrounding social ecology.

Though the concept of pharmecology is essential to any contemporary understanding of substance use patterns and subjective experiences, it is not a sufficient explanatory construct. One must also consider the social ecology of substance use and abuse to fully understand the range of interactive influences on individual and collective drug use patterns.

Social Ecology

Preparation and Maturation

Preparation. Botanical history demonstrates the relevance of preparation for ecological change by providing an example of what happens when a nonendogenous agent is introduced into a population unprepared or without immunity to its effects; consider the plight of the chestnut tree. A Brooklyn botanical garden brought into its rare collection an Asian plant contaminated by fungus. This new fungus rapidly spread throughout the Northern Hemisphere and destroyed a large proportion of chestnut trees. Similarly, the gypsy moth, a foreign insect introduced to an environment without its natural checks and balances (similar to the rituals and sanctions in a social context), exploited the situation with a rapid population influx into the ecosystem. The gypsy moth problem probably will be solved only by nature and, in fact, the many existing gypsy moth diseases may provide the regulating agent.

The history of the American Indians offers a somewhat different illustration of the influence of social ecology on substance use and misuse. The American Indians have a significantly higher rate of alcoholism than the general population. Alcohol, when originally introduced into the Indian culture, was a foreign agent or substance; the Indian culture had little preparation, in the form of social sanctions or rituals, to provide protection against alcohol abuse. Conversely, the Indians had a very controlled pattern of tobacco use that limited smoking to ritualized ceremonies. Their use did not include twenty prerolled, easily accessible, and portable cigarettes offered in a convenient carrying case that might have compromised their social control mechanisms.

Maturation. Environmental geology demonstrates the process of ecological maturation: At the start, a young river is just a muddy water ditch or gully. Eventually, over time and through exposure to a diversity of conditions, the river begins to meander and eventually creates a valley. This mature river valley, with its multiple flood planes, is much more complex, having adapted to many conditions. The mature river valley, unlike the mud wash, can accommodate a wide variety of adverse environmental conditions.

Cocaine use in the United States is like the gypsy moth or the new river: it is a relatively new intoxicant of abuse, not endogenous to this society. Pharmacologically, cocaine is a powerful central nervous system stimulant with a short duration of action; the pharmacologic effects of cocaine vary with site and route of admission. The two most socially prevalent and approved central nervous system stimulants are tobacco and caffeine. Cocaine now represents a third energizing drug that society is being forced to recognize because of its growing popularity, publicity, and use despite its extreme cost and illegal status.

In a new context, intoxicating drugs create conditions similar to the foreign insects introduced to the Northern Hemisphere. Perhaps cocaine was introduced too quickly into a society that had very little immunity or exposure to adapt to and accommodate the situation. Consider our "type-A" society as an unvaccinated culture that has not yet developed the antibodies to protect against compulsive cocaine use. As a system with little or no immunity, we can speculate that adaptive systemic changes will evolve naturally over time to assure survival. The use of alcohol and other psychoactive substances has already been characterized by the evolution of ecological adaptations as evidenced by the decreasing use of psychoactive drugs (Institute for Social Research 1981), with cocaine and other stimulants as the notable exceptions. The following section illustrates further the concept of ecological adaptation by considering the natural history of an illicit drug.

Ecological Adaptations, Illicit Drugs, and Drug Users

The Natural History of an Illicit Drug. Zinberg (1974, 1984) considered the history and social learning processes associated with marijuana. His work illustrates how the interaction of illicit drugs and drug users, within the context of a social ecology, can affect profoundly the social learning process.

When an illicit drug is newly introduced to the social setting, its use is considered deviant. Generally, those who seek out new drugs have strong motives for doing so; they are often perceived as social misfits or psychologically disturbed. Fearing society's disapproval, as well as its legal sanction, new drug users typically experience high levels of anxiety. Their anxiety is also elevated because they have little knowledge of the drug's possible effects. As deviant drug use patterns become more prevalent and popular, as marijuana use did in the mid-1960s, knowledge about the drug and its effects increase. Misconceptions are slowly corrected. New ones may develop, however, such as the idea that all marijuana users are peace loving.

As marijuana became more accepted, important social developments emerged. For example, in the midst of inevitable controversy and questioning that existed between first-generation marijuana users and the "straight" culture, a second generation of users appeared. Instead of attempting to break with the straight society, the second generation user, motivated by curiosity or an objective interest in the drug's effect, stimulated a new, more comprehensive cycle of information acquisition about the drug and its consequences. When this second generation of users supported the arguments of the first generation, they were more likely to be heard. They were greater in numbers, more diverse in background, and their motives were less antagonistic and, therefore, more accepted. Thus, this generation of users had the opportunity to explode many of the stereotypical myths that existed about marijuana use and users. As the second-generation users developed, the larger straight society moved away from its formerly rigid position toward marijuana and became confused. This confusion motivated nonusers in the social setting—those not motivated by drug hunger or social rebellion—to experiment with the drug. The diminished reports of adverse reaction to marijuana from this subgroup had an even greater effect on the larger social setting than either of the other two groups. Furthermore, as more diverse groups of people comprised the using population, it became more probable that various drug-use styles worked better and caused fewer difficulties.

In sum, as each generation of users acquires more knowledge about a drug, and as this information is disseminated, there is less likelihood that users who have antisocial personalities will predominate. Large numbers of people who are experienced with marijuana have children who are beginning to enter adolescence. These parents may play a very different role in socializing their childrens' relationship with marijuana from that of their own parents.

Ecological Unpreparedness and Immaturity: The Role of Advancing Technology and the Inhibition of Social Controls. As drug technology advances, it provides an ever-increasing variety and availability of both licit and illicit substances. This situation inhibits the development of rituals and sanctions like those that accompany the social use of many natural drugs. For example, before Indians use peyote, they take part in the ritual of preparing the drug.

This ritual puts them in the right frame of mind for using peyote, gives them knowledge of the drug, and emphasizes the quality of use, thus providing an opportunity for social learning and the development of social control. Similarly, Segal (1983) suggested that the history of the Eskimos with psychoactive substances reflects the absence of ecological preparation and maturation. The Eskimos had no experience with psychoactive substances until white settlers and gold fortune hunters arrived in their land. Without ecological preparation, that is, cultural heritage, the Eskimos were unable to integrate safely the use of alcohol into their social system.

In our culture, the responsibility for drug preparation has been transfered to the technological expert or manufacturer; this transfer of preparation—from user to provider—has restricted the natural development of social controls. First-time users can be suddenly confronted with a substance they do not understand and have not handled before; for this substance, the rituals, sanctions, or other social controls (for example, Maloff, Becker, Fonaroff & Rodin 1982) have not had time to develop, be disseminated, and be assimilated.

In addition to providing society with new and more powerful drugs that lack built-in social controls, advanced technology has also supplied the means of publicizing the effects of these new drugs. In the 1960s, the various media suddenly introduced the public to the adverse and disastrous effects of a psychedelic "trip." The psychedelic experience of a variety of users was telescoped into a few searing media presentations. These presentations gave the impression (which most of the public believed) that these adverse reactions were normal responses to psychedelic drug use. Those who had personal experience with psychedelic drug use were not convinced by the media accounts. As a result, they were forced into a sharply opposing position. Neither of these reactions to the new patterns of drug use permitted (1) adequate opportunity for social learning about the range of drug responses or how to best cope with them, or (2) the development of social sanctions and rituals that might prevent many of the dysfunctional reactions.

The use of cocaine has changed dramatically since the 1960s. During this period, large-scale drug experimentation took place within a larger spectrum of the American population than ever before. The increase in the number and variety of cocaine and other illicit drug users represented a normalization of the illicit use of psychoactive substances. Though such use remains illicit, the current generation of cocaine users is not restricted to "sociopathic personalities." Rather, contemporary users represent every personality type, and these individuals are typically less deviant than their cocaine using predecessors. As we mentioned earlier, by the 1980s, cocaine has become America's favorite illicit drug and is considered the "Champagne Drug" of drugs and carries with it the implicit motto that "everything goes better with coke".

Ecological Maturation and Styles of Intoxicant Use

In addition to a careful examination of the complex issues associated with drug users' pharmecology and contextual social ecology, it is essential to discriminate among the users' various styles of drug use. Examining the styles of intoxicant use available within a culture may provide an indication of the degree of maturity of the social ecology of the substance. Like the young versus the mature river, perhaps, substances new to a culture are associated with more compulsive styles of use; alternatively, ecologically mature substances may be used in a variety of styles. These styles include controlled patterns of use and multiple social mechanisms that regulate such use. For example, Americans frown on drinking in the morning and drinking and driving.

Currently, a wide range of cocaine-using styles or patterns exists within the cocaine subculture. People may use cocaine experimentally, recreationally, occasionally, abusively, compulsively or addictively, with other drugs, or alone. A "chipper," for example, consumes addictive drug substances but sufficiently regulates his or her use to avoid addiction. Therefore, a cocaine chipper employs styles of controlled substance use that guard against compulsive drug use.

Informal Social Controls

Cocaine, because of its illegal status and relatively recent and rapid growth, provides an additional problem in terms of curtailing abusive consumption. Unlike alcohol, the informal social control mechanisms of cocaine have not evolved rapidly enough to keep pace with its growing popularity and social use. The social rituals and sanctions that have evolved for alcohol use are not as fully developed for cocaine users. Again, unlike alcohol and because of its illegal nature, the mechanisms of cocaine control are not taught through any formalized networks within the user's social milieu (family or school systems). The capacity to regulate cocaine use has not been transmitted from one generation to the next, nor are social rituals and sanctions built into the users' social matrix. The usual social prescriptions and protections against addiction are thus less developed with cocaine; this observation suggests that there is a higher potential for abusive cocaine use in this country. As social control mechanisms for cocaine become more mature, we can expect cocaine abuse and the associated adverse consequences to diminish.

Conclusions

An ecological perspective toward intoxicant use indicates that new substances, along with new ideas about their use, are continually introduced into society. It takes time for a culture to sort out how, when, and where these factors influence personality development and interpersonal relationships. Not only must the drug and the personal need of the user be taken into account but also the subtleties of history and social circumstance. It bears repeating that Edwards, in pointing out the fallacy of trying to separate the specific incident of drug taking from its social matrix, once remarked that "One could not hope to understand the English country gentleman's fox-hunting simply by exploring his attitude toward the fox" (Edwards 1974b). Similarly, Szasz (1974) noted that we could not begin to understand the meaning of baptism just by studying the chemistry of water.

Both Edwards' and Szasz's comments reflect the need for a more Galilean approach to understanding the use of both licit and illicit substances. Aristotelian approaches are no longer sufficient to provide a comprehensive understanding of the pharmecology and social ecology of intoxicant use and abuse.

Implications of Galilean Thinking for the Treatment and Prevention of Cocaine Abuse

A Galilean approach to cocaine abuse suggests it is necessary to investigate how the process of control is developed; cocaine chippers provide a natural population to study that may permit the identification of how they control their drug consumption and under what circumstances these controls break down. In addition, recent evidence (Burglass 1985; Kozel & Adams 1985) suggests that it is essential to include the role of alcohol and other sedative/hypnotic drugs as well as marijuana consumption in any effort to understand the mechanisms of control associated with cocaine use. In the United States, alcoholism is the third leading cause of death and the third leading cause of mental retardation; that is, the fetal alcohol syndrome. Therefore, a better understanding of the relationship between alcohol and these other psychoactive substances is essential to drug abuse treatment efforts.

In terms of cocaine abuse prevention, identification of these evolving control mechanisms, external and internal, might be capitalized on by main-streaming these controls into the new cocaine-using social milieu. Drug education efforts should focus on teaching "styles of control" that will generalize from one substance to another, thereby minimizing adverse consequences to substance use. This approach is not unlike that of our colonial ancestors who consumed large quantities of alcohol but managed to maintain a low level of alcohol-related problems by embracing social standards that were sufficiently powerful to limit the extent to which alcohol was used (Zinberg & Fraser 1979). This was accomplished by defining how, when, and where one could drink as well as sanctioning the "unseemly behaviors" that might be associated with drinking.

The application of an ecological approach to substance use and abuse suggests that active prevention measures be taken by examining individual and personal control styles and injecting effective control mechanisms into society to limit compulsive substance use and abuse. For example, Zinberg & Fraser (1979) identified five sociocultural standards or cultural variables that appear to be associated with controlled drinking behavior:

1. Group drinking is clearly differentiated from drunkenness and is associated with ritualistic or religious celebrations.
2. Drinking is associated with eating or ritualistic feasting, or the beverage is actually consumed with the food.
3. Both sexes, as well as different generations, are included in the drinking situation, whether they drink or not.
4. Drinking is divorced from the individual effort to escape personal anxiety or difficult (intolerable) social situations. Further, alcohol is not considered medicinally valuable.
5. Inappropriate behavior when drinking (violence, aggression, overt sexuality) is absolutely disapproved, and protection against such behavior is offered by the "sober" or the less intoxicated (p. 362).

Although the Revolutionary War disrupted these social rituals so that alcohol consumption gradually became more problematic, we are proposing the restoration and use of social vehicles that might increase the rate of cultural maturation for the social ecology associated with cocaine—or other intoxicant—use and abuse. A complete examination of socially mature treatment and prevention programs is beyond the scope of this discussion. Nevertheless, one can readily extrapolate important lessons from the regulatory mechanisms we've covered. These lessons suggest that the same ecology that encourages excessive behaviors can be gently altered to promote increased social and personal control over the use of intoxicating substances. The social ecological approach that we have advocated should offer, among other benefits, the opportunity to reduce legal, military, and police expenditures and substitute more appropriate social control mechanisms.

Summary

This afterword encourages a more realistic understanding of intoxicant use and abuse than those perspectives that now dominate the field. Instead of taking a unidimensional, categorical approach toward the understanding of intoxicant use and misuse, it is suggested that a more interactive and dynamic view be applied to the entire psychopharmacological menu from which drug users select their substances of use and abuse. The chemical ecology of the drug user is conceptualized in terms of their "pharmecology." In addition, the social and cultural contexts within which intoxicants are used and abused were examined as a critical but neglected factor that influences drug use and abuse. Ecological preparedness and maturation are also recognized as two of the dynamic factors that affect patterns of drug use. The implications of this approach for the treatment and prevention of drug abuse were also discussed.

Notes

Chapter 1

Abelson, H.I., & J.D. Miller. 1985. A decade of trends in cocaine use in the household population. In N.J. Kozel and E.H. Adams (eds.) *Cocaine use in America: Epidemiologic and clinical perspectives*. (DHHS Publication Number ADM 85—1414), 35–49. Washington, D.C.: U.S. Government Printing Office.

Clayton, R.R. 1985. Cocaine use in the United States: In a blizzard or just being snowed? In N.J. Kozel and E.H. Adams (eds.) *Cocaine use in America: Epidemiologic and clinical perspectives*. (DHHS Publication No. ADM 88—1414) 8–34. Washington, D.C.: U.S. Government Printing Office.

Johnson, Vernon E. 1986. *Intervention: How to help someone who doesn't want help*. Minneapolis: Johnson Institute Books.

Orford, J. 1985. *Excessive appetites: A psychological view of addictions*. New York: John Wiley & Sons.

Shaffer, H.J. 1987. The epistemology of "addictive disease": The Lincoln-Douglas debate. *Journal of Substance Abuse Treatment* 4:103–113.

Shah, Idries, 1983. *The Exploits of the Incomparable Mulla Nasrudin*. England: Octagon Press.

Valenstein, E.S. 1986. *Great and desperate cures: The rise and decline of psychosurgery and other radical treatments for mental illness*. New York: Basic Books.

Chapter 2

Abelson, H. I., Miller, J. D. 1985. A decade of trends in cocaine use in the household population. In N.J. Kozel and E.H. Adams (eds.) *Cocaine Use in America: Epidemiologic and Clinical Perspectives*. (DHHS Publication November ADM 85—144), 35–49. Washington, D.C.: U.S. Government Printing Office.

Anderson, H., et al. 1985. The evil empire. *Newsweek*. February 25, 14–18.

Baxter, L.R. 1983. Desipramine in the treatment of hypersomnolence following abrupt cessation of cocaine use. *The American Journal of Psychiatry* 140:1525–1526.

Beck, M. 1985. Feeding America's habit. *Newsweek*, February 25, 22–23.

Berger, G. 1981. *Addiction: Its Causes, problems, and treatments.* New York: Franklin Watts.

Black, C. 1982. *It will never happen to me!* MAC Printing and Publications Division. Denver, Colo.

Boza, R.A., F. Milanes, A. Flemenbaum. 1986. Early diurnal dexamethasone suppression test results in cocaine abuse accompanied by dysphoria. *The American Journal of Psychiatry* 143:1493–1494.

Burglass, M.E. 1983. *Cocaine use: Patterns and outcomes.* Cambridge, Mass: Correctional Solutions Foundation Press.

Burglass, M.E. 1985. The use of marijuana and alcohol by regular users of cocaine: Patterns of use in style of control. In H. Milkman and H. Shaffer (eds.), *The Addictions: Multidisciplinary perspectives and treatments.* Lexington, Mass.: Lexington books, 111–120

Charleston W. Va. mayor admits cocaine guilt. 1987. *New York Times*, November 18, 9.

Chitwood, D. D. 1985. Patterns and consequences of cocaine use. In N. J. Kozel and E. H. Adams (eds.) *Cocaine use in America: Epidemiologic and Clinical Perspectives.* (DHHS Publication No. ADM 85—1414). 111–129. Washington, D.C.: Government Printing office.

Clayton, R.R. 1985. Cocaine use in the United States: In a blizzard or just being snowed? In N.J. Kozel and E.H. Adams (eds.), *Cocaine use in America: Epidemiologic and clinical perspectives.* (DHHS Publication No. ADM 85—1414). 8–34. Washington, D.C.: Government Printing office.

Cocaine in the executive suite? 1985. *Fortune*, December 23, 9.

Drug Enforcement Administration. 1977. *Drugs of abuse.* U.S. Government Printing Office. 28–33.

Drugs and a U.S. pullout. 1985. *Newsweek*, January 28, 37.

Dyke, C.V. 1981. Cocaine. In J. Lowinson & P. Ruiz (eds.), *Substance abuse: Clinical problems and perspectives.* Baltimore: Williams and Wilkins.

Faulstich, M.E. 1987. Psychiatric aspects of AIDS. *American Journal of Psychiatry* 144:551–556.

Flax, S. 1985. The executive addict. *Fortune, 111:* June 24. 24–32.

Freud, S. [1884] 1974. Uber coca. In R. Byck (ed.), S.A. Edminster and F.C. Redlich (trans.), *Cocaine papers.* New York: Stonehill.

From hot tips to hard drugs—another Wall Street Bust. 1987. *U.S. News & World Report*, April 27, 55.

Gay, G.R. 1975. Cocaine: History, epidemiology, human pharmacology, and treatment: A perspective on a new debut for an old girl. *Clinical Toxicology* 8 (2): 149–178.

Gay, G., C. Sheppard, D. Inaba & J. Newmeyer. 1973. An old girl: Flyin' low, dying' slow, blinded by snow: Cocaine in perspective. *The International Journal of the Addictions* 8 (6): 1027–1042.

Gladwell, M. 1986. A new addiction to an old story. *Insight* 2 (October 27) 8–12.

Gold, M. (1983, September). *Psychiatry letter.* p. 2.

———. 1984. *800-COCAINE.* New York: Bantam Books.

Gold, M. Washton, A. & Dackis, C. 1985. Cocaine abuse: Neurochemistry, phenomenology, and treatment. In N. J. Kozel and E. H. Adams (eds.) *Cocaine use in*

America: Epidemiologic and Clinical perspectives. (DHHS Publication No. ADM 85—1414). 130-150. Washington, D.C.: Government Printing office.

———. 1986. *800-COCAINE.* (rev. ed.). New York: Bantam Books.

Goodman, L., & A. Gilman. (eds.) 1985. *The pharmacological basis of therapeutics.* (Seventh Ed.). New York: Macmillan.

Gravitz, H. 1985. Children of alcoholics handbook. South Laguana, CA: The National Association for Children of Alcoholics.

Grinspoon, L., & J.B. Bakalar. 1985. *Cocaine: A drug and its social evolution.* New York: Basic Books.

Isner, J.M., N.A.M. Estes, P.D. Thompson, M.R. Costanzo-Nordin, R. Subramanian, G. Miller, G. Datsas, K. Sweeney, & W.Q. Sturner. 1986. Acute cardiac events temporally related to cocaine abuse. *New England Journal of Medicine* 315:1438–1443.

Iyer, P. 1985. Fighting the cocaine wars. *Time,* February 25, 26–35.

Jaffe, J. H. 1985. Drug addiction and drug abuse. In L. Goodman & A. Gilman (eds.), *The pharmacological basis of therapeutics* (Seventh ed.). New York: Macmillan. 532–581.

Johnson, T., C. Lubenow, M. Miller, D. Gonzales, G. Carroll. 1987. Urban murders: On the rise. *Newsweek,* February 9, 30

Johnston, L.D., O'Malley, P.M. & Bachman, J.G. 1986. *Drug use among American high school students, college students, and other young adults. National trends through 1985.* (DHHS Publication No. ADM 86—1450). 111–129. Washington, D.C.: Government Printing office.

Jordon, N. 1985. Coke abuse: New treatment formula. *Psychology Today* 19:22.

Kauffman, J.F., H.J. Shaffer, & M.E. Burglass. 1985. The clinical assessment and diagnosis of addiction II: The biological basics—drugs and their effects. In T. Bratter and G. Forrest (eds.), *Current treatment of substance abuse and alcoholism.* New York: MacMillan. 107–136.

Keteyian, A. 1987. Dark clouds over sun country. *Sports Illustrated,* 66 (April 27):24–25.

Knox, R.A. 1987. AIDS tally may show just half of addict toll. *Boston Globe,* June 4. 1,15.

Koffend, J. 1979. The case for alcohol. *Atlantic Monthly,* 244, 66–70.

Kozel, N.J. & E.H. Adams. 1985. *Cocaine use in America: Epidemiologic & clinical perspectives.* National Institute of Drug Abuse Research Monograph 61. Washington, D.C.: U.S. Government Printing Office.

Kurkjian, S. 1988. Noriega charges cite $5m bribe. *Boston Globe,* February 6, 1, 24.

Marmor, M., D.C. Des Jarlais, S.R. Friedman, M. Lyden & W. El-Sadr. 1984. The epidemic of acquired immunodeficiency syndrome (AIDS) and suggestions for its control in drug abusers. *Journal of Substance Abuse Treatment* 1:237–247.

McDonald, M. 1986. A war on cocaine. *Maclean's* 99 (August 4) 20.

Merganthau, T., N.F. Greenberg, A. Murr, M. Miller, G. Raine. 1986. Crack and crime. *Newsweek,* June 16, 16–22.

Miller, R. 1985. Richard Hatfield under fire: New drug charges brought against the premier. *Maclean's,* February 18. 12–16.

Mills, J. 1986. *The underground empire: Where crime and governments embrace.* New York: Doubleday.

Musto, D. 1973. *The American disease*. New Haven: Yale University Press.

National Institute on Drug Abuse (NIDA). 1986e. July. Cocaine briefing.

National Institute on Drug Abuse (NIDA). 1986d. May. NIDA notes.

National Institute on Drug Abuse (NIDA). 1986c. May. Capsules.

National Institute on Drug Abuse (NIDA). 1986b. April. Prevention networks.

National Institute on Drug Abuse (NIDA). 1986a. Data from the Drug Abuse Warning Network (DAWN): Semiannual report. Trend data through July–December 1985. Statistical Series (Series G. No. 17, DHSS Publication No. ADM86-1463). Washington, D.C.: U.S. Government Printing Office.

National Institute on Drug Abuse (NIDA). 1985. Data from the Drug Abuse Warning Network (DAWN): Annual data 1984. Statistical Series (Series 1, No. 4, DHSS Publication No. ADM85-1407) Washington, D.C.: U.S. Government Printing Office.

National Institute on Drug Abuse (NIDA). 1984. Cocaine Research: Special research grant announcement for the Department of Health and Human Services (catalogue of Federal Domestic Assistance No. 13-279).Washington, D.C.: U.S. Government Printing Office.

National Institute on Drug Abuse (NIDA). 1983/84. National survey on drug abuse: Main findings 1982 (Contract No. 271-81-1702, DHSS Publication No. ADM84-1263). Washington, D.C.: U.S. Government Printing Office.

National Institute on Drug Abuse (NIDA). 1983. Population projections based on the National Survey on Drug Abuse, 1982 (DHHS Publication No. ADM83-1303). Washington, D.C.: U.S. Government Printing Office.

Nordlund, R. 1987. Is there a Contra drug connection? *Newsweek* 109: (January 26) 26.

Orwell, G. 1949. *1984*. New York: Harcourt Brace.

Paxton, J. (ed.) 1987. *The Statesman's Yearbook*. New York: St. Martin's Press.

Perry, S., & P. Jacobsen. 1986. Neuropsychiatric manifestations of AIDS-spectrum disorders. *Hospital and Community Psychiatry* 37:135–142.

Post, R. 1975. Cocaine psychosis: A continuum model. *American Journal of Psychiatry* 132:225–231.

Ray, B.A. & Braude, M.D. (eds.). 1986. *Women and drugs: A new era for research* (National Institute on Drug Abuse Research Monograph No. 65, DHHS Publication No. ADM 86-1447). Washington, D.C.: U.S. Government Printing Office.

Ryser, J., & B. Javetski. 1986. Can South America's addict economies ever break free? *Business Week*, September 22, 40–44.

Sargent, W.C., H. J. Shaffer, & C. Lawford. 1986. Two cases of misdiagnosis: Some essentials of intake. *Journal of Substance Abuse Treatment* 3:69–75.

Seixas, F. 1981. Alcohol. In J. Lowinson and P. Ruiz (eds.). Substance abuse: Clinical problems and perspectives. 191–208. Baltimore/London: Williams & Wilkins.

Shaffer, H.J. & N. Costikyan. 1988. Cocaine psychosis and AIDS: A contemporary diagnostic dilemma. *Journal of Substance Abuse Treatment* 5: 9–12.

Shannon, E. 1986. The Eastern connection: Coke was a frequent flyer. *Newsweek* 107: (February 24) 63.

Siegel, R.K. 1982. Cocaine smoking. *Journal of Psychoactive Drugs* 14:271–359.

Slice of vice: More Miami cops arrested. 1986. *Time* 127: (January 6) 72.

Smith, D. 1986. Cocaine conference. November 13. Boston.

Smith, D.E. & D.R. Wesson. (eds.). 1985. The medical complications of cocaine abuse. *Treating the cocaine abuser.* Center City, Minn. Hazelden.

Thomas, E. 1986. Drugs: The enemy within, *Time,* September 15, 59–68.

Too little kick from champale: Malt liquor chairman Terence J. Fox faces cocaine charges. 1985. *Time,* December 2, 73.

Trebach, A.S. 1982. *The heroin solution.* New Haven: Yale University Press.

Trebach, A.S. 1987. *The great drug war.* New York: Macmillan.

Wisotsky, S. 1986. *Breaking the impasse on the war on drugs.* Westport, Conn.: Greenwood Press.

Zinberg, N.E. 1984. *Drug, set, and setting: The basis for controlled intoxicant use.* New Haven: Yale University Press.

Zinberg, N.E., & M.H. Bean. (eds.). 1981. *Dynamic approaches to the understanding and treatment of alcoholism.* New York: Free Press.

1-800-COCAINE. 1985. Personal Communication, Public Relations Representative.

Chapter 3

Alcoholics Anonymous World Services, Inc. [1939] 1976. *Alcoholics anonymous* (third ed.). New York: Author.

Alexander, B., P. Hadaway, & R. Coambs. 1980. The rat park chronicle. *The British Columbia Medical Journal* 22:54–56.

American Psychiatric Association. 1980. *Quick reference to the diagnostic criteria from DSM-III* (third ed.). Washington, D.C.: American Psychiatric Association.

———. 1987. *Diagnostic and statistical manual of mental disorders DSM-III-R* (third ed.) Washington, D.C.: American Psychiatric Association.

Apsler, R. 1982. Measuring how people control the amounts of substances they use. In N. E. Zinberg and W.M. Harding (eds.), *Control over intoxicant use.* New York: Human Sciences Press. 37–51.

Backman, J., P. O'Malley, & L. Johnston. 1984. Drug use among young adults: The impacts of role status and social environment. *Journal of Personality and Social Psychology* 47 (3): 629–645.

Bardo, M.T., & M. E. Risner. 1985. Biochemical substrates of drug abuse. In M. Galizio & S.A. Maisto (eds.), *Determinants of substance abuse.* New York: Plenum Press. 65–99.

Bocknek, G. 1980. *The young adult: Development after adolescence.* Monterey, Calif.: Brooks/Cole.

Brown, D., & E. Fromm. 1987. *Hypnosis and behavioral medicine.* Hillsdale, N.J.: Lawrence Erlbaum Associates.

Burglass, M.E., & H. J. Shaffer. 1981. *Classic contributions in the addictions.* New York: Brunner/Mazel.

———. 1983. Diagnosis in the addictions: Conceptual problems. *Advances in alcohol and substance abuse* 3:19–34.

Caetano, R. 1987. Public opinions about alcoholism and its treatment. *Journal of Studies on Alcohol* 48:153–160.

Chein, I., D.L. Gerald, R.S. Lee, & E. Rosenfeld. 1964. *The road to H.* New York: Basic Books.

Chitwood, D.D. 1985. Patterns and consequences of cocaine use. In N.J. Kozel and E.H. Adams (eds.), *Cocaine use in America: Epidemiologic and clinical perspectives.* (National Institute on Drug Abuse Reserch Monograph 61: 111–129. Washington, D.C.: U.S. Government Printing Office.

Collins, A.C. 1985. Inheriting addictions: A genetic perspective with emphasis on alcohol and nicotine. In H.B. Milkman & H.J. Shaffer (eds.), *The Addictions: Multidisciplinary perspectives and treatments.* Lexington, Mass. Lexington Books. 3–10.

Comella, B. 1987. AIDS complicates treatment of drug addiction (Letter to the editor). *Boston Globe,* May 22, 20.

Davies, D.L. 1962. Normal drinking in recovered alcoholic addicts. *Quarterly Journal of Studies on Alcohol* 23:94–104.

Eckholm, E. 1986. Cocaine's vicious spiral: Highs, lows, desperation. *New York Times,* August 17, p. 24.

Edwards, G., A. Arif, & R. Hodgson. 1982. Nomenclature and classification of drug- and alcohol-related problems: A shortened version of a WHO memorandum. *British Journal of Addiction* 77:3–20.

Foreman, J. 1986. Temptation: Chemical short-cuts to internal happiness. In Cries for us and our children; Drugs in our lives. *Boston Sunday Globe Special Section.* Globe Newspaper Company. 16–18.

Frosh, W. 1985. An analytic overview of addictions. In H.B. Milkman and H.J. Shaffer (eds.), *The addictions: Multidisciplinary perspectives and treatments.* Lexington, Mass.: Lexington Books. 39–56.

Gay, G., C. Sheppard, D. Inaba, & J. Newmeyer. 1973. An old girl: flyin' low, dyin' slow, blinded by snow: Cocaine in perspective. *The International Journal of the Addictions* 8 (6):1027–1042.

Gendreau, P., & L. Gendreau. 1971. Research design and narcotic addiction proneness. *Canadian Psychiatric Association Journal* 16:265–267.

Gendreau, P., & L. Gendreau. 1970. The "addictive-prone personality": A study of Canadian heroin addicts. *Canadian Journal of Behavioral Science* 2:18–25.

Gochman, S.I., B.A. Allgood, & C.R. Geer. 1982. A look at today's behavior therapists. *Professional Psychology* 13:605–609.

Gold, M., A. Washton, & C. Dackis. 1985. Cocaine abuse: neurochemistry, phenomenology, and treatment. In *Cocaine use in America: Epidemiologic and clinical perspectives* (National Institute on Drug Abuse Monograph 61:130–150). Washington, D.C.: U.S. Government Printing Office.

Gombosi, P. 1987. Personal communications.

Goodwin, D.W. 1979. Alcoholism and heredity: A review and hypothesis. *Archives of General Psychiatry* 36:57–61.

Green, B. 1985. *Getting over getting high.* New York: Quill.

Grinspoon, L., & J.B. Bakalar. 1985. *Cocaine: A drug and its social evolution.* New York: Basic Books.

Harding, W.M. 1983. Controlled opiate use: fact or artifact? *Advances in Alcohol & Substance Abuse* 3:105–118.

Hartmann, D. 1969. A study of drug-taking adolescents. *The Psychoanalytic Study of the Child* 24:384–398.

Heath, D.B. 1987. Cultural, social and ethnic factors as they relate to genetics and alcoholism. In H.W. Goedde & D.P. Agarwal (eds.), *Genetics and alcoholism.* New York: Alan R. Liss. 21–31.

Heather, N., & I. Robertson. 1981. *Controlled drinking.* London: Methuen.

Helzer, J.E., Robins, L.E., Taylor, J.R., Carey, K., Miller, R.H., Combs-Orme, T., & Farmer, A. 1985. The extent of long-term moderate drinking among alcoholics discharged from medical and psychiatric treatment facilities. *The New England Journal of Medicine, 3/2* 1678–1682.

Hendin, H. 1974. Students on heroin. *The Journal of Nervous and Mental Disease* 156:240–255.

Holmes, T.H., & R.H. Rahe. 1967. The social readjustment rating scale. *Journal of Psychosomatic Medicine* 11:213–218.

Jaffe, J.H. 1985. Drug addiction and drug abuse. In L. Goodman & A. Gilman (eds.), *The pharmacological basis of therapeutics* (seventh ed.). New York: Macmillan. 532–581.

Johnston, L.D., P.M. O'Malley, & J.G. Bachman. 1986. *Drug use among American high school students, college students, and other young adults. National trends through 1985.* (NIDA DHHS Publication No. ADM86-1450). Washington, D.C.: U.S. Government Printing Office.

Jones, S., C. Treece, & E. Hoke. 1981. The context of narcotic initiation. Paper presented at the National Coalition of Alcohol and Substance Abuse. Washington, D.C.

Kandel, D.B., D. Murphy, & D. Karus. 1985. Cocaine use in young adulthood: Patterns of use and psychological correlates. In N.J. Kozel and E.H. Adams (eds.), *Cocaine use in America: Epidemiologic and clinical perspectives* (National Institute on Drug Abuse Research Monograph 61: 76–110). Washington, D.C.: U.S. Government Printing Office.

Kandel, D.B. 1978. *Longitudinal research on drug use: Empirical findings and methodological issues.* Washington, D.C.: Hemisphere.

Kauffman, J.F., H.J. Shaffer, & M.E. Burglass. 1985. The biological basics: Drugs and their effects. In T. Bratter & G. Forrest (eds.), *Alcoholism and substance abuse: Clinical interventions.* New York: Free Press.

Khantzian, E.J. 1975. Self selection and progression in drug dependence. *Psychiatry Digest* 36:19–22.

Khantzian, E., F. Gawin, H. Kleber, & C. Riordan. 1984. Methylphenidate treatment of cocaine dependence —A preliminary report. *Journal of Substance Abuse Treatment* 1:107–112.

Khantzian, E.J., & C. Treece. 1985. DSM-III psychiatric diagnosis of narcotic addicts: Recent findings. *Archives of General Psychiatry* 42:1067–1071.

Khantzian, E.J. 1985. The self-medication hypothesis of addictive disorders: Focus on heroin and cocaine dependence. *American Journal of Psychiatry* 142:1259–1264.

Khantzian, E.J., & J. Mack. 1983. Self-preservation and the care of the self: Ego instincts reconsidered. A. J. Solnit, R.S. Eissler & P.B. Neubauer (eds.) *Psychoanalytic Study of the Child* 38. New Haven: Yale University Press.

Khantzian, E.J. 1978. Personal communication.

Kuhn, T.S. 1962. *The structure of scientific revolutions.* Chicago, Ill.: University of Chicago Press.

Levinson, D. 1978. *The seasons of a man's life.* New York: Ballantine Books.

Levinson, D. 1987. The Cambridge Hospital Grand Rounds announcement.

Lindesmith, A.R. 1981. A sociological theory of drug addiction. In H. Shaffer & M. Burglass (eds.), *Classic contributions in the addictions.* New York: Brunner/Mazel. 203–218.

Mack, J. 1981. Alcoholism, A.A., and the governance of the self. In M.H. Bean & N.E. Zinberg (eds.), *Dynamic approaches to the understanding and treatment of alcoholism.* New York: Free Press. 128–162.

Maloff, D., H.S. Becker, A. Fonaroff, & J. Rodin. 1982. Informal social controls and their influence on substance use. In N.E. Zinberg & W.M. Harding (eds.), *Control over intoxicant use: Pharmacological, psychological, and social considerations.* New York: Human Science Press.

Marlatt, G.A., J.S. Baer, D.M. Donovan, & D.R. Kivlahan. 1988. Addictive behaviors: Etiology and treatment. *Annual Review of Psychology* 39:223–252.

Milkman, H., & W. Frosch. 1973. On the preferential abuse of heroin and amphetamine. *Journal of Nervous and Mental Disorders* 156:242–248.

Milkman, H., & S. Sunderwirth. 1983. The chemistry of craving. *Psychology Today* 20 (10):36–44.

Miller, W.R. 1985. How prevalent are controlled drinking outcomes? A commentary on Helzer et al. 1985. *Bulletin of the Society of Psychologists in Addictive Behaviors* 4:207–212.

Mirin, S.M., & R.D. Weiss. 1986. Affective illness in substance abusers. *Psychiatric Clinics of North American* 9:503–514.

Newmeyer, J. 1987. Personal communication. January 14.

Orcutt, J.D. 1976. Ideological variations in the structure of deviant types: A multivariate comparison of alcoholism and heroin addiction. *Social Forces* 55:419–437.

Orford, J. 1985. *Excessive appetites: A psychological view of addictions.* New York: John Wiley & Sons.

Pace, N.A. 1984. *Guidelines to safe drinking.* New York: McGraw-Hill.

Peele, S. 1987. A moral vision of addiction: How people's values determine whether they become and remain addicts. *The Journal of Drug Issues* 17:187–215.

Peele, S. 1986. The implications and limitations of genetic models of alcoholism and other addictions. *Journal of Studies on Alcohol* 47:63–73.

Peele, S. 1984. The cultural context of psychological approaches to alcoholism: Can we control the effects of alcohol? *The American Psychologist* 39:1337–1351.

Rado, S. 1933. The psychoanalysis of pharmacothymia. *The Psychoanalytic Quarterly* 2:1–23.

Robins, L.N. 1974. *The Vietnam drug user returns.* Special Action Office Monograph, Series A, No. 2. Washington D.C. U.S. Government Printing Office.

Robins, L.N., J.E. Helzer, M. Hesselbrock, & E.D.Wish. 1977. Vietnam veterans three years after Vietnam: How our study changed our view of heroin. In L. Harris (eds.), *Problems of drug dependence* (proceedings of the Committee on Problems of Drug Dependence). Richmond, Virg. Committee on Problems of Drug Dependence.

Rohman, M.E., P.D. Cleary, M. Warburg, T.L. Delbanco, & M.D. Aronson. 1987. The response of primary care physicians to problem drinkers. *American Journal of Drug and Alcohol Abuse* 13:199–209.

Shaffer, H.J., & B. Gambino. 1983. Addiction paradigms III: From theory-research to practice and back. *Advances in Alcohol and Substance Abuse* 3:135–152.

Shaffer, H.J., & J. Kauffman. 1985. The clinical assessment and diagnosis of addiction I: Hypothesis testing. In T. Bratter & G. Forrest (eds.), *Alcoholism and substance abuse: Strategies for intervention*. New York: The Free Press. 225–258.

Shaffer, H.J., & B. Gambino. 1979. Addiction paradigms II: Theory, research, and practice. *Journal of Psychedelic Drugs* 11:299–304.

Shaffer, H.J. 1986. Conceptual crises and the addictions: A philosophy of science perspective. *Journal of Substance Abuse Treatment* 3:285–296.

Shaffer, H.J. 1987. The epistemology of "addictive disease:" The Lincoln-Douglas debate. *Journal of Substance Abuse Treatment* 4:103–113.

Shaffer, H.J., & M.E. Burglass. 1981. *Classic contributions in the Addictions*. New York: Brunner/Mazel.

Shaffer, H.J., & R. Schneider. 1985. Trends in behavioral psychology and the addictions. In H. Milkman and H. Shaffer (eds.), *The addictions: Multidisciplinary perspectives and treatments*. Lexington, Mass.: Lexington Books. 39–55.

Shaffer, H.J. 1985. The disease controversy: Of metaphors, maps, and menus. *Journal of Psychoactive Drugs* 17:65–76.

Siegel, R.K. 1985. New patterns of cocaine use: Changing doses and routes. In N. J. Kozel and E. H. Adams (eds.) *Cocaine use in America: Epidemiologic and clinical perspectives*. (DHHS Publication No. ADM 85—1414). 204–220. Washington, D.C.: U.S. Government Printing Office.

Smith, D.E. 1986. Cocaine, "crack" and designer drugs. Paper presented at the November LifeCycle Conference. Newton, Mass.

Sobell, M.B., & L. Sobell. 1976. Second-year treatment outcome of alcoholics treated by individualized behavior therapy: Results. *Behavior Research and Therapy* 14:195–215.

———. 1973. Individualized behavior therapy for alcoholics. *Behavior Therapy* 4:49–72.

Stone, N., M. Fromme, & D. Kagan. 1984. *Cocaine, seduction and solution*. New York: Clarkson N. Potter.

Szasz, T. 1974. *Ceremonial chemistry. The ritual persecution of drugs, addicts, and pushers*. New York: Anchor Press/Doubleday.

Treece, C.T., & E.J. Khantzian. 1986. Psychodynamic factors in the development of drug dependence. *Psychiatric Clinics of North America*, 9:399–412.

Treece, C. 1984. Assessment of ego function in studies of narcotic addiction. In Bellak, L. & Goldsmith, L.A. (eds.) *The broad scope of ego function assessment*. New York: John Wiley & Sons. 268–290.

Vaillant, G. E. 1983. *The natural history of alcoholism*. Cambridge: Harvard University Press.

Weil, A. 1972. *The natural mind*. Boston: Houghton Mifflin.

Wieder, H., & E. Kaplan. 1969. Drug use in adolescents. *Psychoanalytic Study of the Child* 24:399–431.

Wikler, A. 1965. Conditioning factors in opiate addiction and relapse. In D.I. Wilner & G.G. Kassebaum (eds.), *Narcotics*. New York: McGraw Hill. 85–100.

Wurmser, L. 1974. Psychoanalytic considerations of the etiology of compulsive drug use. *The Journal of the American Psychoanalytic Association*. 22:820–843.

Wurmser, L. 1978. *The hidden dimension: Psychodynamics in compulsive drug use.* New York: Aronson.

Young, E. 1987. Co-alcoholism as a disease: Implications for psychotherapy. *Journal of Psychoactive Drugs* 19:257–268.

Zinberg, N.E. 1975. Addiction and ego function. *Psychoanalytic Study of the Child* 30:567–588.

———. 1984. *Drug, set, and setting: The basis for controlled intoxicant use.* New Haven: Yale University Press.

Zinberg, N.E., & H.J. Shaffer. 1985. The social psychology of intoxicant use: The interaction of personality and social setting. In H. Milkman and H. Shaffer (eds.), *The Addictions: Multidisciplinary perspectives and treatments.* Lexington, Mass.: Lexington Books.

Zinberg, N.E., & W.M. Harding. 1982. Introduction—control and intoxicant use: A theoretical and practical overview. In N.E. Zinberg & W.M. Harding (eds.), *Control over intoxicant Use: Pharmacological, psychological, and social considerations.* New York: Human Sciences Press. 13–35.

Zinberg, N.E., W.M. Harding, and M. Winkeller. 1977. A study of social regulatory mechanisms in controlled illicit drug users. *Journal of Drug Issues* 7:117–133.

Chapter 4

Carras, E. 1988. AHS noted for self-help programs. *Andover Townsmen,* March 17, 18.

Diamond, E., F. Accosta, & L.J. Thornton. 1987. Is TV news hyping American's cocaine problem? *TV Guide,* 35 (February 7):4–10.

Esterly, G. 1987. Should TV be a weapon in the war against drugs? *TV Guide,* 35. (March 21):4–7.

Frisby, M.K. 1987. Youths say no to antidrug ads. *Boston Globe.* May 22, pp. 23, 28.

Gladwell, M. 1986. A new addiction to an old story. *Insight* 2 (October 27): 8–12.

Henry, W.A. 1986. Reporting the drug problem: Have journalists overdosed on print and TV coverage? *Time,* October 6, 73.

Kaplan, J. 1983. *The hardest drug: Heroin and public policy.* Chicago: University of Chicago Press.

Kaplan, J. 1985. Personal communication.

Macintyre, A. 1980. Epistemological crises, dramatic narrative, and the philosophy of science. In G. Gutting (ed.), *Paradigms and revolutions.* London: University of Notre Dame Press.

Trebach, A.S. 1987. *The great drug war.* New York: Macmillan.

Turning in your parents. 1986. *Newsweek,* 108. (August 25):34.

Weil, A.W., & W. Rosen. 1983. *Chocolate to morphine.* Boston: Houghton Mifflin.

Weisman, A.P. 1986. I was a drug-hype junkie. *The New Republic,* October 6, 14–17.

Chapter 5

Baer, P., J. Foreyt, & S. Wright. 1977. Self-directed termination of excessive cigarette use among untreated users. *Behavioral Therapy & Experimental Psychiatry* 8:71–73.

Bailey, M.B., & J. Stewart. 1966. Normal drinking by persons reporting previous problem drinking. *Quarterly Journal of Studies on Alcohol* 27:30–41.

Barcha, R., M.A. Stewart, S.B. Guze. 1968. The prevalence of alcoholism among general hospital ward patients. *American Journal of Psychiatry* 125:681–684.

DiClemente, C.C. & J. O. Prochaska. 1979. Self-change and therapy change in the successful cessation of smoking behavior. Paper presented at the annual meeting of The Rocky Mountain Psychological Association, Los Vegas.

DiClemente, C.C., & J.O. Prochaska. 1982. Self-change and therapy change of smoking behavior: A comparison of processes of change of cessation and maintenance. *Addictive Behaviors* 7:133–142.

Goodwin, D.W., J.B. Crane, & S.B. Guze. 1971. Felons who drink: An eight-year follow-up. *Quarterly Journal of Studies on Alcohol* 32:136–147.

Graeven, D., & K. Graeven. 1983. Treated and untreated addicts: Factors associated with treatment and cessation of heroin use. *Journal of Drug Issues* 13 (2):207–218.

Hecth, E. 1978. A retrospective study of successful quitters. Paper presented at the annual meeting of the American Psychological Association, Toronto, Canada.

Johnson, Vernon E. 1986. *Intervention: How to help someone who doesn't want help.* Minneapolis: Johnson Institute Books.

Jorquez, J. 1983. The retirement phase of heroin-using careers. *Journal of Drug Issues* 13 (3):343–365.

Kendall, R.E., & M.D. Stanton. 1966. The fate of untreated alcoholics. *Quarterly Journal of Studies on Alcohol* 27:30–41.

Khantzian, E.J. 1985. The self-medication hypothesis of addictive disorders: Focus on heroin and cocaine dependence. *American Journal of Psychiatry* 142:1259–1264.

Kissin, B., S.M. Rosenblatt, & K. Machover. 1968. Prognostic factors in alcoholism. *American Psychiatric Association Research Reports* 24:22–43.

Ludwig, A.M. 1985. Cognitive processes associated with "spontaneous" recovery from alcoholism. *Journal of Studies on Alcohol* 46 (1):53–58.

Marlatt, G.A., J.S. Baer, D.M. Donovan & D.R. Kivlahan. 1988. Addictive behaviors: Etiology and treatment. *Annual Review of Psychology* 39:223–252.

Miller, M.M. 1942. Ambulatory treatment of chronic alcoholism. *Journal of the American Medical Association* 120:271–275.

National Institute on Drug Abuse (NIDA). 1984. *Cocaine research: Special research grant announcement for the Department of Health and Human Services.* (Catalog of Federal Domestic Assistance No. 13–279). Washington, D.C.: U.S. Government Printing Office.

O'Donnell, J., H. Voss, R. Clayton, G. Slatin, & R. Room. 1976. *Young men and drugs: A nationwide survey.* NIDA Research Monograph. Washington D.C.: U.S. Government Printing Office.

Perri, M., Richards, C., and Schultheis, F. 1977. Behavioral self-control and smoking reduction: A study of self-initated attempts to reduce smoking. *Behavior Therapy* 8:360–365.

Prochaska, J.O., & C.C. DiClemente. 1986. Toward a comprehensive model of change. In W.R. Miller & N. Heather (eds.), *Treating addictive behaviors: Processes of change.* New York: Plenum. 3–27.

Robins, L.N., & G. Murphy. 1967. Drug use in a normal population of Negro men. *American Journal of Public Health* 59 (9): 1580–1596.

Robins, L. 1973. *The Vietnam drug user returns.* National Institute of Drug Abuse Monograph, Washington, D.C.: U.S. Government Printing Office.

Schachter, R. 1982. Recidivism and self-cure of smoking and obesity. *American Psychologist* 37 (4):436–444.

Smart, R. 1975/1976. Spontaneous recovery in alcoholics: A review and analysis of the available research. *Drug and Alcohol Dependency* 1:277–285.

Stall, R., & P. Biernacki. 1986. Spontaneous remission from the problematic use of substances: An inductive model derived from a comparative analysis of the alcohol, opiate, tobacco, and food/obesity literatures. *The International Journal of the Addictions* 21 (1):1–23.

Vaillant, G.E. 1983. *The natural history of alcoholism.* Cambridge: Harvard University Press.

———. 1966. A twelve-year follow-up of New York narcotic addicts: Some characteristics and determinants of abstinence (original study, 1966). In H. Shaffer & M. Burglass (eds.), *Classic contributions in the addictions* (1981). New York: Brunner/Mazel.

———. 1973. A twenty-year follow-up of New York narcotic addicts. *Archives of General Psychiatry* 29:237–241.

Vaillant, G.E., & E.S. Milofsky. 1982. Natural history of male alcoholism: IV. Paths to recovery. *Archives of General Psychiatry* 39:127–133.

Waldorf, D. 1983. Natural recovery from opiate addiction: Some social-psychological processes of untreated recovery. *Journal of Drug Issues* 13 (2):237–280.

Waldorf, D., & P. Biernacki. 1979. Natural recovery from heroin addiction: A review of the incidence literature. *Journal of Drug Issues* 9(2): 281–289.

———. 1981. The natural recovery from opiate addictions: Some preliminary findings. *Journal of Drug Issues* 9 (1):61–74.

Winick, C. 1964. The life-cycle of the narcotic addict and of addiction. United Nations Bulletin Narcotics, 16 (1):1–11.

Chapter 6

Marlatt, G.A., J.S. Baer, D.M. Donovan, & D.R. Kivlahan. 1988. Addictive behaviors: Etiology and treatment. *Annual Review of Psychology* 39:223–252.

Chapter 8

Doyle, Sir A.C. [1887] 1984. A study in scarlet. In *The illustrated Sherlock Holmes.* New York: Crown/Avenel. 635–712.

Marlatt, G.A. 1985. Determinants of relapse and skill-training interventions. In G.A. Marlatt & J.R. Gordon (eds.), *Relapse prevention: Maintenance strategies in the treatment of addictive behaviors.* New York: Guilford Press. 71–127.

———. 1983. The controlled-drinking controversy: A commentary. *American Psychologist* 38:1097–1110.

Marlatt, G.A., & J.R. Gordon (eds.). 1985. *Relapse prevention: Maintenance strategies in the treatment of addictive behaviors.* New York: Guilford Press.

Marlatt, G.A., & J.R. Gordon. 1980. Determinates of relapse: Implications for the maintenance of behavioral change. In P.O. Davidson & A.M. Davidson (eds.), *Behavioral medicine: changing health lifestyle.* New York: Brunner/Mazel.

McAuliffe, W., & J. Ch'ien. 1986. Recovery training and self-help: Relapse-prevention programs for treated opiate addicts. *Journal of Substance Abuse Treatment* 3:9–20.

Weil, A. 1972. *The natural mind.* Boston: Houghton Mifflin Company.

Chapter 9

Bean-Bayog, M. 1988. Psychotherapy and alcoholism. Presented at a symposium on *Treating the addictions.* March 3–4. Harvard Medical School, Cambridge, Mass.

Marlatt, G.A., J.S. Baer, D.M. Donovan, & D.R. Kivlahan. 1988. Addictive behaviors: Etiology and treatment. *Annual Review of Psychology* 39:223–252.

Marlatt, G.A., & J.R. Gordon. 1980. Determinates of relapse: Implications for the maintenance of behavioral change. In P.O. Davidson & A.M. Davidson (eds.), *Behavioral medicine: Changing health lifestyle.* New York: Brunner/Mazel.

Marlatt, G.A., & J.R. Gordon (eds.). 1985. *Relapse prevention: Maintenance strategies in the treatment of addictive behaviors.* New York: Guilford Press.

Vaillant, G.E. 1966. A twelve-year follow-up of New York narcotic addicts: Some characteristics and determinants of abstinence (original study; 1966) In H. Shaffer & M. Burglass (eds.) *Classic contributions in the addictions* (1981). New York: Brunner/Mazel.

Afterword

Bateson, G. 1979. *Mind and nature.* New York: Dutton.

Burglass, M.E. 1985. The use of marijuana and alcohol by regular users of cocaine: Patterns of use and style of control. In H. Milkman and H. Shaffer (eds.), *The addictions: multidisciplinary perspectives and treatments.* Lexington, Mass: Lexington Books.

Edwards, G.F. 1974. Drugs, drug dependence, and the concept of plasticity. *Quarterly Journal of Studies on Alcohol* 35:176–195.

Edwards, G.F. 1974b. Personal communication. Cited in Zinberg, N.E. and H.J. Shaffer (1985). The social psychology of intoxicant use: The interaction of personality and social setting. In H. Mllkman and H. Shaffer (eds.), *The addictions: Multidisciplinary perspectives and treatments*. Lexington, Mass.: Lexington Books.

Harding, W.M. 1983. Controlled opiate use: Fact or artifact? *Advances in Alcohol & Substance Abuse* 3:105–118.

Hartford, R.J. 1978. Drug preferences of multiple drug abusers. *Journal of Consulting and Clinical Psychology* 46:908–912.

Institute for Social Research. 1981. *Drug and alcohol use among high school seniors.* Ann Arbor: University of Michigan.

Kauffman, J.F., H.J. Shaffer, & M.E. Burglass. 1985. The biological basics: Drugs and their effects. In T. Bratter and G. Forrest (eds.), *Alcoholism and substance abuse: Clinical interventions*. New York: The Free Press.

Kozel, N.J., & E.H. Adams. 1985. Cocaine use in America: Epidemiologic and clinical perspectives. National Institute of Drug Abuse Research Monograph 61, Public Health Service, Alcohol, Drug Abuse & Mental Health Administration, (DHHS Publication No. ADM 85—1414). Washington, D.C.: U.S. Government Printing Office.

Lewin, K. 1931. The conflict between Aristotelian and Galileian modes of thought in contemporary psychology. *Journal of Genetic Psychology* 5:141–177.

Maloff, D., H.S. Becker, A. Fonaroff, & J. Rodin. 1982. Informal social controls and their influence on substance use. In N.E. Zinberg & W.M. Harding (eds.), *Control over intoxicant use: Pharmacological, psychological, and social considerations*. New York: Human Sciences Press.

National Institute of Drug Abuse. 1984. Cocaine research: Special research grant announcement for the Department of Health and Human Services. Public Health Service. Alcohol, Drug Abuse and Mental Health Administration.

Segal, B. 1983. Alcohol and alcoholism in Alaska: Research in a multicultural and transitional society. *The International Journal fo the Addictions* 18:379–392.

Shaffer, H.J. 1983. The natural history and social ecology of addictive behaviors. *Advances in Alcohol and Substance Abuse* 3:1-6.

Shaffer, H.J., & N.E. Zinberg. 1985. The social psychology of intoxicant use: The natural history of social settings and social control. *Bulletin of the Society of Psychologists in the Addictive Behaviors* 4:49–55.

Szasz, T. 1974. *Ceremonial chemistry. The ritual persecution of drugs, addicts, and pushers.* New York: Anchor Press/Doubleday.

U.S. Department of Health, Education, and Welfare. 1979. *Smoking and health: A report of the surgeon general.* U.S. Department of Health, Education, and Welfare, Public Health Service, Office of the Assistant Secretary for Health, Office on Smoking and Health. SHEW Publication No. (PHS)79-50066.

U.S. Department of Health and Human Services. 1982. *The health consequences of smoking.* U.S. Department of Health and Human Services, Office on Smoking and Health, DHHS Publication No. (PHS)82-50179.

Zinberg, N.E. 1974. *High states: a beginning study.* Washington, D.C.: Drug Abuse Council. Also in H.J. Shaffer & M.E. Burglass (eds.), *Classic contributions in the addictions* (1981). New York: Brunner/Mazel.

————. 1975. Addiction and ego function. *Psychoanalytic Study of The Child* 30:567–588.

————. 1984. *Drug, set, and setting: The basis for controlled intoxicant use.* New Haven: Yale University Press.

Zinberg, N.E., & K.M. Fraser. 1979. The role of the social setting in the prevention and treatment of alcoholism. In J. Mendelson and n. Mello (eds.), *The diagnosis & treatment of alcholism.* New York: McGraw-Hill.

Zinberg, N.E., & H.J. Shaffer. 1985. The social psychology of intoxicant use: The interaction of personality and social setting. In H. Milkman and H. Shaffer (eds.), *The addictions: Multidisciplinary perspectives and treatments.* Lexington, Mass.: Lexington Books.

Zinberg, N.E., & W.M. Harding. 1982. Introduction—control and intoxicant use: A theoretical and practical overview. In N.E. Zinberg & W.M. Harding (eds.), *Control over intoxicant use: Pharmacological, psychological, and social considerations.* New York: Human Sciences Press.

Zinberg, N.E., W.M. Harding, & M. Winkeller. 1977. A study of social regulatory mechanisms in controlled illicit drug users. *Journal of Drug Issues* 7:117–133.

Index

About the Authors

Howard J. Shaffer, Ph.D., is an assistant professor of psychology in the department of psychiatry at Harvard Medical School. In addition, he is the director of the Center for Addiction Studies at Harvard Medical School and the Department of Psychiatry at the Cambridge Hospital, as well as chief psychologist at the North Charles Institute for the Addictions.

Dr. Shaffer is a licensed clinical psychologist in Massachusetts and New Hampshire. He is a certified health care provider in psychology by the Council for the National Register of Health Care Providers in Psychology.

Currently, Dr. Shaffer serves as an Associate Editor of *The Psychology of Addictive Behaviors* and *The Journal of Substance Abuse Treatment*. He is also an editorial board member of the *Journal of Psychoactive Drugs* and *Advances in Alcohol and Substance Abuse*.

Dr. Shaffer contributes extensively to the professional literature. His research influences the way addictive behaviors are conceptualized, assessed, and treated. In addition to research, his interests include teaching, conducting psychotherapy, and consulting.

Stephanie B. Jones, Ed.D, is an instructor in psychology in the department of psychiatry at the Cambridge Hospital and Harvard Medical School. In addition, she is a research fellow at the Center for Addiction Studies at Harvard Medical School and the Department of Psychiatry at the Cambridge Hospital.

Dr. Jones is a clinical psychologist who maintains an active psychotherapy practice. Her interests include the psychodynamics of addictive behavior as well as the process of natural recovery.